RELIGIONS OF
THE SILK ROAD

RELIGIONS OF
THE SILK ROAD

Premodern Patterns of
Globalization

Second Edition

RICHARD FOLTZ

palgrave
macmillan

First edition published in 1999 by
PALGRAVE MACMILLAN™
175 Fifth Avenue, New York, N.Y. 10010 and
Houndmills, Basingstoke, Hampshire, England RG21 6XS
Companies and representatives throughout the world.

PALGRAVE MACMILLAN is the global academic imprint of the Palgrave
Macmillan division of St. Martin's Press, LLC and of Palgrave Macmillan Ltd.
Macmillan® is a registered trademark in the United States, United Kingdom
and other countries. Palgrave is a registered trademark in the European
Union and other countries.

ISBN: 978–0–230–62125–1

Library of Congress Cataloging-in-Publication Data is available from the
Library of Congress.

A catalogue record for this book is available from the British Library.

Design by Newgen Imaging Systems (P) Ltd., Chennai, India.

Second edition: May 2010

To Manya, Shahrzad, Persia, and Bijan
with love

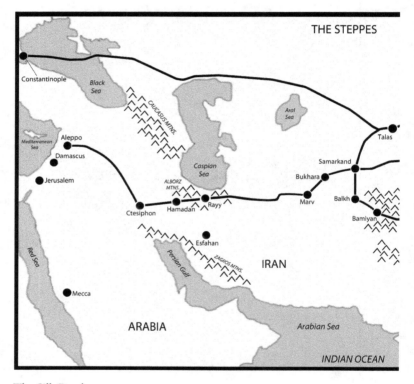

The Silk Road

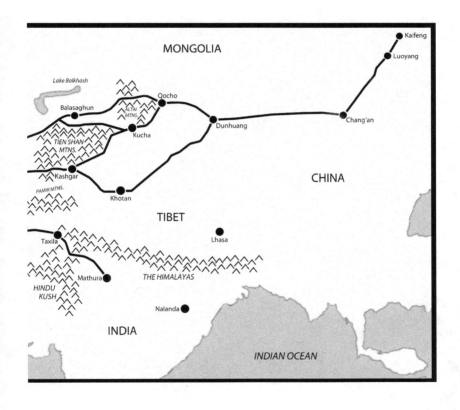

MONGOLIA

Lake Balkhash

Balasaghun

ALTAI MTNS.

Qocho

Kucha

Dunhuang

Kaifeng

Luoyang

Chang'an

CHINA

TIEN SHAN MTNS.

Kashgar

PAMIR MTNS.

Khotan

TIBET

Lhasa

Taxila

Mathura

THE HIMALAYAS

HINDU KUSH

Nalanda

INDIA

INDIAN OCEAN

Contents

Preface   xi

One   The Silk Road and Its Travelers   1

Two   Religion and Trade in Ancient Eurasia   23

Three   Buddhism and the Silk Road   37

Four   A Refuge of Heretics:
          Nestorians and Manichaeans on the Silk Road   59

Five   The Islamization of the Silk Road   85

Six   Ecumenical Mischief   105

Seven   A Melting Pot No More   127

Epilogue: The Religion of the Market   137

Notes   141

Bibliography   165

Index   181

Preface

The decade since this book was first published has brought considerable feedback, much of it positive, some critical, but—significantly I think—it has not yet abated. The fact that the book continues to reach new readers is deeply gratifying, yet it also brings a sense of obligation. The intervening years have seen much new research on the history of cultural movement along the Silk Road, and anyone choosing to start off with an overview such as this one deserves an up-to-date introduction to the sources available should they wish to pursue their own studies further. I am therefore grateful to have been given the opportunity to prepare this revised, tenth anniversary edition.

As should be obvious from the broad sweep of the title, this book takes a generalist approach. It was and remains an attempt to weave some 2,000 years of Asian history around a particular thread—that of the movement and transformation of religious ideas—into a readable and informative account. It is more concerned with presenting a reasonably coherent overall pattern than with resolving disputes over fineries of detail in the design; these I have left to the specialists in the many fields which such a survey necessarily encompasses.

I have never claimed expertise in any of these fields, but rather begged those more knowledgeable than myself to indulge me for my trespasses into their various territories, much as the Silk Road traveler was bound to solicit the goodwill of the many authorities through whose lands he would pass. Although I continue to hope that specialists will find some interest and value in my effort to compose a meaningful "big picture," this book was written first and foremost with the student and general reader in mind. For this reason I tried to keep transliterations as simple as possible, simplifying diacritics. For Chinese I have used the pinyin system except where a more familiar English version exists.

My original inspiration on the topic of religions in Central Asia followed a lecture by the late Hans-Joachim Klimkeit at the Harvard Center for World Religions, when I was beginning my graduate studies back in the early 1990s. I am grateful to his memory, first for sparking my interest nearly two decades ago and later for his encouraging comments as I came to complete the first edition of this book. Jerry Bentley, Richard Bulliet, and Nicola DiCosmo also read the typescript of the first edition and offered many useful suggestions. Richard Frye's remarks improved an early version of chapter Two, and Jan Nattier helped guide me through a much-needed overhaul of chapter Three. The criticisms of two anonymous reviewers for *The Journal of Early Modern History* helped me to strengthen my discussion of the Islamization of Inner Asia. In updating the first edition I have attempted to address a number of points raised in published reviews by Thomas Allsen, Jason Neelis, Frantz Grenet, Jason BeDuhn, and Denis Sinor. For any remaining errors of fact or interpretation, I alone remain responsible.

Some of the material in this book first appeared in the form of journal articles. These are: "When Was Central Asia Zoroastrian?" in *The Mankind Quarterly* 38/3 (1998), "Ecumenical Mischief under the Mongols," in the *Central Asiatic Journal* 43/1 (1999), and "Judaism and the Silk Route," in *The History Teacher* 32/1 (Nov. 1998). I thank the editors of those journals for permission to incorporate this material into the present work.

Susan Roach of interlibrary loan at Gettysburg College patiently and efficiently dealt with my unending requests throughout the academic year 1997–1998. Michael Flamini, my original editor at St. Martin's Press, was instrumental in bringing the book's first edition to publication. I am indebted to İbrahim Özdemir and Aydın Aslan for making the book available to Turkish readers, and to Ali Ferdowsi and Askari Pasha'i for bringing it to the Persian audience. More recently, my thanks go to Chris Chappell at Palgrave for inviting me to undertake this revised second English edition.

In my experience at least, no personal achievement is realized without a supportive network of family and friends. Among all those many individuals who have been a positive force in my life, I am especially grateful to my parents for being there since the beginning, to Shahrzad, Bijan, and Persia for giving me hope for the future, and to Manya for choosing to share this journey with me.

Montréal
26 April 2009

Chapter One

The Silk Road and Its Travelers

During the latter decades of the nineteenth century, popular European fascination with the world beyond reached an all-time high. The British and French empires spanned the globe, and their colonial agents sent home exotic goods and stories. Poets and painters put their own visions of the seductive Orient onto paper and canvas.

The last remote corners of the world were completing the list of European discoveries; mountains were measured, and the sources of great rivers determined and mapped. Tibet and other far-off lands were penetrated for the first time by Europeans, as British, Russian, and German agents ventured into the most inaccessible reaches of Central Asia, attempting to pave the way for colonial claims.

The Silk Road dates from this romantic period, in name if not in reality. In fact the trans-Asian trade network linking the Mediterranean with East Asia had been past its prime for over 400 years,[1] when a late nineteenth-century player in that web of intrigue known as the Great Game,[2] Ferdinand von Richthofen, invented the term "Silk Road" (*Seidenstraße*, in his native German). This term came to epitomize a sense of exoticism and adventure that still holds today.

In fact the "Silk Road" was not one road but many; it was actually a network of roads, generally going East and West, but with spurs into southern Iran, the northern Eurasian steppe, and south over the Hindu Kush to the Indian subcontinent. It must be confessed that in all of history Richthofen appears to have been the first to conceptualize the land routes across Asia in such a singular way—no one else, at least, had come up with such a catchy label.

Yet, in the century since its invention as a concept, the Silk Road has captured and captivated the Western imagination. It has given us images of fabled cities, exotic peoples, awe-inspiring mountains and deserts, and the death-defying feats of hardy long-distance travelers. Novels have been written, feature films and documentaries produced, travel packages sold, archaeological expeditions funded, and international conferences held, all using the Silk Road as their theme. In 1998 the world-famous cellist Yo-Yo Ma founded The Silk Road Project, a nonprofit cultural organization represented musically by the Silk Road Ensemble, which performs concerts all over the world. In the summer of 2002 the Smithsonian Institution held a Silk Road festival on the Mall in Washington, D.C., and in 2006 the city of Chicago launched an even bigger, year-long event. A slew of travel books has come out in an attempt to satisfy the urges of modern readers hoping to replicate the adventures of travelers past, and many of the old explorers' accounts have been reprinted for those content to experience them vicariously from home. There is now even a vegetarian Silk Road cookbook! All proof that like any catchphrase of vaguely defined beauty, the Silk Road can be whatever we wish it to be—it can serve as the projection screen for anything we dream.

A Premodern Globalization Network

Human movement across Inner Asia dates back to prehistoric times.[3] How the route we call the Silk Road first came into being can be guessed at simply by considering a physical map of Eurasia. The human inhabitants of the Central Asian steppes, covering the broad region spanning what is now eastern Ukraine and western Kazakhstan, north of the Caspian Sea, live in one of the world's most extreme ecological climates. Scorching summers, frigid winters, and scant water sources meant that human groups in premodern times were constrained to a marginal existence, dependent on a pastoral-nomadic economy supplemented by intertribal raiding. The Rig Veda, a collection of hymns brought by one of these warlike groups of Central Asians to India more than 3,000 years ago, evokes the culture and values of these ancient people, whom we refer to as the "Proto-Indo-Europeans" because so many modern languages from Europe to India descended from theirs. The name by which they called themselves was "Aryans" (*airyo*), which meant "the noble ones."

While fortune may have denied the ancient Aryans a mild climate and fertile lands for agriculture, it did favor them with an abundance of grazing wildlife, notably cattle and horses. These two species would play a huge role in their culture, their religion, and ultimately their success in overrunning much of Eurasia within little more than a millennium. The key event was their domestication of the horse, which likely occurred between 5,000 and 6,000 years ago.[4] This gave the Aryans both the means to flee their harsh homeland in search of better opportunities and a distinct advantage in confronting other human groups they encountered along the way. Aryans thus spread outward from Central Asia in successive waves over a period of many centuries, bringing their patriarchal culture and warrior values, as well as their language, to lands as far afield as the British Isles to the West, China to the East, and India to the South.

Returning now to our physical map of Eurasia, we can see that there is a more or less continuous ecological transition zone between mountain ranges and plains stretching from Hungary in the West all the way across to Mongolia and northern China in the East. Of course the prehistoric Aryans had no maps, so whenever a group of them decided to leave their homeland they were literally striking off into the unknown. Their most vital need, as for all living things, was water, and the most reliable way to stay close to water sources was to follow the edge of mountain chains, where runoff from snowmelt comes down in the form of streams. To actually enter the mountains was difficult and dangerous, while straying too far out onto the steppes meant the streams would likely run dry. Thus, not surprisingly, the Silk Road develops along this mountain-hugging West-East corridor all the way across the center of the Eurasian continent. Since the western steppes are lower and less arid than the eastern, on the whole there was more westward migration than there was toward the East, which explains why most of the Indo-European languages are found in Europe.

The written history of Central Asia begins long after the Aryans began their migrations, when they had taken their places among the settled, urban-agricultural cultures. Modern-day Silk Road storytellers usually begin their tale with the mission of Zhang Qian, who was sent by the Han emperor of China, Wudi, to the "Western Regions" in 139

BCE to propose an alliance with a nomadic Indo-European people known to the Chinese as the Yuezhi (known in Western sources as the Tocharians) against another steppe confederation which they called the Xiongnu (probable predecessors to the Huns), who constantly harassed the Chinese with sporadic raids that even the Great Wall could not prevent. Zhang did not succeed in his appointed task but learned quite a bit from his travels, which lasted 13 years and may have taken him as far as northwestern India. During the course of this time he was captured and imprisoned by the Xiongnu, escaped, and was imprisoned by them again on his way home before finally managing to return and offer his report to the emperor.

One writer has suggested that Zhang's mission was less an official embassy than "an intelligence mission staffed with expendable personnel."[5] Whatever the case, the traveler's tales of lands and peoples to the west suggested to Wudi tempting opportunities for trade. Within a few years Chinese merchants were regularly braving the difficult journey west through the Gansu corridor, around the forbidding Takla Makan desert, and into Central Asia.

For the next 20 years or so this trade seems to have thrived. Wudi was particularly keen on obtaining horses from a place called Dayuan, probably the Ferghana valley in modern Uzbekistan, which Zhang had visited. The Chinese referred to these mounts as "heavenly horses" that "sweat blood."[6] The people of Dayuan were reluctant to part with large numbers of them, however, and eventually in 104 BCE the Han emperor sent his general, Li Guangli, at the head of a large army with instructions to acquire these horses by force. Supplies were insufficient and much of the army starved en route. Massively reinforced by Wudi, the Chinese reached their destination only after two years and finally succeeded in getting the inhabitants of Dayuan to capitulate. In the end the Chinese only managed to bring home 30 or so of the "heavenly horses," but the trade route had been definitively opened and its eastern portion put under Han control.

Despite the prominence of these events, which are detailed in the Chinese sources, trans-Asian overland trade probably linked the West with China much earlier than Han times. (Silk, used in China since at least 3600 BCE, has been found in Egypt from around 1000 BCE, and in Europe from around 300 years later.[7]) Few, if any, individuals ever made the long and dangerous transcontinental journey as a single trip, however. Silk and other high-value goods were transported in contiguous stages, each part of more or less distinct economic systems and under the control of various political ones.

In the thirteenth century Marco Polo's claim to have covered the whole distance from Venice to China and back was so unusual as to have sounded utterly unbelievable to his fellow Italians, and indeed his account has been questioned by some contemporary scholars. In any case during the subsequent decades, others, Asian as well as European, certainly did make this great journey, thanks to the *pax mongolica,* which had brought most of Eurasia under one political administration for the first time in history. One fourteenth-century Italian merchant, Francesco de Balducci Pegolotti, even wrote a sort of Asian travel guide for businessmen![8] Overall, however, this kind of direct personal contact between East and West was rare.

The historical norm was that most participants in the moving of goods across Asia played relay roles. Central Asian middlemen might travel East or West into foreign lands, and even set up trading offices there, but of individuals who personally conveyed silk or anything else from China to the Mediterranean in the pre-Mongol period, history has given us no confirmed examples.[9] Still, the overall connections are apparent in hindsight. Therefore, having admitted that the Silk Road nomenclature is a recent invention, we will retain it as a general term to represent the complex network of land routes across Asia.

This network, which existed first and foremost to facilitate trade, at the same time provided a means of cultural exchange that connected peoples over much of the world, conveying not just goods but fashions, traditions, and ideas. Thus, the phenomenon referred to today as "globalization" is actually nothing new, but merely an accelerated form of patterns going back more than 3,000 years.[10]

Scholars or Scoundrels?

If it is to the explorer-agents of the turn of the century that we owe the Silk Road as a concept, then it is likewise to them that we owe much of our knowledge of its history. Many of these individuals—Aurel Stein, Albert von le Coq, Paul Pelliot, and Langdon Warner (the Harvard professor who was the model for Steven Spielberg's Indiana Jones)— were scholars, and had a real interest in the histories and cultures of the regions they visited. Often armed not only with government funding and diplomatic support but connections with museums and universities as well, they were keen (if not always careful) archaeologists. By diligence and skill, by means and ruse, they uncovered long-lost treasure troves of architecture, art, and literature, much of it religious in nature.[11]

One example of the lasting contribution of these men to the history of religions is that prior to their activities, next to nothing was known of the once-great tradition of Manichaeism. During its early life from the third through the ninth centuries, this chameleon-like religion enjoyed massive appeal throughout the Mediterranean and Western Asia, to the extent that defenders of Christianity, Zoroastrianism, and Islam all saw it as the single greatest threat to the very survival of their own faiths. Manichaeism was rooted out and eradicated by force in the West, and all remnants of its existence destroyed by the end of the sixth century. By the tenth century few Manichaeans survived in the Muslim heartlands. Further east along the Silk Road, however, the religion survived another 700 years.

For many centuries Manichaeism was known only through the polemics of its enemies (such as St. Augustine, himself a former Manichaean), and it was not until the beginning of the twentieth century that actual Manichaean written works were found to have survived, locked up in forgotten vaults and buried beneath the deserts of East Turkestan, modern Xinjiang. (A few decades later, further Manichaean texts would turn up in Egypt.) These writings, along with architectural ruins and fragments of wall paintings, were the relics of a Manichaean kingdom of the ninth and tenth centuries after the religion had briefly served as the official faith of the Uighur Turkish Empire.

This is not to say that the noble intentions of the turn-of-the-century adventurer-scholars haven't been questioned. In fact in China today they are considered little more than bandits; tour guides point out the bare spaces that used to hold frescos or manuscripts and say, "Stolen!" And indeed, while many of these relics had been damaged or neglected for centuries,[12] the methods employed by Europeans to acquire them were sometimes shady.

For example, Aurel Stein, finding that a large cache of ancient manuscripts had been inadvertently discovered by a Daoist monk while restoring a grotto shrine, gained access to the site by persuading the monk that although European in outward appearance, he was really a spiritual disciple of the famous Buddhist traveler Xuanzang. Stein insisted that just as that seventh-century pilgrim had "saved" so many

Sanskrit works by bringing them from India, he now had a mission to preserve these works by carting them off to England. "I was performing a pious act," Stein rationalized, "in rescuing for Western scholarship those relics of ancient Buddhist literature and art which local ignorance would allow to lie here neglected or to be lost in the end."[13]

Von le Coq used similar reasoning but with more tragic results. He had his workers attempt to chip off entire walls of medieval Buddhist and Manichaean fresco work, but they did a somewhat careless job, and in the process of removal and transportation to Germany many of the paintings were severely damaged. The final blow came at the end of World War II, when most of them were destroyed in the allied bombing of Berlin. Today the lost paintings survive only in the color reproductions that von le Coq published in 1923.[14]

The somewhat cavalier nature of Stein's claim notwithstanding, it is true that the bulk of subsequent research on Silk Road texts has been done by Westerners, albeit with notable contributions from Japanese and Chinese scholars. The manuscripts were found to have been written in 17 different languages, many of which were unknown to anyone alive at the beginning of the twentieth century. The majority are Buddhist works, but a substantial number are Manichaean and Nestorian Christian. A Jewish business document in Hebrew letters from the eighth century unearthed at Dunhuang by Stein has provided the earliest known example of the "Islamic" New Persian language.[15]

European philologists have succeeded in deciphering most of these long-forgotten tongues, and begun the process of translating them into modern ones.[16] In addition, today there are numerous active archaeological digs in western China, now under the sponsorship and surveillance of the Chinese government. Much of the material in this book owes itself to these twentieth-century finds preserved by the dry desert air of western China, and to the efforts of contemporary scholarship to explain their content and meaning.

The religious texts and paintings found in East Turkestan (or Xinjiang, as it is now called in Chinese), together with archaeological and written evidence from elsewhere in Central Asia, attest to a bizarre amalgamation of religious ideas drawn from Christianity and Judaism, Buddhism, and Zoroastrianism. Often this mixture is expressed in the deliberate, peculiar syncretism of Manichaeism.

It would seem, in fact, that eastern Central Asia in the premodern period became a melting pot of religious traditions because it served as a remote refuge for heterodox beliefs, and that well into the Mongol period it was one of the most religiously diverse places on the globe. How this very pluralistic religious environment came to be one of the world's most uniformly Muslim regions is one of the more intriguing questions of Silk Road history.

Religion and Trade

It is no coincidence that throughout history ideas and technologies have spread along trade routes, and that merchants have been among their prime transmitters. One only has to think about it to realize that traveling businessmen do not simply convey, sell and acquire goods, and move on. They socialize, interact, and observe while on the road, and they take their impressions home with them.

Nor are businessmen the only utilizers of trade routes; many other kinds of travelers benefit from the networks fostered by commercial activity. In the modern world business travelers are the driving force behind the airline industry, even if the average flier thinks little about that connection. Likewise, while freeways are now a way of life for most North Americans, in fact, the interstate highway system in the United States was originally devised in the 1950s as a hidden public subsidy to support the development of the trucking industry (at the expense of trains).

Among academics, increasing attention has been given in recent years to the role of long-distance trade in the cross-pollination of cultures and ideas.[17] Taking as its theme the specific example of the spread of religious ideas, the book you are now reading tells the story of how religions accompanied merchants and their goods along the overland Asian trade routes of premodern times. It is a story of continuous movement, encounters, mutual reactions and responses, adaptation and change. This is part—though, the reader is cautioned, only a part—of a much broader historical dynamic of cultural interaction, exchange, and conversion. While long-distance trade is not in and of itself an "explanation" of how religions spread across Asia or why Asians converted to them, a case will be made here that it is an important factor, important enough to serve as the theme of a book-length treatment.

Although some of the religious traditions in this story (Christianity, Islam, Judaism, and Buddhism) are familiar to us living today, it would be misleading to project too much of what we know of their modern manifestations into the Silk Road context. Religions are not monolithic, fixed institutions existing each in their own realm of dominance, although we often speak of "Christendom," "the Islamic World," and so on. In reality, religions are like organisms: they are born into this world at a point in time, they grow, develop, undergo diverse influences, and adapt to their environment. They quibble with their neighbors, experience periods of painful soul searching, have good days and bad. At some point they may split like cells, each taking on a new life. Over time, having proven themselves, they may settle into the self-confident stasis of maturity. Sometimes, eventually, they die. In China, especially, they are more often simply absorbed. Nothing could better illustrate the organic nature of religious traditions than the example of their experiences along the Silk Road.

The Silk Road was more than just a conduit along which religions hitched rides East; it constituted a formative and transformative rite of passage. No religion emerges unchanged at the end of that arduous journey. Key formative influences on the early development of the Mahayana and Pure Land movements, which became so much a part of East Asian civilization, are to be sought in Buddhism's earlier encounters along the Silk Road. Manichaeism, driven underground in the West, appears in the eighth century as a powerful political force in East Turkestan, then gradually blends into the amorphous mass of Chinese popular religion. Nestorian Christianity, expelled as a heresy from the Byzantine realm, moves eastward, touches hundreds of thousands among the Eurasian steppe peoples, and appears centuries later like a bad dream to the first Catholic missionaries in China who find it comfortably entrenched there as the recognized resident Christianity of the East.

Islam, carried along by the momentum of the Arabs' military success, makes its appearance on the Silk Road in the eighth century but comes to a temporary halt after the Battle of Talas in 751. Directly and indirectly, Islam would be carried further east through trade, just like its predecessors. Nor would the new tradition remain Arab property: it would belong instead to the Persians, the Turks, the Indians, the Chinese—and it would feed from their cultures. Ideas, after all, like individuals, need to acquire new tastes and new sponsors if they are to thrive in foreign climes.

The existence of trade routes and constant commercial activity linking diverse cultures from ancient times meant that religious ideas (like technology, and other aspects of culture) could easily spread along trade networks that spanned Eurasia. Indeed, like running water finding open channels, this spread was probably inevitable. But the religion-trade relationship was mutually reinforcing. For example, the expansion of Buddhism brought an increased demand for silk, which was used in Buddhist ceremonies, thereby further stimulating the long-distance trading activity that had facilitated the spread of Buddhism in the first place.[18]

The Caravan Experience

If one needed or wanted to travel from one place to another in premodern Asia, the most prudent way (indeed, virtually the only way) of ensuring one would survive the trip was to join up with a caravan heading in the direction one wished to go. Travel was an exceedingly expensive and dangerous proposition, especially the further one got from areas of dense population.

As noted earlier, Inner Asia contains vast tracts of inhospitable land, often with little water, and sparse human settlements frequently separated by great distances. The road from the Mediterranean to China is barred by some of the world's highest and most rugged mountain ranges, some of its driest, most expansive deserts, and an extreme continental climate that makes both winter and summer travel extremely difficult. The most physically challenging regions also tended to be those furthest from the reach of governmental administrations, making them prime grounds for banditry. And where local government did exist, it might be hostile to outsiders.

Caravans coped with all of these problems in a variety of ways. There is safety in numbers, and caravans could be made up of anything between several dozen and several thousand travelers at a time. They followed established routes, so were unlikely to get lost, and they traveled in set daily stages, stopping in places where the locals expected them and were prepared to meet their needs. They were usually led by professional caravaneers who had made the trip before, and attempts were made to secure the approval and protection of all the authorities through whose lands the caravan was to pass. Occasionally caravans would receive military escorts through particularly dangerous or unruly areas.

The oases of the Silk Road—Marv, Balkh, Bukhara, Samarkand, Kashgar, Turfan, Khotan, Kucha, and others—owed their prosperity and often their very existence to the regularity of passing caravans. They offered way stations, or caravansarays (from the Persian *kārvān sarā*), where large numbers of travelers could stop and rest for a night or more, stock up on food and supplies, buy local goods, and sell the locals imported ones. Travelers would also often exchange their beasts of burden, to either obtain fresh, healthy, and rested animals or trade in one type of animal for another more suitable for the next stage of the journey.

Caravan travelers transported their goods and personal belongings mainly on horses, mules, and donkeys. For desert regions camels were used: dromedaries in southwestern Asia and Bactrians in the colder, higher elevations of Inner Asia. In the most extreme conditions the choice was rather a yak or a *hainag,* which was a cross between a bull-yak and a cow. Donkeys and mules carried packs, while horses, oxen, and camels often drew carts. The pace, set by the camels, was tediously slow: four miles an hour unloaded, and two-and-a-half to three miles an hour when loaded up. The average load was around 300 pounds per camel. At this pace, a caravan might cover 30 miles a day.[19]

Even with the protection and regularity provided by a caravan, disasters were not uncommon. Dehydration, starvation, and exhaustion could befall even the best-planned expedition. Snowstorms or sandstorms could make a caravan lose its way, and even large caravans were not immune to attack from highwaymen. All in all, to travel was to assume an immense amount of risk, not to mention the expense. Exotic tales notwithstanding, a reasonable person would hope as much as possible to *avoid* romance and adventure, and pray just to arrive home again safely one day! The copious travelers' donations that enriched local religious institutions existing along the Silk Road are prime evidence of this mind-set.

Caravan traffic existed primarily by and for long-distance trade. For the most part nobody but a merchant would have the means, the motivation, or the mettle to undertake travel when its conditions were so rigorous and its outcome so uncertain. This also explains why it was mainly goods of high value in proportion to their bulk that were carried along the Silk Road: one had to stand to make a considerable profit from his wares for such a daunting endeavor to seem at all worthwhile.

(It may be noted that in terms of its weight-to-value ratio, the spice saffron was even more advantageous as a travel currency than silk.)

Still, there were people who joined caravans for other than purely commercial reasons. Diplomatic missions attached themselves to them. Sometimes people who had some special talent, or thought they did, would travel to distant courts in the hope of receiving patronage. A few hardy souls traveled merely to satisfy their own curiosity. Others had scholarly interests, and traveled for purposes of research.

With the appearance of proselytizing religions came missionaries. First Buddhists, then Christians and Manicheans, and finally Sufi Muslims latched onto caravans that would take them and their "spiritual goods" into new lands. As new religious traditions carried by the Silk Road disseminated eastwards and took root along the way, travelers were increasingly able to find coreligionists in even the most far-flung and out-of-the-way places who could provide them with assistance and fellowship, and to whom in return they could bring some contact (and often cash donations) from the outside world.

The spread of religious traditions across Asia also stimulated religious pilgrimage. For example, once Buddhism had established itself in China, Chinese Buddhists began to feel the need for direct contact with the sources of their tradition in India. Chinese monks, the most famous of whom are Faxian in the fifth century and Xuanzang in the seventh, traveled the Silk Road through Central Asia and down into the Indian subcontinent. Over time, Korean and Japanese Buddhist pilgrims also appeared.[20] And by the thirteenth century, Christian Turks from Mongolia such as Rabban Sauma and his disciple Markos were undertaking the pilgrimage west to Palestine and beyond.

From the tenth century or even earlier, Sufi masters attached themselves to Silk Road caravans in order to spread their often esoteric interpretations of Islam eastward into Inner Asia and China. They frequently won large local followings, converting people more by their own personal charisma than through the canonical teachings of the faith. Often such figures were attributed with miraculous powers, and when they died their disciples would typically erect a shrine in their honor, which might later become a focus of pilgrimage.

It was not only, or even primarily, through missionary activity that religious ideas spread along the Silk Road, however. The earliest of the "mobile" religious systems to take this eastward path, the Iranian and the Jewish, were not proselytizing faiths. Even the later so-called missionary religions won converts at least as much through their prestige as foreign, cosmopolitan traditions as they did through active proselytization.

This is a phenomenon that historian Jerry Bentley has aptly characterized as "conversion by voluntary association."[21] According to this interpretation local communities, especially in remote areas, would tend to see foreign traders as being their link to the outside world, a world that wasn't hard to imagine as being far more advanced and civilized than the isolated settlement one lived in. Likewise, any local who adopted the cultural trappings of the foreigners (religion being a particularly visible example) could feel and might be considered by others as being more connected to that greater outside world.

A significant aspect of this tendency for anyone involved in commerce was the practical consideration of maintaining the strongest and broadest connections possible with one's business associates. Numerous cases in world history serve as illustration. For example, the spread of Islam through the Sahara and around the Indian Ocean basin is generally attributed to the success of Muslims in dominating the trade networks of those regions, with the resulting dominance of Sharia law in the marketplace and favorable concessions and taxation terms being extended to Muslim traders in areas under Muslim control.[22] The same pattern applies to Central Asia beginning in the eighth century, but even before Islam a similar process was at work there. It is surely no coincidence that the periods in which Buddhism, Manichaeism, and Nestorian Christianity experienced their most active spread through Inner Asia were connected with the adoption of those traditions by merchant communities.

For the most part, merchants and other travelers along the Silk Road were linguistically Iranians, whether Persian, Parthian, Bactrian or Sogdian, Zoroastrian, Jewish, Buddhist, Christian, Manichean, or Muslim. Mentions in Chinese sources of "Westerners" (usually *Hu*) therefore can usually be taken as referring to individuals of Iranian background. As Thomas Allsen noted in reviewing the first edition of this book, "The extent to which religious and commercial activity was integrated (if not fused) on the Silk Road is well illustrated by the Zoroastrian communities in Tang China [618–917 CE] whose religious establishments, commercial and diplomatic interests were overseen by a government bureau headed by an official called a *sa-po* or *sa-pao*, a title derived from the Sanskrit word *sārthavāha*, 'caravan leader.'"[23]

The Sogdians

The prime actors in this cross-cultural scenario are the people of Transoxiana, roughly modern Uzbekistan. This is a dry but fertile region of Central Asia lying between two great rivers: the Amu Darya (known to the Greeks as the Oxus and to the Muslims as the Jayhun) and the Syr Darya (the Jaxartes or the Sayhun, respectively). Early inhabitants of this arid land were among the first peoples to develop irrigation. For over three millennia agriculture thrived there, until the Russians imposed their rule late in the nineteenth century and turned the land over to a soil-destroying, water-depleting cotton monoculture, which the post-Soviet governments of Central Asia have so far chosen to maintain.

Irrigation ensured Transoxiana's survival, but its prosperity depended on trade. Situated halfway between the Mediterranean and East Asian centers of civilization, the peoples of this region were ideally situated to be middlemen, and throughout history they have answered this call. From the earliest times it is the natives of Transoxiana who appear as the central figures in trans-Asian trade, and with their role as traders, comes their role as transmitters of culture and ideas.[24]

From ancient times the principal inhabitants of Transoxiana were an Iranian stock known as the Sogdians.[25] A sedentary Indo-European people related to their nomadic neighbors the Sakas, or Scythians, they spoke an Iranian language, Sogdian, which survives today as Yaghnobi in parts of central Tajikistan. It is often claimed that their religion in ancient times was Zoroastrianism, but there is little absolute evidence for this. More likely their religious beliefs and practices were drawn from the broader pool of old Iranian religion, including a range of local deities and hero cults.

The Sogdian merchants were for centuries among the most successful in Asia, and their trading activities formed the major link connecting East and West. They were like cultural bees, cross-pollinating ideas and traditions from one civilization to another. In the centuries immediately before the Common Era, Buddhism took hold among the Bactrians, another Iranian people living to the northwest of India in what is now Afghanistan. Sogdians living or trading in Bactria adopted Buddhism and spread its teachings throughout their trading colonies all along the Silk Road as far as China. Later Sogdians were enthusiastic converts to Manichaeism or Nestorian Christianity, and became the representatives of these faiths through their string of merchant communities across the Asian interior.

With their international connections Sogdian merchants knew foreign languages, and uncharacteristically for the time, some were even literate. They were often engaged as interpreters and translators. It was Sogdian scribes who translated most of the religious texts of Buddhism, Manichaeism, and Christianity into the various languages of the Silk Road, from Indian Prakrits (vernacular dialects), Aramaic, or Parthian into Bactrian, Tocharian, Khotanese, Turkish, or Chinese, either via Sogdian or directly. For that matter, it was Sogdians who brought the technology of paper production from China to the West, and well into the Islamic period their capital, Samarkand, was known throughout the world for the quality of its paper.

Some 90 years ago the British agent-explorer Sir Aurel Stein found the earliest known example of rag paper, dating from the fourth century, in the Tarim basin of modern China; it consisted of business letters written in the Sogdian language in Aramaic script.[26] In his account of his expeditions, Stein remarks in connection with his discovery of Sogdian Buddhist texts, "What a large share this Iranian element must have had in the propagation of Buddhism along the old 'Northern Route' to carry its particular language and writing to these marches of China proper!"[27] Stein's observation about the Sogdians' connection with Buddhism remains valid for their role in spreading other religious traditions as well.

During the eighth century Muslim armies based in Khurasan, composed of Arab settlers and native Iranian converts, gradually conquered and absorbed the Sogdian lands in Central Asia and brought them into the fold of the Muslim empire under the Caliph of Baghdad. First the ruling elite and aristocracy, then over time the general population, converted to Islam in increasing numbers, to such an extent that since the fifteenth century the native sedentary population of Central Asia has been almost completely Muslim.

It would seem that even before Muslim power was fully consolidated in Central Asia, Sogdian merchants were among the earliest and most enthusiastic converts to the new religion. The practical element lurking beneath this trend is not hard to see. Muslims had taken over control of the trade networks that connected Central Asia with the Mediterranean world; if Sogdian traders wished to maintain business in that direction, the advantages of being part of the dominant tradition were obvious.

Once their own Central Asian homeland had come under Muslim rule and Islamic law as well—a process that took several centuries and was marked by rebellions—merchants would have had particular incentives not to cling to the old ways.

As Sogdians in Western and Central Asia gradually turned to Islam, following the established pattern, this led to the conversion of their fellow Sogdian trading partners further east. This in turn facilitated the participation of non-Sogdian Muslims in the Sogdians' trading activities beyond the lands under Muslim rule, so that when Islam came to China it was not only Sogdian but also Persian and Arab Muslims who were its bearers.

Thus, from the eighth century onward, Sogdians and others in Central Asia adopted Islam and became active participants in the formation of Muslim culture. But Islam came to Central Asia through the filter of Persian civilization, which it had already absorbed and which was its most prominent non-Arab influence. The Arab Muslims' most dramatic accomplishment was the defeat and absorption of the entire Persian Sasanian Empire during the 640s. In 750 the so-called Abbasid revolution displaced the center of Muslim power and administration eastward into the Persian world. The new Abbasid Empire then in many respects merely maintained the preexisting Persian cultural and political realities under a new Islamic identity. Islam became increasingly Persian in character: Islamic law, philosophy, literature, art, and mysticism all developed to a large extent in the Persian cultural sphere.[28]

It was therefore a very Persianized form of Islam that penetrated and transformed Central Asia over the next several centuries. It was mainly in the Persian language that Islamic religion and Muslim culture were communicated to Central Asians. Just as in Egypt and in Syria the local Semitic languages gradually gave way to Arabic, in Central Asia, Sogdian and other Iranian languages ceded to Persian. Although Central Asia had been incorporated at times into previous Persian empires, from the Achaemenids to the Parthians to the Sasanians, it was under the Islamic Caliphate that local identity essentially disappeared and Central Asia became an integral part of the Persian world. Indeed, by the tenth century, a new Bukhara-based Persian dynasty, the Samanids, had made Central Asia the center of that world,[29] and it would remain so for several centuries to come.

Language and Proselytization

Attitudes and choices about language are central to questions about the spread of religions. The Iranian and Hebraic traditions apparently did not proselytize along the Silk Road, but remained the faiths of expatriate Iranian or Jewish communities. Coincidentally, the sacred texts of Zoroastrianism and Judaism remained bound to languages that were no longer spoken or understood by the majority of their adherents, whereas actively proselytizing movements such as Buddhism, Manichaeism, and Christianity consciously attempted to reach potential converts through both preaching in and translating texts into vernacular languages.

Yet, in the wake of the first translation of Hebrew texts into a popular language, the Greek Septuagint, throughout the Roman period the Hebraic tradition that would evolve into Judaism did win many converts; it would seem, in fact, that at no time in its history did it experience such growth. By contrast, the story of Judaism along the Silk Road at a later stage in its life is one of far-flung, and over time, increasingly isolated communities struggling to maintain their religious identity. The tragedy of this trend underlies contemporary treatments by Jewish scholars of the demise of the ancient Chinese Jewish community in the middle of the twentieth century.[30]

When and why conversion to Judaism began to decline is beyond the scope of the present work, but the issue may be pursued briefly. It may be that the Talmudic approach represents Judaism on the defensive, following the destruction of the Second Temple by the Romans in 70 CE. This case highlights the importance of noting, in any discussion pertaining to a religious tradition, where that tradition stands within its own historical life cycle of development.

The spread of Islam across Central Asia presents a special case with regard to language, but one that perhaps ultimately fits the pattern. It has been argued that no religious tradition is more scripture-bound than Islam, and since Muslims do not believe a translation of the Qur'an remains the Qur'an, Islam has tended to be seen as strongly tied to the Arabic language.

While in theory such a tie certainly exists, in reality Arabic played less of a role in the transmission of Islam to the peoples of the Silk Road than Persian did. An early twelfth-century Bukharan translator into Persian of an Arabic work on local history explains in his preface that "[s]ince most people do not show a desire to read an Arabic book, friends of mine requested me to translate the book into Persian."[31] Similarly, among the illiterate steppe nomads Islam was learned not so much from Arabic texts as through the often highly personalized teachings of charismatic individuals who preached in local languages such as Turkish.

In general, there would appear to be a connection between the success of a religion in winning converts and the readiness with which the substance of that religion was communicated through local vernaculars. It should be noted that successful translation is not merely linguistic; meaningful analogues must be found for symbols and concepts. In many cases such analogues between one cultural vocabulary and another simply do not exist, and must be invented. It is thus easy to see how the substance of religious traditions was often transformed along the Silk Road, sometimes radically, as a result of the translation process.

Women's Roles in Cultural Transmission

For the most part long-distance travelers were men, for whom travel frequently entailed liaisons or marriages with local women. Formally speaking in most cultures the offspring of such mixed unions tended to be considered members of the father's community, but in reality it was often the mothers who exercised greater influence on their children's cultural education.

This informal level of passing on tradition is far less documented than that reflected in standard male history, and must often be reconstructed from secondary evidence. It is therefore difficult to make assertions about women's roles and influence that can be clearly substantiated; nevertheless, a growing number of historians are attempting to round out the picture drawing on whatever sources they can.

The anthropological fieldwork of Sergei Poliakov conducted in Tajikistan during the last four decades of the Soviet period has shed much light on the roles of women in passing on religious tradition to their children.[32] At a time when even men were cut off from the influence of the mosque, Poliakov demonstrates how Islam—or more accurately, a popular local expression of it—survived 70 years of enforced official atheism by being preserved through a culture of shrine visitation, a culture that was largely the province of women.

Although the shrine custodians who acted as teachers and transmitters were men, it was mainly the women who came to the shrines, often to pray for offspring. An American friend of mine visited such a shrine in Uzbekistan in the company of his wife; the attendant assumed they were there to pray for children, and recited the *fatiha* (the opening chapter of the Qur'an) for them. My friends joked about it afterwards—they had no plans for children. But four months later the wife was pregnant!

Normally women visit such shrines alone, and in the course of such visits the custodian usually serves as a religious instructor. The knowledge passed on through this type of system belongs more to oral culture than it does to canonical texts, and it was this oral culture, transmitted principally by women to their children, that formed the backbone of Central Asian religious life throughout the Soviet period.

Richard Eaton has described a similar system for the transmission and dissemination of Islamic vocabulary and symbolism in southern India dating back at least to the sixteenth century and probably earlier.[33] The folk literature of this region suggests that the spread of Islam—or perhaps more accurately, Islamic ideas and symbols—among the Indian masses was facilitated to a large extent by Sufi shrine attendants who composed "Islamic" songs in the local language and taught women to sing them while spinning, cooking, as lullabies, or at weddings. Since merely singing such songs did not require any kind of formal conversion or profession of faith, they spread widely and became a significant element of popular culture. As Islamic concepts and symbols worked their way into Indian society in this way it would not always be easy to tell Muslims from Hindus on the basis of their religious vocabulary. In fact such distinctions acquired importance mainly beginning with the British period, when the colonial government began conducting censuses and applying their own social categories to the subject population.

Still, even to this day in India one finds ostensible Hindus, Christians, Jains, and Sikhs visiting the shrines of Muslim saints, and vice versa. While men too participate in shrine culture, especially festivals, on a daily basis the normative influence of the mosque is more open to them, whereas women's access to "Islamic" teaching is more through the shrines.

At the upper end of society, women often appear as key figures in giving space to new religious ideas. Foreign missionaries are often given audiences with royal wives—whether because their husbands were too busy or the women simply more spiritually curious is unclear—and wealthy women are often memorialized as patrons of religious endowments. The problem for us is that women left few written records of their own; thus, as for the masses in general, we must attempt to recover their voices and experiences mostly by reading between the lines of the historical texts written by elite males, apart from rare exceptions.[34]

One such exception is found among the fourth-century Sogdian letters from Dunhuang discovered by Aurel Stein—two of them are from the stranded wife of a traveling businessman. The picture is a sad one: her first letter is to her wayward husband, who has left her in a far off land with no means of subsistence. "Surely the gods were angry with me on the day when I did your bidding," she tells him. "I would rather be a dog's or a pig's wife than yours!" In a second letter, addressed to her mother back in Samarkand, she complains, "I live wretchedly, without clothing, without money; I ask for a loan, but no one consents to give me one, so I depend on charity from the priest."[35]

While women's history is only recently beginning to emerge as a corrective to the established male-oriented view, it is likely that female-centered patterns of religious education within the family existed in many different historical contexts. That is a matter for future research, but women's roles may be borne in mind as one seeks to understand the various expressions of religious syncretism that continuously emerge from within the multicultural and cosmopolitan societies of the Silk Road.

Other Historical Problems

The largely unwritten history of women and nonelite men—most of whom were not literate and did not leave texts representing their views—is not the only obstacle to reconstructing the history of premodern cultures. Another fundamental problem, especially acute in the study of religious traditions, is determining which ideas can be attributed specifically to each of them. Especially as we go further back into prehistory and perceive borrowings between traditions, it is far from clear in many cases which culture borrowed from which. Such is the case with the many shared ideas found among the ancient Semitic Israelites and the Indo-European Iranians.

A related problem is determining the very nature of any given tradition. Religious belief and behavior varies inevitably even over brief stretches of space or time, often even within the boundaries of what we consider to be a single tradition; thus, any attempt to circumscribe belief and practice within a particular definition is bound to be to some degree arbitrary. Students of religion are often no less prone than practitioners to seek a reified, "authoritative" version of a tradition, usually derived from a particular interpretation of key texts. We should recognize that an overly text-centered approach not only tacitly supports elite, often hegemonic views at the expense of the nonliterate majority, it also does little to help us reconstruct what it is that the majority actually did and believed.

Moreover, while some texts remain physically unchanged over many centuries, they are always interpreted through the filters of diverse and ever-evolving cultural lenses. We are stretching things, and possibly seriously anachronizing, if we refer to ancient Yahweh worshippers as Jews or Ahura Mazda devotees as Zoroastrians. By the same token, the beliefs of second-century Parthian Buddhists or thirteenth-century Turkish Nestorians may be hard to reconcile with standard modern definitions of Buddhism or Christianity.

A third dimension to this problem of categorization is that in any given place and time people more likely than not exhibit beliefs and practices that are to some degree heterogeneous. Where we perceive evidence of the presence of a recognizable tradition, we nevertheless often lack evidence that the people in question thought of themselves as adherents to that tradition in any way that matches what we project back onto them.

When we find, for example, material from fifth-century Central Asia that we associate with Buddhism, and other evidence we deem to be Zoroastrian, we may draw a variety of conclusions:

(1) That both Buddhist and Zoroastrian native communities existed there
(2) That both communities existed, but one was foreign and the other native
(3) That *local* religion was a mixture of Buddhism and Zoroastrianism
(4) That the original local religion, though surviving, had incorporated Buddhist and Zoroastrian elements

In actual fact it is very difficult, if not impossible, to settle on any of these interpretations definitively. What we can observe is that in general, the further a community is from centers of religious authority, the more localized and heterogeneous its forms of expression.

This brings us to yet another unresolved question, which concerns the extent of conversion to a given tradition in any particular place and time, or its proportional representation within the society. Even when we can obtain strong evidence for the presence of an identifiable tradition—say, a monastery containing canonical works in its library and bearing standard iconography on its walls—we often cannot extrapolate with any real accuracy how pervasive that tradition was.

We know that under the Uighur kings in the eighth and ninth centuries Manichaeism attained official status for the only time in its career. But despite its being the state religion, the mass of the population cannot have converted to it, for we see simultaneous evidence for the presence of Buddhists, Christians, and for the persistence of the traditional Turkic shamanistic religion in Uighur society.

Likewise, the decline of Zoroastrianism, Buddhism, Manichaeism, and Christianity along the Silk Road, though a historical fact, is very difficult to trace with any sort of precision. Once the absence of evidence is complete, we can say with relative certainty that by that point a tradition has been extinguished. But if, for example, we find no Nestorian relics in Central Asia that date later than the mid-fourteenth century, neither does that tell us how numerous the Christians were who produced those last relics, nor does it tell us when the last practicing Nestorian died or converted to Islam.

Manichaeism in China ceases to be identifiable as a distinct tradition by the sixteenth century; yet, in recent years, a Manichaean temple has been found in Fujian province. (The locals thought it was Buddhist, until a team of Swedish archaeologists informed them otherwise.)[36] Clearly, any observations regarding the existence and the survival of religious ideas, along the Silk Road or anywhere else in world history, ought to be advanced with humility.

Chapter Two

Religion and Trade in Ancient Eurasia

Archaeological evidence suggests that urban-based political structures in the Oxus region began to develop from the early part of the first millennium BCE. To the north, within the vast swath of steppelands reaching across the Asian continent from above the Black Sea all the way to the frontiers of China, the culture was mainly nomadic or seminomadic. As urbanization developed, the pastoral peoples of the Eurasian steppe entered into a long, rocky partnership with settled civilization that lasted for well over 2,500 years, until the present century when "modernizing" governments began forcibly resettling nomadic groups and bringing their age-old way of life to an end.

In a 1928 book Harold Peake and Herbert John Fleure conceptualized this symbiotic relationship as "the Steppe and the Sown," a framework that remains popular among many who study the social history of Central Asia. According to this model, Central Asian history is defined largely by the dynamics of nomadic-sedentary relations, often hostile, even violent, but always mutually interdependent.[1]

Specifically, the relationship meant that pastoral peoples would provide raw materials, such as wool and leather from their herds, to be processed by the oasis dwellers who would offer back manufactured goods in exchange. On a different level, the nomads would often attack and plunder the settled folk, like wolves raiding chicken coops.[2] Having taken their fill, they might then recede again to the steppes. Or, seduced by the fleshpots of civilization, they might stay on and assimilate, often taking their place as the new ruling class, thereby injecting new blood and new energy into a decadent society. Inevitably conquerors from the steppe who chose to settle in the cities would adopt the culture of those they had conquered, and become in their turn the champions and defenders of that culture. This pattern repeats itself again and again over the course of three millennia.

In most cases the dominant peoples of the Eurasian steppe have belonged to either the Iranian or Turkic language families. Although the Iranian tongues, being Indo-European, are distinct from the Altaic Turkic dialects, the speakers themselves have often been less easy to distinguish, since their shared history has provided them with many shared traits, ideas, and ways of life. This includes the Iranian and Turkic languages themselves, as can be seen in the bilingualism that remains in some parts of Central Asia to this day.

The same is true for religious beliefs, practices, and myths. Many of the religious concepts of the ancient Iranian peoples can be fitted more or less neatly into the scheme of Indo-European religion and social structure, as reconstructed by Georges Dumézil and others.[3] But in many cases the same phenomena are observable among the Ural-Altaic peoples as well. It has been suggested that such widespread phenomena as horse nomadism, fire worship, exposure of the dead, and the concept of universal dominion granted by a sky god were all borrowed from the Indo-European Aryans by other steppe peoples further east—but this is largely a matter of speculation.[4]

In ancient Eurasian as in other primal societies, religion manifested itself mainly through rituals of daily life, such as in preparation for hunting, funeral rites, and so on.. Archaeological remains are the primary source for reconstructing these ancient religious rites and beliefs. The tripartite pyramidal structure of Indo-European society posited by Dumézil, consisting of priests, warriors, and pastoralists, seems to be reflected in the earliest building foundations uncovered at Dashly (in northern Afghanistan) and elsewhere. These appear to take the form of sacred triads: three gates, nine towers.[5] Burial sites also show evidence of animal sacrifice, especially horses, but also dogs and oxen. The graves often have wooden covers held up by posts, just as described in the Rig Veda text of the ancient Indo-European migrants to India, often referred to as the Indo-Aryans.[6]

In another parallel with the Indian culture depicted in the Rig Veda, proto-Iranians of the steppes relied heavily on horse-drawn chariots, especially in warfare. This was likely the same vital technology that enabled the Indo-Aryans to subdue the northern Indian subcontinent, and other Indo-European groups to overrun Europe. As noted earlier, it was upon the steppes of western Central Asia that the horse was first domesticated and hitched up to a chariot—probably in the area of modern Ukraine—although riding horseback appears to have been a later innovation.[7] Significantly, a horse-drawn chariot is the means by which the ancient Iranians believed the soul departs this world, while in Greek myth it is the means by which Apollo conveys the sun across the sky.

Other beliefs characteristic of the ancient Iranians are described in classical Greek accounts of various Iranian tribes known to them, especially the Sakas, or Scythians.[8] The Sakas believed that the implements they considered most important—the yoke, the plow, the spear, and the chalice—were divine gifts. They had a cult of the horse, believing the horse to be an intermediary between this world and the next. The steppe Iranians' reverence for horses is seen in the frequency of horse motifs in Saka art, a theme that is found in the funerary art of the steppes at least as late as the sixth century CE. Horse sacrifice among the Sakas is mentioned by Herodotus, as is a water taboo and the making of drinking vessels from the skulls of slain enemies; all these customs are found later among various Turkic peoples.[9]

The Sakas also had a fire cult, and a related cult of the sun. Herodotus quotes Tomyris, queen of the Massagatae tribe, as swearing "by the Sun our master" and says of them that "The only god they worship is the sun, to which they sacrifice horses: the idea behind this is to offer the swiftest animal to the swiftest of gods."[10]

Herodotus elsewhere states that the supreme Saka god was named Tabiti, whom he equates with the Greek Hestia.[11] The Greeks observed religious images, altars, and temples to be in use among the Sakas. They noted the existence of a figure known as an *enaree*, a sort of effeminate divination expert. Greek writers commented on the Sakas' elaborate funeral and burial rites, and on their efforts to protect ancestral tombs.[12] One Saka tribe, the Argippaei, were mentioned by Herodotus as having a special sacred status that protected them from attack by neighboring tribes and enabled them to serve as arbitrators in disputes.[13]

As in ancient Greece, local religious activity in the Iranian world often centered on worship of a mythical hero. In Bukhara the major cult focused on the heroic figure of Siyavash. He appears later as a character in the Persian national epic, the *Shāh-nāmeh,* or "Book of Kings," which the tenth-century poet Abo'l-Qasem Ferdowsi, like his Greek counterpart Homer, redacted from a variety of ancient oral traditions.

Generally speaking the Iranian tribes tended to dominate the western part of the Eurasian steppe, and the Altaic peoples the east, although there were Altaic groups in the region of the Ural mountains and elsewhere and Indo-Europeans at least as far east as the Tarim basin of modern Xinjiang.[14] Thus, we must turn to Chinese sources for references to the Altaic peoples. The earliest mentions of the Xiongnu (third century BCE to second century CE) state that, like the Chinese, they offered sacrifices to their ancestors, and to the gods of heaven and earth, according to a seasonal ritual calendar. Furthermore, they consulted the stars and the moon before embarking on military maneuvers.[15]

A much later Western source from a sixth-century Greek envoy to Central Asia describes a Turkish funeral ceremony in which mourners lacerated their faces, and like the ancient Iranians, sacrificed horses and also servants.[16] More elaborate information is given in the earliest known inscriptions in a Turkic language, found on stone pillars by the banks of the Orkhon River in modern Mongolia, which date from the seventh century. These inscriptions specifically refer to a sky god, Tangri, and to a sacred mountain called Ötükän. Tangri comes to be identified as the supreme god of the Altaic peoples, and survives as a synonym for Allah in modern Muslim Turkey.

Zoroaster

At some point in prehistory—exactly when is not known—a religious reformer appeared among the Iranian pastoralists of Central Asia. Zarathushtra, or Zoroaster as he is known to Westerners, is believed by some to have lived as early as the thirteenth century and by others as late as the sixth BCE. His home has been placed as far west as Azerbaijan and as far east as Mongolia.[17] Zoroastrianism, the religious tradition that traces its foundations back to his teachings, is represented today by small communities of believers in India (especially Mumbai), Iran, and North America. Some compositions, actually hymns, attributed to Zoroaster himself are preserved in the sacred book of the Zoroastrians, the Avesta, in which they are known as the Gathas. These hymns are in a very old and unique Iranian dialect, close to Vedic Sanskrit, and were passed down orally for centuries before being included in the Avesta sometime in the early centuries of our era.

Zoroaster was a preacher, probably of priestly family background, who sought to reform the religious practices of his community. He opposed certain tendencies common to various Indo-European peoples, such as bull sacrifice and the ritual drinking of *haoma* (Skt. *soma*), an intoxicating beverage that perhaps accompanied bloody sacrifices.[18] (In the Rig Veda, Soma is the second most important god after Indra.) Zoroaster also singled out one god or *ahura* (Skt. *asura*) from among the Iranian pantheon for exclusive worship, and referred to this god as Ahura Mazda, or "Lord Wisdom." The other Iranian gods, the ahuras and the *daēva*s (Skt. *deva*), he demoted to demons: the English word "devil" is ultimately, like the concept itself, of Iranian origin.[19]

Thus, Zoroaster, like Moses, who may have been his contemporary, seems to have been among the earliest of the world's major religious figures to sow the seeds of monotheism. His vision differed from that of the ancient Israelites, however, in that it accounted for evil by positing the existence of an evil deity, Angra Mainyu (Ahriman). For this reason Zoroastrianism is sometimes characterized as a dualistic, rather than a monotheistic religion.

A general assumption is often made that the various Iranian peoples of "greater Iran"—a cultural area that stretched from Mesopotamia and the Caucasus into Khwarazm, Transoxiana, Bactria, and the Pamirs and included Persians, Medes, Parthians, and Sogdians, among others—were all "Zoroastrian" in pre-Islamic times. As one writer recently put it, "After the conversion of King Vishtasp [by Zoroaster], all of Iran is thought to have become Zoroastrian, and it continued to be so up to the end of the Sassanian empire."[20] This view, though common even among serious scholars, is almost certainly overstated.[21] While the various Iranian peoples did indeed share a common pantheon and pool of religious myths and symbols, in actuality a variety of deities were worshipped—particularly Mithra, the god of covenants, and Anahita, goddess of the waters, but also many others—depending on the time, place, and particular group concerned.

The fact is that while Zoroastrianism, like Judaism, has ancient roots, both religions are essentially products of the Christian era. Zoroastrianism was first codified only from the third century CE as the official state religion of the Iranian Sasanian Empire, anywhere from 1,000 to 1,500 years after the life of Zoroaster. Rabbinical Judaism began to take shape around the same time, as did canonical Christianity, and in all three cases the process was a dynamic one lasting several centuries.

Thus, what is known of Sasanian Zoroastrianism does not necessarily describe the religious beliefs and practices of ancient Iran. In fact, no known Achæmenid sources even mention the prophet Zoroaster, though, curiously, contemporary Greek sources do. One should be wary of projecting back onto Achæmenid- and Parthian-era Iranians the "Zoroastrian" tradition in its Sasanian form.[22] The same is all the more true for Central Asia. It is perhaps safer to speak of "Mazda-worshippers" when referring to peoples—including the Achaemenids and many others—who venerate Ahura Mazda (indeed, historically that is how Zoroastrians have called themselves), but this would not necessarily include many Iranian groups who held Mithra or other gods in higher esteem.

We can in any case speak of Iranian religion in a broad sense, by identifying certain elements that clearly belong to an Iranian religious "pool" of myths, deities, symbols, and rituals. Iranian religion can then be understood in its various local contexts to be made up largely of elements drawn from this pool. The mix varies depending on the time and locale, with different elements having greater or lesser relative weight, or none at all, and with diverse non-Iranian regional elements filtering in.

It appears that before as well as after Zoroaster many Iranian communities considered the sun to be the visible form of Ahura Mazda. Assyrian inscriptions give the form Asara Mazas (proto-Iranian *Asura mazdas*), and in the Saka language *urmaysde* is the word for sun.[23] The sun, and its earthly analogue, fire, both served to purify. It is worth noting that the Indo-Aryans worshipped Agni, the god of fire, and that the Indian practice of purifying the bodies of the dead on funeral pyres has at its root the same purpose as the Iranian practice of exposing their remains to the sun. As one scholar has remarked, " . . . fire and light are purifying agents, destroying dead matter and releasing the nonmaterial soul to paradise. Paradise itself is conceived of, in both cases, as a place of light."[24]

A moon cult also figured in the Iranian religious world. The moon was equated with the figure of a heavenly bull, which was widespread in ancient times, especially in Mesopotamia. In the Avestan language the moon is called *gao chithra*, "having bull semen." According to Iranian myth all earthly animals were born of this semen, while plants were created from its dripping onto the ground. Evidence of bull worship from the early second millenium BCE has been found at Altin Tepe in present-day Turkmenistan. It has been suggested that the Makh temple at Bukhara mentioned in early Islamic sources was originally a temple of the moon (cf. Pers. *māh*, "moon").[25]

Perhaps the most visible element of Iranian religion is the festival of the new year, called *Nō rūz* ("new day"), held at the vernal equinox. This pan-Iranian festival seems to have originally been connected with Jamshid (Av. Yima), the "Primordial Man" figure in Iranian mythology, though its distant origins are likely Mesopotamian.

In Achæmenid times quite a few of the Iranian deities that Zoroaster had attempted to demote to demons were still present in the Iranian religious pantheon even in the central Persian lands. The royal inscriptions of Darius I criticized the Sakas and Elamites for not worshipping Ahura Mazda,[26] indicating the official primacy the Achæmenid elites accorded to that god, but we have little record of the religious beliefs and practices of the Iranian masses. An abundance of evidence from the later Achæmenid period indicates that the most popular deity became Anahita, goddess of the waters, originally the Mesopotamian goddess Ishtar.

In Central Asia, the Achæmenid rulers attempted to impose a calendar based on their own religious festivals, but this does not appear to have been a great success. The Sogdians substituted names of their own for most of the months, and invented new names for the intercalary days, which, in the words of W.B. Henning, "shows little regard for the Amesha Spentas ['Bounteous Immortals,' considered in Zoroastrianism to be aspects of Ahura Mazda] and lack of familiarity with the Gathas."[27] Moreover, Sogdian and Bactrian texts and inscriptions indicate the worship of a range of Iranian and non-Iranian deities, including the Greek goddess Demeter and the Indian god Shiva. As Nicholas Sims-Williams observes, "[O]ne of the most notable features of the traditional east Iranian religion revealed by the discoveries of the twentieth century is the extent to which it differs from that of the Avestan and Pahlavi books."[28]

Among the divinities popular in Central Asia was Baga (cf. Skt. Bagha, Rus. Bog), a god associated with wine and marriage.[29] The Sogdian "Ancient Letters," documents from near Dunhuang, which probably date to around 313 CE, before Buddhism, Christianity, or Manichaeism took hold among the Sogdians, mention only "the lord of the temple" *(Vgnpt)* and not the chief of the magi *(mogrt)*, leading us to understand that the former was more important in the Sogdian world even in the early Sasanian period.[30] The goddess Nanai, a local analogue to Anahita imported from Mesopotamia, is frequently mentioned . The figure of the devil carries a distinctly Sogdian name, Shimnu, which is derived independently of the Avestan Angra Mainyu.[31] In light of so many local differences, applying the term "Zoroastrian" to the religion of Central Asia's Iranian peoples hardly seems justified.

The Encounter of Iranian and Judean Religion

The Israelite monarchy established in Palestine by King David in the tenth century BCE was obliterated by powers from the East in two major stages, beginning in the eighth century BCE and concluding in the sixth. The Assyrians crushed the northern kingdom of Israel in 722 and forcibly relocated its inhabitants to other parts of their empire. The Book of II Kings states that Ten Tribes of Israel were exiled to "Halah and Habor by the River Gozan and in the cities of the Medes" (18: 11). Since the former locations have been situated in the eastern Iranian region of Khurasan, the Israelite presence in Central Asia can be considered as originating at that time.[32] It has accordingly been proposed that these earliest exiles may have engaged in long-distance overland trade.[33] Such hypotheses are not implausible, but solid evidence is lacking.

The southern kingdom of Judah managed to survive for another century and a half through diplomacy, but in 586 a new power, the Babylonians, put an end to Judean independence, destroying Jerusalem and its Temple, which had been the center of the priest-dominated sacrificial religion of the Israelites since the time of King Solomon. Like the Assyrians, the Babylonians deported the Judean survivors to Mesopotamia to work as slaves.

Less than 50 years later, in 539 a Persian army under Cyrus the Great conquered Babylon and freed the various enslaved peoples there, including the Judeans. Allowed to return home to Judah, most Judeans chose instead to stay in Babylon as free citizens of the new Persian Empire, or elected to try their luck elsewhere in the Persian-controlled lands. Many relocated eastward to Iran proper and laid the foundations for Jewish communities that have survived there to the present day, especially in the cities of Hamadan (ancient Ecbatana) and Esfahan.

As Cyrus had also made conquests to the east, as far as Bactria and Sogdiana, it is likely that some of the Babylonian Jews relocated to those provinces as well. The Book of Esther states in several places (3:6, 8; 8:5, 12; and 9:20) that the Jews lived "in all the provinces" of the Persian Empire. The modern-day Jewish communities of Bukhara and Samarkand, in particular, like to trace their history back to Assyrian times, and consider themselves to be descended from the Ten Tribes.[34] Though this origin is affirmed by Saadia Gaon of Fayyum in the tenth century,[35] there is no direct evidence for Jewish presence in Central Asia earlier than the Achæmenid period as described in the Book of Esther.

It does seem likely that many of the post-exilic Judean settlers in Persian lands took up commerce. It would have been consistent with later patterns for them to set up trade networks with relatives or other Judeans in other parts of the Persian Empire or elsewhere. Roman sources show that by Parthian times both Palestinian and Babylonian Jews were involved in the silk trade from China. Hebrew names appearing on pottery fragments from Marv dating from the first to the third centuries CE attest to the presence of Jews living along the Silk Road at that time.[36] Because Jews were spread across a wide geographical area spanning both the Parthian and the Roman lands, they were ideally situated to participate in trade between the two empires.[37]

Iranian Influences on Judaism

Influences picked up by Jewish communities in one cultural environment could easily travel to connected communities in another. Beginning in the Persian period and continuing through Hellenistic and Parthian times, a number of Iranian beliefs and concepts began to work their way into the religious outlook of the Judeans, a tradition that would later evolve into Judaism.[38]

Eschatological ideas such as warnings of the "last days" and belief in a messianic savior, a bodily resurrection, and a last judgment are just some of the notions that Judaism (and subsequently Christianity and Islam) seems to have borrowed from the Persians. The concepts of a heavenly paradise (Old Pers. *pairi daēza*) and a hell of punishment for the wicked are also seen in ancient Iranian religion, but not in Israelite sources prior to the Babylonian period. The Iranian evil spirit Angra Mainyu, or Ahriman, evolves into the Christian and Muslim devil, who first appears in the book of Job as *ha-satan*, "the accuser." The concept of angels and demons, likewise, seems to derive from Iranian beliefs. Ancient Iranian cosmology, with its numerology based on the number seven, may be the precedent for later evolutions in Greek philosophy and in Jewish, Christian, and Muslim mysticism.[39]

The biblical Book of Esther, composed apparently in Iran sometime in the fourth century before the Common Era, provides one of the most explicit examples of interaction between the Iranian and Israelite religious traditions. It also provides the earliest record of numerous Iranian cultural traditions, such as court protocol, which continue to be attested through the Islamic period. The drinking custom mentioned in Esther 1: 8 and echoed in the tenth-century Arab writer al-Jahiz, is one example. Others are the function of the chamberlain in Esther 6: 4-5, and the role of eunuchs in 1: 10.[40]

The Book of Esther has been shown to contain numerous elements derived from Iranian religion. The plotter Teresh and the disloyal minister's evil wife, Zeresh, appear to be reflections of the demons Taurvi and Zairik in the Avesta. Together they can be seen to represent the Iranian paradigm of "the lie" (drūj) opposed to the king's law (dātā), and by extension lewdness versus chastity, and violence versus the pacifism of the righteous.[41]

The Jewish festival of Purim, which comes out of the Esther story, was likely derived from the ancient Iranian springtime festival of Fravardigan, which, like Purim, began on the fourteenth day of the month of Azar and included an exchange of gifts.[42]

Like some other Indo-European peoples, Iranians believed time would end in a great apocalyptic event. This final catastrophe (which is known as Ragnarök in later Scandinavian mythology) was called Frasho-kereti ("the making glorious"), or Fraoshkart, by the ancient Iranians. It is surely no coincidence that the apocalyptic writings of Jewish tradition, such as those found in the books of Ezekiel and Daniel, appear in the context of the Babylonian captivity and after.

Iranian origins have even been seen in aspects of the Christian apocalypse of St. John the Divine. The passage in Revelation 11: 1-2 prophesying that Jerusalem, but not its Temple, would be destroyed is derived from an earlier Jewish apocalyptic text written in Greek, the Oracles of Hystaspes. The latter work, composed most likely in Parthia, was in turn based on an old Iranian story about King Vishtaspa, the royal convert won over by Zoroaster; the anonymous Jewish author presumably sought thereby to imbue his tale with the authority of an ancient Iranian prophecy.[43] Eventually the "Great King" of the original magian story evolved into the figure of Christ in the Revelation of John. Thus, over a period of centuries, what had originally been a uniquely Iranian eschatology was developed into a Hellenic, and eventually Christian concept.[44]

It has been observed that concepts apparently Iranian in origin become most evident in Jewish sources not from the Persian period (the sixth to the fourth centuries BCE), but later during the Hellenistic period, when they become evident in Greek-ruled Palestine.[45] This supports the theory that Iranian ideas found their way into Jewish culture through the agency of Jews who had settled in the Iranian world, and were thus immersed in Iranian culture. Iranian Jews would then have transmitted these ideas westward to the Jewish communities of the Mediterranean lands with which they remained in contact. We have seen that the basis of this preserved contact was, to a significant extent at least, Jewish involvement in long-distance trade.

Judaism in East Asia

A single stone inscription from a synagogue in Kaifeng along the lower reaches of the Yellow River offers a tantalizing suggestion regarding the earliest Jewish presence in East Asia. The inscription, which dates from 1663, reads:

> The religion started in *T'ien-chu* (lit. "India," but probably just meaning the West), and was first transmitted to China during the Chou (the Zhou dynasty, ca.1100-221 BCE). A *tz'u* (ancestral hall) was built in Ta-liang (Kaifeng). Through the Han, Tang, Sung, Ming, and up till now, it has undergone many vicissitudes.[46]

If we are to believe this inscription, the Jewish community discovered at the turn of the twentieth century in eastern China would appear to have been founded by traders who came to East Asia, presumably via the Silk Road, prior to the end of the third century BCE. It has even been suggested that this process was already occurring in the time of King David! Supporters of the latter theory point to terms in the Hebrew Bible that they take to mean "silk," although detractors point out that these meanings are far from established.[47] For a long time enthusiasts identified "the land of Sinim" in Deutero-Isaiah with China, a connection since disproven.[48] In 1993 archaeologists in Egypt found a sample of silk dating to the tenth century BCE,[49] and Israelite traders are perhaps as likely as anyone to have played a role in bringing it there. One might say that to argue Jews *may* have participated in trans-Asian trade from the earliest times is fine, but so far the more extreme dates are purely speculative.

Unfortunately the Kaifeng inscription is uncorroborated by any other piece of evidence, and may just reflect the Chinese Jewish community's boldest claim to antiquity in its own origin myth. An earlier inscription from 1512 and a slightly later one from 1679 both date the Jews' first arrival in China to the Han period (202 BCE–221 CE). Consistent with this dating, some Chinese Jews told a Jesuit missionary in the early eighteenth century that according to their own oral tradition, their ancestors had first come from Persia during the reign of Mingdi (58–75 CE).[50] The Kaifeng community, meanwhile, appears to have arrived by sea no earlier than the ninth century CE, separately and distinctly from the Jews who had come overland into Chinese territory much earlier.[51]

Iranians and Judeo-Persians on the Ancient Silk Road

Although firm evidence is lacking, it is not unlikely that both Iranian and Judeo-Persian merchants were active along the Silk Road from a very early time. Naturally their religious ideas would have accompanied them on their travels, and therefore would have become familiar to peoples encountered by these merchants along the way. Based on a study of foreign loanwords in ancient Chinese, Sinologist Victor Mair has suggested that Iranian soothsayers were employed by the Western Zhou dynasty of China, that is, prior to the eighth century BCE.[52]

So we can say that in ancient times certain religious ideas may have spread geographically eastward, in the sense that the *possessors* of those ideas physically went there. This is not to say, however, that Iranian or Judaic religious systems "grew" or won converts. The great missionary religions had not yet entered the stage of world history.

In traditional societies, religions, like people, are generally considered as being attached to a particular locality or region, and by extension to their own local culture. From an Inner Asian or Chinese point of view, whatever religion a foreign merchant of Iranian or Israelite origin practiced was simply the home religion of the Iranians or of the Israelites; one would no more think of embracing such religion oneself than of pretending to be from Iran or Palestine.

Still, as Turks, Chinese, and other East Asian peoples came into contact with these merchants from the West and became familiar with their ways of thinking, subtle influences must have penetrated in both directions through everyday encounters and conversation. For example, it has been suggested that Daoists of the late Han period borrowed their term for "the highest heaven," *daluo,* from the Iranian *garo-dmana,* the "house of praise," the highest of the four heavens, associated with Ahura Mazda who is referred to in parts of the Avesta as Dadhvah.[53]

It has been argued by a Japanese scholar that the so-called ghost festival, an annual ritual for "feeding" untended souls that became extremely popular during the Tang period, actually had Iranian origins. The Chinese name for the festival, *Yulanben,* may be derived from the Sogdian *rw'n* ("soul"; cf. Pers. *ravān*), and a popular tale associated with the festival, in which a monk, Mulian, descends into hell to retrieve his mother, seems to be based on the Greek myth of Dionysos and Semele.[54] There is evidence for other such influences from the early centuries of our era,[55] but similar exchanges of ideas may have been going on much earlier, and if Iranian soothsayers did serve the Zhou, they probably were.

Chapter Three

Buddhism and the Silk Road

Sometime from the seventh to the fourth century BCE in northeastern India lived a man named Siddhartha Gautama, who came to be known as the Buddha, or "Enlightened One."[1] A spiritual reformer who sought a "Middle Path" between worldliness and asceticism, the Buddha preached a message based on Four Noble Truths: that life is suffering, that there is a cause of that suffering, namely, desire, that there is a way to end suffering, and that the way is by following an Eightfold Path of right opinion, right thought, right speech, right activity, right livelihood, right effort, right attention, and right concentration. In contrast to a localized approach to religion that seems to have pertained in ancient human societies, the Buddha taught that his analysis was universal, that it was true for all people everywhere regardless of their culture.

During his lifetime the Buddha founded a quadrapartite community of followers, called the *sangha*, divided between male and female monks and laity. In practical terms, the role of the laity was to support financially the monastic class. Soon Buddhist monks and merchants were traveling throughout India and beyond, spreading the Buddha's universal message. This was the first large-scale missionary effort in the history of the world's religions, and its spread was tied to that of economic networks.

Though marginal at first, Buddhist activity received a boost under Emperor Ashoka of the Maurya dynasty (r.ca. 268-239 BCE). According to the popular version of the story, Ashoka came to feel remorse for all the death and suffering his military conquests had caused, and became attracted to Buddhism, raising it to official status (though not state religion) within his vast northern Indian empire. Whether or not he actually became a Buddhist himself, or whether he had motivations other than ethical ones, is not entirely clear.[2]

Since the time of the Buddha the leading Buddhist monks had held two councils in an attempt to resolve disagreements over correct doctrine and practice.[3] A surviving legend states that Ashoka, troubled by these disputes, called a third council in 244 BCE in order to formulate a Buddhist orthodoxy.[4] In the event this third council, if it happened, only intensified the divisions.

Traditional views have it that the dispute within the sangha centered on a controversy regarding the nature of the monks who had attained Enlightenment, referred to as *arhats*. Five theses were proposed, purportedly by a monk named Mahadeva, that challenged the status of the arhats by suggesting that they were still subject to worldly distractions such as erotic dreams, residue ignorance, lingering doubts, and so forth.

Another argument was that the arhats' approach restricted the possibility of Enlightenment to a very small group of people. Yet another layer of disagreement had to do with the infiltration of popular religious practices into the tradition, especially the veneration of relics of the Buddha. The more "conservative" monks felt that this type of innovation was a threat to the purity of the Buddha's message and to the rigor of commitment to a Buddhist lifestyle.

The conservatives, according to the traditional view, defended the arhats' exalted status as leaders within the community, while the majority supported the five theses that aimed at bringing the arhats down from their pedestal of privilege. The conservative party came to be known as the Sthaviras, and their opponents, the Mahasanghikas, or "the majority community."[5]

Recently some scholars of early Buddhism have sought to revise this version of history, suggesting that much of the disagreement may actually have come later, and gotten projected backward as a "historical" explanation for existing schisms. It may be that the central point of tension within the early sangha was over additions to the body of rules governing the monastic lifestyle, called the *vinaya*. A majority of monks rejected the adding of new rules, accepting as binding only those laid down by the Buddha himself. According to this more recent interpretation the Sthaviras were those seeking to "reform" the vinaya by adding to it; the Mahasangikas, who claimed to possess the older, shorter version, were therefore the "conservative" party.[6]

To complicate matters further, there evolved diverse schools of commentary on the Buddha's teaching. Each of these schools, which were collectively known as *nikaya*, compiled its own canon of texts purporting to be the Buddha's teaching, along with the particular interpretations of it that they considered to be authentic and authoritative. Legend states there were 18 such schools. Many have left texts, but the only school surviving to the present day is the Theravada (Skt. Sthaviravada, lit., "the way of the elders"), which is the dominant form of Buddhism in Sri Lanka and Southeast Asia.

Buddhism has produced a body of texts more vast than any other movement in human history, making the study of even one school a potentially lifelong task. A Chinese colleague relates that when beginning his graduate study he was issued the following warning by his professors: "The serious study of Buddhism is a Black Hole—if you enter, you will never re-emerge!"[7]

Buddhist Schools of the Silk Road

Since most of the early Buddhist schools no longer exist, their thought must be reconstructed on the basis of surviving texts. The available texts even of defunct schools date to hundreds of years after these schools arose, so it is difficult to know the positions of the various early schools and their relationship to each other with any certitude.

The major Nikaya schools connected with the regions traversed by the Silk Road were the Dharmaguptakas and the Sarvastivadins. The Mahasanghikas were also active early on. The alternative approach, a more inclusive movement that came to be known as the Mahayana, or "Great Vehicle," first gained influence in Central Asian regions such as Khotan, before eventually displacing the Nikaya schools from the Silk Road altogether.

The Mahasanghikas

The Mahasanghika attempt to reduce the singular importance of the arhat ideal, or perhaps simply their resistance to innovations in the vinaya, created the first great schism within the Buddhist community.

Many of the Mahasangikas also believed that intuition *(prajñā)* happened instantaneously, and not gradually as the Sarvastivadins and others taught; this idea later became central in the Mahayana as well, especially in its Zen form.

The famous colossal Buddha statues at Bamiyan in Afghanistan, which until their destruction by the Taliban in 2001 stood 150 feet high carved into a rock cliff face, may have been the work of Mahasanghikas in the northwest.

The Dharmaguptakas

The Dharmaguptaka school was probably the most influential along the Silk Road up to the time of the Kushan Empire in the first centuries of the Common Era. The Dharmaguptakas wrote their texts mainly in Gandhari Prakrit, the dominant vernacular language of the Kushan heartland in northwestern India. Many Dharmaguptaka texts were transmitted to China by early Central Asian missionaries. By the seventh century, however, the school had disappeared from India completely and had very few representatives left in Central Asia.

The Dharmaguptaka school appears to have been distinguished primarily by its doctrine that the Buddha was separate from, and superior to, the Buddhist community, and not a part of it as other schools believed. A practical ramification of this attitude was the belief that only gifts given to the Buddha could bring merit, and not gifts to the community. Since the monastic community depended for its survival on gifts from lay followers, this doctrine may have played a role in the school's ultimate decline.

The Sarvastivadins

The name of this school derives from the phrase *sarvam asti*, "everything exists," which characterized its theory of time. According to this view, the past, present, and future all exist simultaneously. According to Theravada tradition, one of the main accomplishments of the third Buddhist council called by Ashoka was the rejection of the Sarvastivadins.

If true, this may have been a factor in pushing the Sarvastivadin school into Central Asia. By the second century the Dharmaguptakas were losing ground to the Sarvastivadins there. Unlike other schools that used Pali or other regional languages, the Sarvastivadins wrote their texts for the most part in Sanskrit, the ancient priestly language, in an archaizing attempt to give their works a higher authoritative character. (It is worth noting here that in most traditional societies the past holds great weight, so when it comes to models of authority, "the older the better." Religious thinkers seeking to propagate new ideas and interpretations—Jewish rabbis of the Talmudic period are a good example—usually try to present them as the "authentic" teaching of some remote historical figure, rather than as something original. This can make it difficult to assign a precise date to written texts, which are often claimed to be much older than their written forms.)

The Mahayana

The Mahayana was not a school per se, but rather a "pan-Buddhist movement" defined mainly by the acceptance of new scriptures.[8] The origins of the self-styled "Greater Vehicle" to Enlightenment are not fully clear, and may never be. The interpretation of earlier scholarship that saw the tradition as growing out of the Mahasanghika school is no longer generally accepted, but the question of whether the Mahayana arose primarily within the lay or the monastic community continues to be debated.[9]

The Mahayana movement, which appears to have been rather small at first, probably began in northwestern India or Central Asia during the first century BCE. Although a few Mahayana scriptures were recently discovered in northern Pakistan, many of what would later become the main Mahayana texts were probably composed in Central Asia along the Silk Road, where the constant mixing of cultures and ideas must have contributed diverse influences. As one contemporary scholar has cautiously put it, "[I]t is just possible that the popularization of the Mahayana was a phenomenon which took place outside the Indian subcontinent, for reasons connected perhaps with the transmission of Buddhism to other cultures."[10]

Among the distinctive themes of the new scriptures was an elevation of the Buddha to the "supramundane" *(lokattara)*, reflected in the belief that his death was a mere appearance (an idea adopted from the Mahasanghikas). There was also an emphasis on compassion for the less fortunate, and most importantly, the idea that all beings contain "the buddha-nature" *(tathagatha)* and should aspire to no less than full buddhahood. One who embarked upon this quest toward becoming a buddha was known as a *bodhisattva*, a state considered superior to that of an arhat.

A bodhisattva can be defined as one who vows to be reborn as many times as it takes to work toward becoming a full buddha, for the sake of helping all sentient beings to salvation. This is contrasted in the Mahayana "Perfection of Wisdom" literature *(Prajñāparamita)* with the narrower goal of purely personal salvation that characterized the traditional approach.[11] An additional element of early Mahayana works is a strong hostility toward those who wouldn't accept the new texts as authentic.[12] Eventually Mahayanists began to derisively refer to the traditional schools as *Hinayana,* the "Lesser Vehicle."

Furthermore, while schools such as the Theravada can be considered atheistic, the Mahayana expression eventually allowed for treating buddhas and bodhisattvas as divinities. According to some Mahayana interpretations, bodhisattvas who acquired more merit than they needed could pass it on to others. Devotees would therefore often pray to the Buddha or boddhisattvas to help save them from the cycle of rebirth into the world *(samsāra).*

The Mahayana did not develop its own vinaya, however. Instead, monks followed the rules laid down by the Nikaya school of their preference. Thus, while the Mahayana tradition largely displaced Nikaya schools from China, Chinese monks continued to follow the vinaya of either the Sarvastivada or the Dharmaguptaka school, precisely those that were the first to dominate the Silk Road.[13]

What is true of all the schools is that their activities had an important economic dimension. Traveling Buddhists, whether monks or businessmen, would come to the attention of local elites who would perceive advantages in associating themselves with the international networks these Buddhists were creating. Often they would support them through the building of monasteries, which became centers for the increasingly global Buddhist economy, enriched by the lands they controlled and by the donations of passing travelers seeking blessing and protection. This symbiotic relationship pattern was followed by Christians, Manichaeans, and Muslims later on.

The Gandhara Synthesis and the Kushans

It is certainly consistent with this later reality that according to a legend preserved in Pali, the language of the Theravada canon, Silk Road merchants began spreading the Buddha's teaching even in his lifetime. This legend relates that two brothers from Bactria (medieval Balkh, in the north of Afghanistan), named Tapassu and Bhallika, visited the Buddha in the eighth week after his Enlightenment and immediately became his disciples. According to the story, the brothers then returned to Bactria and built temples dedicated to the Buddha.[14]

While there is no evidence to confirm the legend of Tapassu and Bhallika, edicts inscribed on rock pillars set up by Ashoka several centuries later state that he sent missionaries into his northwestern territories.[15] Over the following centuries Bactria did become a major Buddhist region, and remained so up to the Muslim conquests. In the seventh century, on the eve of the Arab invasions, the Chinese Buddhist pilgrim Xuanzang found that Balkh had some 100 Buddhist monasteries and 3,000 priests. These monasteries received substantial donations from business travelers and controlled large tracts of productive land, such that by the time of Xuanzang they formed the major economic nodes of the Silk Road.

The northwestern part of the Indian subcontinent was home to a diverse mix of cultures. It was the meeting ground between the Indian and Iranian worlds, and from the latter part of the fourth century BCE there was added a Greek presence as well. Alexander of Macedon conquered much of this territory between 332 and 327 BCE, and left in his wake a Hellenic administration that would survive in parts of Asia for another two centuries as the Seleucid dynasty.

Greek settlers in Bactria and Gandhara (what is now north-central Pakistan) brought with them the gods of the classical Greek pantheon, and have left coins and other archaeological evidence in testimony. (Bactrian, an Iranian language, was written using the Greek alphabet.) Some Greeks adopted local religions, such as the Seleucid ruler Antialcidas's ambassador Heliodoros, who erected a pillar to Vishnu at Besnagar.[16] Although evidence of widespread conversion in either direction is lacking, religious ideas must have been exchanged on some level with the native Iranian and Indian populations of those areas. Greeks in Asia, as elsewhere, attempted to identify local deities as corresponding to their own.[17]

A tale of the blinding of King Ashoka's son Kunala relayed by Xuanzang appears to be a Buddhist recasting of the Greek tragedy of Hippolytus and Phaedra. Xuanzang reports that in the seventh century blind pilgrims would pray at the stupa of Kunala, near Taxila, in what is now Pakistan, for the restoration of their sight.[18] In a remarkable example of cultural continuity, a modern-day hospital there is known for the excellence of its eye facilities.[19]

As one would expect, cross-cultural influences in Gandhara went in both directions. In some cases there is evidence that local cults adopted Greek forms of worship, as at a Greek-style sanctuary to the god Vaxshu (Gk. Oxus) at Takht-i Sangin in northern Afghanistan. Or, alternatively, both Greek and Bactrian rites may have been practiced at the same temple, since it appears to be dedicated to both fire and water gods.[20] Likewise, certain Indian notions may have made their way westward into the budding Christianity of the Mediterranean world through the channels of the Greek diaspora.

Religious tolerance appears to have been the norm. The Græco-Bactrian general Menandros, who conquered part of northern India and ruled there as king from around 150 to 135 BCE, treated Buddhist communities under his control with benevolence. His memory is preserved in a Buddhist treatise called the Milindapañha, or "The Questions of Menander," a dialogue in the Platonic style between the king and an Indo-Greek monk named Nagasena.[21]

Herakles with a lion skin served as an artistic model for the Buddhist Vajrapani, a protector of the Buddha. The image of Ganymede's abduction by Zeus in the form of an eagle was taken up by Gandharan artists and recast onto a Buddhist tale, the Sussandi-jataka story of a bodhisattva who falls in love with a married woman and takes the form of the bird Garuda in order to carry her off. ("Garuda" is now the name of the national airline of predominantly Muslim Indonesia.) This image appears in Buddhist paintings and sculptures throughout the Indian subcontinent and all across the Silk Road into China; it also finds its way into Sasanian art, where it acquires a Zoroastrian interpretation.[22]

By around 130 BCE, Greek rule in Bactria had succumbed to nomadic incursions from Sakas and other steppe peoples. The Sakas too absorbed some Buddhist influence and left a number of Buddhist inscriptions. After a century or so of Saka rule, a new power, the Kushans, arose in what is now northwestern Pakistan.

The Kushans' origins are not entirely clear, although it appears they were an ethnically mixed group consisting partly of Indo-European immigrants from further east along the Silk Road, a people known to the Chinese as Yuezhi who probably spoke Tocharian.[23] They moved into the Gandhara region and seized control from the local Indo-Parthian rulers from the mid-first century onwards, and thus came to rule over a population that included native Indians, Iranian-speakers, and Greek settlers. From there they moved into northern India, giving them control over the trade routes connecting the Indian subcontinent with the Silk Road to the northwest.

Kushan coins bear images of a variety of deities, Iranian, Indic, and Buddhist, suggesting that the new ruling elite had a tolerant attitude toward diverse religions. They held the Iranian goddess Ardoxsho and the Indic god Shiva both in particularly high regard.[24] Votive figures of Hariti, the Indian goddess of smallpox, are an ominous presence of this time; the smallpox epidemic that hit the Mediterranean world during the second century BCE probably started in the Kushan lands and spread west via the trade routes.[25]

From the beginning of their rule, the Kushans adopted the symbol of the Greek Nike, goddess of victory, a clear attempt to appropriate the royal ideology of their Græco-Bactrian predecessors. Yet, the second Kushan ruler, Vima, was a devotee of Shiva. It has been suggested that Vima's sympathy for Indic religion was a reflection of his desire to gain control over the Silk Road, since by that time Indians were active in trade throughout the Oxus region and even as far as China.[26]

Vima's successor, Kanishka I (r. ca. 127–151 CE), while presumably maintaining the desire to become master of the Silk Road, turned his attention toward mustering the support of his Iranian subjects to the west. During his rule the Iranian forms of divine names reemerge from beneath the Greek ones, although Shiva retained a high official status. Buddhist legend appears to confuse him with his grandson, Kanishka II, who helped the spread of Buddhism through the building of viharas (monasteries) and stupas (temples to house relics). He is also said to have called a Buddhist council in Kashmir, in which it was decided to rewrite the original Gandhari vernacular, or "Prakrit" texts in the high literary language of Sanskrit, a turning point in the evolution of the Buddhist literary canon. Though Kanishka was not himself a convert to Buddhism, Buddhist sources refer to him as a "second Ashoka."

It is in the Kushan period that the Buddha is first depicted in human form, a development that some scholars have attributed to Greek influence. Statues and busts of the so-called Gandhara school, which developed under the Kushans, show a marked blending of Indian and Greek elements, and formed the basis for the later development of Buddhist art in China and elsewhere. A late first-century statue of the Buddha flanked by two bodhisattvas, with an inscription mentioning the transferral of merit, may be the earliest explicit evidence yet discovered of Mahayana ideas.[27]

Greek as well as Iranian influences appear to have shaped the evolution of Mahayana images (and perhaps thought as well) during the Kushan period. The most popular representation of the Buddha in Kushan art is Maitreya, the "future Buddha," some of whose soteriological and eschatological qualities seem to echo those of the Zoroastrian Saoshyant and the Jewish and Christian Messiah. In a particularly striking parallel, in Buddhist mythology, Maitreya will be welcomed by a disciple named Kasyapa; the name of a similar figure in Zoroastrianism, awaiting the Saoshyant, is Karashaspa.[28]

Later, in Manichaeism, Maitreya becomes connected with the Iranian god Mithra and with Jesus. The buddha Amitabha and bodhisattva Avalokitesvara, who figure prominently in later Chinese and Japanese expressions of Buddhism, bear features that have been associated with the Iranian gods Zurvan and Mithra. In some cases, Amitabha (which means "infinite radiance") seems to be simply understood as the Iranian god of light, equated with the sun.[29]

Stories about the life of the Buddha containing Jewish and Christian elements appear.[30] Even the Trojan horse turns up in an Indian Buddhist story—now it is a wooden elephant, however, and the besieged bodhisattva, unlike the Trojans, is not fooled.[31] All of these commonalities may reflect the attempts of Indian Buddhist missionaries to present their message through figures, terms, and symbols familiar to a Western, Græco-Iranian audience.

A third-century Chinese Buddhist source states that the Kushan lands were one of the main centers of Buddhism.[32] The Kushans may have had Buddhist texts translated into their own language and later into Sogdian for the benefit of Central Asian converts; no such translations have survived, however. Extant Sogdian translations are later, and they were done from Chinese, not Indian versions.

Sometime during the Kushan period, a monk by the name of Sutralanka, who was a native of the Kushan capital, Puskaravati (modern Charsadda, near Peshawar), traveled to Shash (modern Tashkent) in Central Asia in order to decorate a Buddhist vihara there.[33] This implies the existence of a Buddhist host audience in that part of Central Asia at the time.

Sogdiana does not appear ever to have experienced widespread conversion to Buddhism, however. Xuanzang was disappointed to see how poorly the faith was represented when he visited Samarkand in the seventh century, and a Korean Buddhist passing through several decades later found only one Buddhist monk living in a monastery.[34] Buddhism seems to have been carried further east along the Silk Road by small groups of Parthian, Sogdian, and Bactrian converts associated with diaspora merchant communities. We are faced with an apparent irony, that while Sogdians were among the principal agents in the eastward spread of Buddhism, the faith seems never to have taken root in their homeland.

By the fifth century most of the former Kushan lands were being raided and plundered by nomadic armies from the steppes to the north, known as Hephthalites or White Huns. The Hephthalites looted Buddhist monasteries, dealing a severe blow to the Buddhist culture of western Central Asia by taking away the financial base that had enabled it to thrive.

Parthian Buddhism

The Greek Seleucids were displaced in Iran and Central Asia by an eastern Iranian dynasty, the Parthians, at the beginning of the second century BCE. The Parthians became the new middlemen on the Silk Road, controlling the overland trade from China at a time when Romans were becoming passionate customers for silk.

The Silk Road city of Marv (Grk. Margiana), situated in the eastern part of the Parthian Empire, appears to have had a Buddhist community by the middle of the second century of the Common Era.[35] Several scholars have been reluctant to concede the importance of Iranian Buddhism at this early date,[36] but this appears to be for lack of familiarity with the wealth of evidence turned up in Turkmenistan by Soviet archaeologists beginning in the early 1960s.[37]

Inscriptions using the Kharosthi Indian script found in the Oxus region further east date from 58 BCE to 129 CE, attesting to the presence of Mahasangikas there.[38] Later inscriptions found in the Oxus valley belonging to the fourth and fifth centuries are in Brahmi, another Indian script. This together with the discovery of fifth-century Sarvastivadin texts in Marv suggest that the latter school, though coexisting with the Dharmaguptakas, eventually predominated in western Central Asia.[39]

The picture of Gandharan and Parthian Buddhism painted by archaeological finds from the region is dominated by various Nikaya schools. This poses an historical problem, in that a number of Parthian Buddhists who went to China are mentioned as having translated Mahayana texts there. If there was an early Mahayana presence in western Central Asia, evidence by which it can be reconstructed is still awaited.[40]

The Tarim Basin

Buddhist missionaries probably reached Khotan on the southern loop of the Silk Road skirting the Takla Makan desert sometime in the first century, although legend has it that a monk from Kashmir came there during Ashoka's reign. Khotan was inhabited by Iranian peoples. The people of Kucha north of the desert were also Indo-Europeans, whose highly archaic language, Tocharian, suggests that they were among the first Indo-European groups to leave the ancestral homeland further west.[41] Buddhist paintings found in Kucha during the early twentieth century are derived from the Gandharan style, indicating close contact between the two regions at that time. The light-complexioned figures seen in these paintings are distinctly Europoid, often blue eyed. Further east, in Miran, has been found the work of a Buddhist painter named Tita (Titus?), perhaps a Roman artist who traveled east along the Silk Road in search of employment.

The major source of Buddhist influence on Khotan in the early centuries of the Common Era seems to have been Kashmir, a predominantly Sarvastivadin region at that time. The kings of Khotan played an important role in sponsoring Buddhist schools, first the Sarvastivadins and the Mahasanghikas and later, by the fourth century, the Mahayana, which became dominant there. Still later, in the seventh century, the presence of Tantric schools can be detected.[42] In Kucha, meanwhile, the Sarvastivadins remained the favored school, and when Xuanzang visited in the seventh century he found the local monks scornful of Mahayana texts.

It may be asked, why did the kings of these oasis city-states in the Tarim basin welcome and even solicit Buddhist monks from India? While spiritual factors need not be discounted, it is certainly likely that they also saw this as a way of encouraging contact with a larger, more prosperous civilization. As we have seen, cultural exchange tends to be good for business, and vice versa.

The Arrival of Buddhism into China

During the first half of the first century before the Common Era, the Han dynasty of China succeeded in extending its power westward well into Central Asia. The pretext for this westward expansion is said to have been the Han emperor's desire for Central Asian "horses of heaven," as mentioned in chapter One. Once the Chinese controlled the eastern half of the Silk Road, Western merchants and other travelers would have had increased access to China. Thus, it is probable that foreign Buddhists entered China sometime before the Common Era.

The first clear mention of Buddhism in a Chinese source is a reference in the *Hou Han shu* (Late Han History) to a Buddhist community at the court of the governor of Chu province that included some Chinese lay followers. The governor is described as observing both Buddhist and Daoist rituals; this indicates that from its earliest penetration into Chinese culture, Buddhism had begun to blend with and adapt itself to local religion.[43] When the governor sent a gift of silk to Ming, the Han emperor, as a token of submission, the emperor sent the following reply:

> The king of Ch'u recites the subtle words of Huang-lao [a Taoist cult], and respectfully performs the gentle sacrifices to the Buddha...Let [the silk which he sent for] redemption be sent back, in order thereby to contribute to the lavish entertainment of the *upasaka*s and the *sramana*s.[44]

The fact that the emperor uses the Indian terms for lay followers and monks indicates that he was familiar with Buddhism, which must therefore have been established in China by that time. Buddhist legend has it that in that same year Emperor Ming dreamed of a "golden man." Told that he had dreamed of the Buddha, the emperor is said to have sent a request to India for Buddhist missionaries.

The first Buddhist missionary named in Chinese sources is a Parthian monk who arrived in the capital Luoyang in 148. An Shigao, as he is called in Chinese, may have been the first to organize the systematic translation of Buddhist (in his case, Nikaya) texts into Chinese. He may also have been one of the first teachers in China of the system of mental exercises known in Sanskrit as *dhyana* (Ch. *chan*, Jap. *zen*). And, consistent with the ancient pattern of royal interest in fortune-tellers, his knowledge of Western astronomy is mentioned.

Another Parthian Buddhist, a traveling merchant referred to as An Xuan, came to China in the year 181 and joined An Shigao's translation team. He is best known for participating in the translation of a Mahayana text, the *Ugrapariprccha* (Ch. *Fajing jing*). From this early date therefore Mahayana and Nikaya schools appear to have coexisted at Luoyang.

The early Mahayana in China is most commonly associated with the efforts of a translator of Kushan origin, Lokaksema, who was active at Luoyang in the last decades of the second century. The 11 earliest known Mahayana texts are Chinese translations, most of which were probably done by Lokaksema or his students.[45] Two of his three principal Chinese assistants were members of a local Daoist sect, giving further evidence of the process of syncretism at work.[46]

Other translators associated with Lokaksema included several Indians and Sogdians. Later figures bearing the Parthian surname (An), such as An Faxian and An Faqin in the third century, may also have come from Transoxiana, where a remnant Parthian administration survived through the fifth century (the western part of the empire having been conquered by the Sasanians from 226).[47]

The oasis town of Kucha on the northern branch of the Silk Road was another Buddhist center from which missionaries traveled to China proper. One Kuchean monk of mixed Indian ancestry, Kumarajiva (born in 344), became the first major translator of Mahayana texts into Chinese. Although Kucha itself was predominantly Sarvastivadin, Kumarajiva had studied Mahayana works in Kashmir as a youth, and became a proponent of the Mahayana approach on his return to Kucha. He was taken to the Chinese capital Luoyang in 402, where he stayed until his death in 412 or 415. Some 300 translations of Buddhist texts into Chinese are attributed to him.

Some scholars have doubted the Iranian role in early Buddhist penetration into East Asia, emphasizing the more direct transmission from India to China northward over the Karakorum mountains to Kashgar and the Tarim basin, and thence back again to the Iranian-inhabited regions of western Central Asia.[48] This view, however, is probably overstated. The abundance of Buddhist remains from the area of Marv dating to as early as the first century CE, as well as linguistic evidence showing the evolution of Buddhist terminology via Parthian, demonstrate that Buddhism traveled first northwest out of the subcontinent into the Iranian world, and then eastward along the Silk Road into China.[49]

This does not preclude a more or less contemporary additional channel via the Karakorum route to the Tarim basin and thence to China (as we have seen, Khotan in particular had direct links with Kashmir). And once Buddhist presence was established in China, the Silk Road offered a natural conduit by which Chinese Buddhist influences could later travel westward again through Central Asia.

The existence of Chinese Mahayana texts translated into Sogdian, by Sogdian merchants in China who had learned Chinese, suggests that this too was sometimes the case.[50] Indeed, the very idea of translating Buddhist texts into local vernaculars appears to have come to Central Asians from the Chinese; prior to the sixth century, when Buddhist texts were first translated into Central Asian tongues, Central Asians were apparently content to read them in Indian languages.[51] Xuanzang, in the seventh century, personally introduced at least one Chinese apocryphal text into India. Finding that the monks of Nalanda, one of the great Buddhist universities, were unfamiliar with The Awakening of Faith in the Mahayana, he "re-translated" this "lost" text into Sanskrit.[52]

If, in fact, the Sogdians and other West Asians began to translate sacred texts as a result of Chinese influence, we may have an example of how "language policy" can play a major role in the success of a religion. Our first evidence for mass conversion to Buddhism along the Silk Road does not come until we reach China, and if early Sogdian Buddhists, indeed, did not translate sacred texts into their native language, that may be a reason why large-scale conversions to Buddhism in the Sogdian homeland did not occur.

Political factors also affected the spread of Buddhism in China. During the rule of the Tang dynasty from 618 to 917, several emperors exhibited a marked taste for the exotic. At such times Westerners as well as Western customs and ideas were unusually welcome in China. Military successes by the Tang likewise extended the influence of Chinese culture and civilization in the direction of the West. At the greatest point of Tang expansion in the eighth century, the Silk Road was under Chinese control as far as modern-day Kyrgyzstan. The Chinese built garrison towns there as elsewhere, and the ruins of an eighth-century temple at Aq Beshim attest to the westward extension of Chinese Buddhism.[53]

Later Buddhist Movements

Pure Land

The early Buddhist idea of a "Buddha land," a paradise where the teachings of the Buddha prevail, was broadened in the Mahayana interpretation to mean that the various boddhisattvas would purify the lands where they resided. One such purified realm, called Sukhavati, the "land of bliss" (which, significantly perhaps, is located in the West), is described in two late first-century texts from northwestern India and a third compiled in Central Asia.

This land of splendor is presided over by the Buddha of Light, Amitabha, who leads his followers to salvation through his own excess of acquired merit. The devotee of Amitabha must focus on him, especially at the moment of death, in order to be transported into the Pure Land. Some have argued that this soteriology has more in common with Western notions of the time than with Indian ones, and that Iranian ideas in particular were formative in the Pure Land tradition.

The Pure Land movement spread along the Silk Road to China and Japan, where it became widely popular, especially among the lower classes to whom its very simple message of salvation appealed. To those who would criticize such an "easy" method to salvation, Pure Land teachers replied that while in the past many could follow a more rigorous path, the darkness of the present age required an easier means.

Tantra

Tantrism began sometime around the fifth or sixth century CE as a movement in eastern India. It combined rituals such as the chanting of incantations, called mantras, and the burning of sacrificial offerings, with yoga. All of these practices had precedents in Brahmanism, but were employed now in a Buddhist context. An esoteric tradition, Tantrism was transmitted secretly from teacher to disciple, at first orally.

During the early eighth century Indian monks such as Subharkara Simha, Vajrabodhi, and Amoghavajra introduced Tantra into China. The teaching briefly interested the court, but among the general populace it could not compete with sects such as the Pure Land, and Tantrism did not survive in the Tang Empire once the Indian missionaries were no longer present.[54] By contrast, Tibet proved particularly receptive to Tantrism, which became the dominant form of Buddhism there beginning in the eighth century.

Chan

A legend states that in the sixth century a Buddhist monk named Bodhidharma, who was from southern India (or possibly Iran), traveled to China in order to bring a new teaching: that the usual rituals, texts, and practices of Buddhists were ultimately useless. Instead, he offered the example of spontaneous Enlightenment, which could be attained through meditation on paradoxes, called *gong'an*s (Japanese *koan*). *Chan* (from Skt. *dhyana*, meditation), as this approach was known, shows considerable influence from Daoism, and is thus an exemplary case of Chinese culture transforming Indian ideas into Chinese ones. The tradition became known in Japan as Zen, and provided a philosophical basis for arts as diverse as samurai swordplay, haiku poetry, and the painting of watercolor landscapes.

Buddhist Pilgrims

As Buddhism won increasing numbers of native converts in China, many Chinese Buddhists came to feel dissatisfied with learning their religion through foreign intermediaries and third-hand translations of texts by Central Asians. It does, indeed, appear that in attempting to make Buddhist concepts palatable to the Chinese, missionaries and translators often took liberties in their translations of key terms and the pairing of Indian with Chinese concepts.

For example, the Indian terms *dharma* (the Buddha's teaching), *bodhi* (Enlightenment), and *yoga* were all at times rendered in Chinese as *dao* ("the way"), a word that Daoists and Confucians had each already endowed with very strong connotations of their own. The term *arhat*, similarly, was translated as *zhenren*, or "True Man," which in Daoism represented one who had mastered the arts of immortality. The ineffable *nirvana* was translated as *wu-wei* ("not-force"), a Daoist term for the ethic of passivity.[55] Ordinary phrases acquired new shades of meaning as well, as in one case in which "husband supports wife" became in Chinese "husband controls wife."

Beginning no later than 260 CE, Chinese Buddhist monks began to travel to India in order to discover for themselves the sources of their faith. Fifty-four of these pilgrims are mentioned in Chinese sources, although there were probably many more who remain anonymous. The desire of these monks to experience India firsthand went beyond the desire to acquire original texts, however. They also wished to visit personally the sites associated with the life of the historical Buddha. Additionally, they hoped to find authoritative teachers of the Buddhist tradition, doubting the orthodoxy in some cases of Buddhist proponents in China. Many pilgrims brought home relics as well, such as teeth or bones believed to be the Buddha's.

One of the most celebrated of these travelers was Faxian, who lived at the turn of the fifth century. From his home in Chang'an (modern Xi'an), Faxian traveled westward to Dunhuang, then via Turfan, Qara Shahr, and Khotan southward over the Karakorum to the Swat valley in what is now northern Pakistan, and from there to India proper. After spending six years in India, from 405 to 411, he returned to China by sea.[56]

Another well-known Chinese Buddhist who traveled to India was Song Yun, a native of Dunhuang who set out in 518. Like Faxian, Song Yun took the relatively direct but exceedingly difficult Karakorum route south from Khotan to Kashmir. According to his account the dangers of this mountain journey were compounded by the presence of a dragon near some mountain lakes below the Zongli Mountains. This dragon was known to cause travelers "all sorts of inconveniences," such as blinding snowstorms, but, according to Song Yun, "if they pay some religious service to the dragon, they find less difficulty afterwards."[57]

Faxian's travels inspired a young man who would become the most famous Chinese Buddhist of all time, Xuanzang.[58] Born near Luoyang in 602, Xuanzang was raised in a traditional Confucian family but came under the influence of an elder brother, a Buddhist monk who inclined toward Pure Land beliefs. At 12 he was admitted to his brother's monastery, and he spent the next 15 years studying the teachings of various Buddhist schools in Chengdu and Chang'an. During this time he grew increasingly frustrated by the apparent errors and inconsistencies he detected in the available Chinese translations of key Buddhist texts. He resolved to go to India, and to bring back a copy of the original Sanskrit version of a text to which he was particularly attracted. This was Asanga's *Treatise on the Stages of Yoga*

Practice, the main text of an intellectualistic Mahayana sect known as the Yogacara.

Xuanzang quite naturally followed the Silk Road westwards, and perhaps in doing so retraced in reverse the original path of the religion from the northwestern Indian subcontinent to China. His route took him first through Dunhuang at the edge of the Takla Makan desert and then through the oasis towns of Agni, Kucha, Aqsu, and Nujkand. From there he traveled to Transoxiana, through Talas to Tashkent and Ferghana, Samarkand, Bukhara, and Khwarazm. He then turned south and passed through Kish, Qunduz, and Termez before crossing the Pamirs through Garm, Kulab, and Wakhsh to Balkh in Bactria. The last leg of his long journey to India took him to Bamiyan and over the Hindu Kush into India. Xuanzang spent the following years traveling throughout the subcontinent, visiting Buddhist sites, debating with scholars, and collecting manuscripts. He returned to China via Khotan after an absence of 13 years.

Xuanzang personally brought back to China 657 Sanskrit manuscripts, many of which he then translated into Chinese.[59] During his travels he played the role of teacher to Central Asian Buddhists he encountered, in many cases expressing dismay and even outrage at their deviance from what he saw as the orthodox tradition.

Beginning in the eighth century Muslim armies began to win control of the Central Asian Silk Roads as far as Talas in modern Kyrgyzstan. Although Islamic law offered protection to "peoples of the Book," namely, Christians, Jews, and by some interpretations Zoroastrians, the early Muslims were generally hostile toward Buddhists. They referred to Buddhists as "idol-worshippers," which had unfortunate associations with the portrayal of Muhammad's Meccan enemies in the Qur'an. This may account in part for the often harsh treatment reserved by Muslims for the Buddhists they encountered in the course of their conquests, but it may also have been largely pretext.

The fact is that the Muslims were aiming to control trade routes that had for centuries been firmly in the hands of Buddhists, who were therefore their primary economic competitors. Thus, claims in Muslim sources that military campaigns were motivated by a desire to spread Islam should perhaps be taken in the same light as those of Western nations today that invade countries on the pretext of "bringing democracy." A thousand years ago, just as today, ideological rhetoric was used to give a righteous face to acts of mundane aggression.[60]

In any case, with the increasing Muslim dominance of the Silk Road, it became more and more difficult for Buddhist monks and pilgrims to travel between India and China.[61] By the second half of the eleventh century this contact ceases, and Buddhism in East Asia, cut off from its Indian sources, is left to go its own way.

Buddhism and Zoroastrianism in Central Asia

Certain passages in the account of Xuanzang's travels have led scholars to perceive a Central Asian Buddhism in decline vis-à-vis Sasanian-sponsored Zoroastrianism. For example, Xuanzang's biographer, Huili, who was one of his disciples, comments sadly that in Samarkand, "[t]he king and people did not believe in Buddhism but worshipped fire. There were two monastery buildings but no monks lived in them. If a guest monk attempted to stay in them, the native people would drive him out with fire."[62]

It seems the Sogdian king was impressed by Xuanzang's piety, however. When two of Xuanzang's accompanying disciples were chased from the temple by fire-worshipping priests, the king ordered the priests to be punished. Xuanzang then "turned the other cheek" by intervening on the priests' behalf. According to Huili, Xuanzang thereby won the respect of the local people, and "the king and people believed in Buddhism and a great meeting was held to ordain some people, who afterwards lived in the monasteries."[63]

Since Huili's work is as at least as much hagiography as biography, his assertions regarding the success of Xuanzang's efforts should be taken with a grain of salt. The Chinese traveler was certainly a charismatic individual, and such figures are often able to generate personal followings wherever they go. This account does not in itself require us to conclude, however, that the Sogdian population had converted from Buddhism to Zoroastrianism and that Xuanzang had managed to set them once again on the straight path.

Furthermore, even if Huili's assertions about his master's successes in Sogdiana are true, the "converts" may have been at least partly made up of individuals who were already Buddhists (or at least to some degree "Buddhistic"), and who merely saw in him an authority whose corrective instruction they were willing to accept. There were numerous schools of

Buddhism as well as variants in local belief and practice spread out across Asia at that time, and if Buddhists existed in Sogdiana (which is certainly possible), it may simply have been their local version of Buddhism that Xuanzang saw as heretical.[64] Huili's phrasing about "correcting evil customs" would seem to be consistent with this interpretation.

Even more likely, perhaps, is that with the rise in Sasanian influence from Iran, any existing local form of Buddhism, which would probably have been colored by local Iranian religiosity to begin with, had increasingly taken on aspects of the newly institutionalized Sasanian Zoroastrianism. The eastern Iranian world has provided documented examples of Zoroastrian influence on the evolution of Buddhism there. One such case can be seen in the layout of the circumabulatory corridor around Buddhist stupas, which is modeled on that of fire temples.[65]

Again, we cannot assume that the population of Sogdiana was ever in any uniform sense Zoroastrian or Buddhist as we understand the terms. For one thing, they lived at some remove from the centers of both Zoroastrian and Buddhist institutionalizing forces. Furthermore, we have evidence of the persistence of strictly local elements, such as the cult of the hero Siyavash at Bukhara, which included the sacrifice of a rooster (symbol of the Iranian god Sraosha) every new year.[66] Most probably, the local religiosity of Sogdiana was made up of many elements drawn from the Iranian/Indo-Aryan pool from which both major religions had evolved, and any attempt to categorize this religiosity at any period as specifically Zoroastrian or Buddhist is bound to be misleading.

Tibet and the Silk Road

The Silk Road skirted the forbidding highlands of the Tibetan plateau, but spur routes connected Tibet to the busier overland tracks. Paintings and rock inscriptions along the upper Indus River in Ladakh at the southwestern corner of the Tibetan world indicate the passing of Christian and Manichaean Sogdian merchants there. Sogdians of various faiths probably carried their business into the Tibetan interior.[67] Buddhism reached Tibet both from India via Nepal to the south, and from China via the eastern Silk Road. Interestingly, Tibet's pre-Buddhist local religion, called Bön, claims in certain texts to have originated in eastern Iran.[68]

From around 655 until 692 a short-lived Tibetan empire gained control over the oasis towns of the Tarim basin, bringing the passing Silk Road trade under its jurisdiction. A century later, from just before 794 until 851, the Tibetans controlled predominantly Buddhist Khotan.[69] This meant temporary increases in traffic channeled off into Tibet proper, which allowed for a greater penetration of Buddhist ideas from China. The first Buddhist temple in Tibet was constructed in around 779 at Samye. There, as in the Tarim region and elsewhere, monks prospered from the contributions of lay devotees engaged in trade.

Tibet's relations with China, which from the late seventh century made them rival competitors for control of the eastern Silk Road, tempered the influence of Chinese Buddhism. Although it is not entirely clear why or how Tibetan Buddhists came to look more to Indian sources, especially Kashmiri Tantrism, Tibet's political need to limit Chinese cultural hegemony was likely a factor. Khotan, with its long-standing Buddhist connections to Kashmir, was probably a major transmission point, especially during the periods when it was under Tibetan control.

Chapter Four

A Refuge of Heretics: Nestorians and Manichaeans on the Silk Road

It was during the first five centuries of the Common Era that the major religions of West Asia defined themselves and began to take the shape in which we recognize them today. To a large extent this was a process resulting from mutual antagonisms: in the Eastern Roman world between Christians and Jews and among proponents of diverse interpretations of Christianity, and in the Iranian sphere, between the caretakers of traditional Ahura Mazda-based worship and the emergent threat of Manichaeism.

Human groups tend to hasten toward self-definition mainly when challenged by something they could conceivably be, but, for fear of losing their identity, must demonstrate they are not. (That is why belief systems in traditional societies often appear so frustratingly flexible and inclusive to modern, description-minded observers.) In religion, preoccupation with "us/them" distinctions is characteristic of the priestly class. We see evidence for this in the legalistic sources of the Hebrew Bible, and in the Talmud of the rabbis who succeeded the priests as guardians of Hebraic tradition; we see it in the polemics of the Church Fathers, and we see it in the merciless efforts of the Zoroastrian magi in suppressing the Manichaean alternative.

The doctrinal disputes of the early Common Era are inseparable from the political sponsors with which they aligned themselves. When one party proved stronger, rivals were branded heretics. This left the way open to persecution, banishment, or even execution. In the case of two movements that proved highly significant for world history, the losers chose exile. What is striking is that they each followed a similar pattern, and headed eastward out of harm's way. In both cases exile ensured their survival for another 1,000 years, and even some periods of success. The logical channel for this eastward migration, as we have seen, was to join up with the caravans of the Silk Road.

Both Christian and Manichaean sources attest to the close relationship between mercantile and missionary activity. Syriac, the lingua franca of West Asian trade, became the liturgical language of the Eastern Church. Among the early Christians the Syriac word for merchant, *tgr'*, was often used as a metaphor for those who spread the gospel. A fourth-century Syriac hymn includes the following stanza:

> Travel well-girt like merchants,
> That we may gain the world.
> Convert men to me,
> Fill creation with teaching.[1]

The Church of the East

The religion we now call Christianity first emerged as a movement within the Jewish society of Roman Palestine. The interpretations that Jesus's followers gave to Jewish history, as expressed in text and legend, were sufficiently radical to cause most Jews to reject them. In the process of doing so, Jewish scholars developed a method for determining and stating what their heritage correctly was and did mean; this was eventually institutionalized as the rabbinical tradition, which became normative for Jews and is the basis of Judaism today.

Similarly, among the Christians there were disagreements over interpreting what they should believe and how they should practice their faith. One of the touchiest problems facing the early Christian theologians was to resolve the issue of Christ's true nature, whether divine or human or somehow both.

Doctrinal disputes within the early Christian church were a reflection of the struggle for supremacy between the highly placed advocates of various interpretations, and thus tended to be identified with particular regional power bases. The "diophysite" position of the so-called School of Antioch was that Christ consisted of two distinct persons, one human and one divine, which were brought into coexistence in the person of Jesus, much as the Spirit of God had descended onto the Hebrew prophets. The rival "monophysite" position, associated with the theologians of Alexandria, was that Christ was the eternal Divine Logos, incarnate as a human being—that He was God living under human conditions.

During the early fifth century this controversy expressed itself in terms of a dispute over how Mary should be described, whether as the "Bearer of Christ" *(christotokos)*, or as the "Mother of God" *(theotokos)*. When a Syrian bishop named Nestorius was appointed Patriarch of Constantinople in 428, he taught the Antiochan view, which he summarized with the remark that he "could not imagine God as a little boy." Nestorius's privileged position at Constantinople as spokesman for the Antiochans resulted in a hostile response led by Cyril, Patriarch of Alexandria.

The Byzantine emperor Theodosius II personally liked Nestorius, but his elder sister, Pulcheria, despised him. Pulcheria had enormous influence over the emperor, and knowing this, Cyril made her a focus of his propaganda campaign against Nestorius. In 431 the emperor called a council at Ephesus to settle on an appropriate terminology for Mary. Cyril was appointed to preside over this council, so it is no surprise that the Antiochan position was denounced as heretical. (In fact, the Antiochan party refused to attend.) The emperor, under pressure from his sister, supported Cyril, and Nestorius was deposed and banished to Egypt.

The Antiochan teaching being dominant in Syria and lands to the east, however, a large part of the diocese chose not to recognize Cyril's authority and seceded to form the Church of the East, with its seat at Ctesiphon (near modern Baghdad), capital of the Persian Sasanian Empire. This implied a rejection of the Byzantine emperor's authority as well, and from that point onwards, the Nestorian church came to be identified with the Persian world in opposition to the Byzantine.

In 451 the Council of Chalcedon proposed a compromise between the monophysite and diophysite positions, namely, that Christ combined two natures but not two persons. The Nestorians tended to see this as something like an acknowledgment of their position, but it didn't go far enough. At a synod in 486 the bishops of the East declared their church explicitly Nestorian, repudiating both

monophysitism and the Chalcedonian "compromise" and expressing
their belief in "one divine nature only, in three perfect persons...."
They went on to state that "(Christ had) two natures, divine and
human...without confusion in their diversity...(yet with) perfect
and indissoluble cohesion of the divine with the human...." A major
problem for the Nestorians seems to have been what living under
human form would imply for God; for example, they held that it was
only the human aspect of Jesus that died on the cross. Their statement
continued, "...if anyone thinks or teaches that suffering and change
inheres in the divinity, and if, when speaking of the unity of the person
of our Saviour, he does not confess that He is perfect God and perfect
man, let him be anathema."[2]

The synod and a subsequent one in 497 put Persian monophysites
on the defensive, and Nestorianism became henceforth the official
(though not the only) doctrine of Christian Asia.

Christianity in Iran

In the Acts of the Apostles (2: 9) it is stated that Iranian Jews from
Parthia, Media, Elam, and Mesopotamia were witness to the miracle
of the Pentecost. Since Christianity arose within the Jewish world, it is
only natural that its eastward spread from Palestine would have been
facilitated first and foremost through existing contacts across the Jewish
diaspora.[3] Since these contacts were to a large degree commercial in
nature, it can safely be assumed that Christianity's first link with the Silk
Road was via the Babylonian Jews.

The Parthian Arsacid dynasty, which ruled Mesopotamia and Iran
during the first two centuries of the Common Era, did not consider
religion a particularly important political issue. As a result there is little
mention of religious sects in Parthian sources, and we can only guess at
the spread of Christian ideas in the East on the basis of analysis of later
materials. It would seem that in the western part of the Parthian realm
Christian communities grew among various Jewish and other sects, local
cults, and varieties of Iranian religion.

The earliest reference to Central Asian communities in a Christian
source is the approving comment of Bardaisan around 196 CE: "Nor do
our sisters among the Gilanians and Bactrians have any intercourse with
strangers." The apocryphal Acts of Thomas, written around the same
time, mentions the "land of the Kushans" *(baith kaishan)*.[4]

In 224 the Sasanians from southwestern Iran overthrew the Parthians and founded a new dynasty. By then Christians were fairly numerous in the Iranian world: an early church history states that in 225 there were 20 bishoprics throughout the Persian-controlled lands.[5] Following the Sasanian emperor Shapur I's victories over the Byzantines in 256 and 260, Greek-speaking as well as Syriac-speaking Christian captives were deported to Iran and thus added to the numbers of Christians there.

The first three Sasanian emperors largely maintained the Parthian tolerance of non-Iranian religions. Under Bahram II (r. 276–93), however, the Sasanian royal house tightened its ties to the Zoroastrian priesthood, whose chief priest, Kartir, had been waging a campaign to make Zoroastrianism the official religion of the new empire. To do this, Kartir felt obliged to eliminate any potentially rival religious organizations. In an inscription from the year 280, he names Christians among those groups he believes should be put down. (Though Kartir also names Jews among those groups he opposes, there is no evidence that Jewish communities were persecuted.[6] They were presumably not numerous enough to constitute a threat.) Essentially the fortunes of Iran's Christians, even more than other religious communities, were tied to the ebb and flow of politics at court.[7]

Christians, like other religious minorities under Sasanian rule, lived a precarious existence. The impulse of individual emperors was more often than not to tolerate them; Christians served in the Sasanian army, and one Christian general even led the Sasanians into battle against the Byzantines. But the magi, who sought to bind up their religious authority with the political authority of the emperor, were always lobbying against Iran's non-Zoroastrian religious communities. The periods when the magi most succeeded in their political aims (such as under Shapur II from 309 to 379, Bahram V from 421 to 439, and Yazdigard II from 439 to 457) were those in which Christians, Jews, and Manichaeans suffered most harshly. A royal decree issued by Shapur II lists a variety of points on which Christians seemed at odds with the state and with Zoroastrian values:

> The Christians destroy our holy teachings, and teach men to serve one God, and not to honor the sun or fire. They teach them, too, to defile water by their ablutions, to refrain from marriage and the procreation of children, and to refuse to go out to war with the Shahenshah. They

have no scruple about the slaughter and eating of animals, they bury
the corpses of men in the earth, and attribute the origin of snakes and
creeping things to a good God. They despise many servants of the
King, and teach witchcraft.[8]

Conversely, when the state and the magi drifted apart (as under
Narseh from 293 to 303, Yazdigerd I from 399 to 421, Balash from 484
to 488, Kavad from 488 to 531, and Hormizd IV from 579 to 590),
Christians and Jews were able to live among the Zoroastrian majority
in peace, and often prospered. In 383 Emperor Shahpur III issued
an edict stating that "Magi, Zandiks (Manichaeans), Jews, Christians
and all men of whatever religion should be left undisturbed and at
peace in their belief." The religious leaders from each community,
meanwhile—magi, priests, and rabbis alike—worked hard to keep
religious identities distinct, as is evident from the many polemical
tracts they wrote against each other.[9] (The vociferousness of these
tracts is an indication that the people themselves were not so averse to
mixing across communities.)

The adoption of Christianity as the official religion of the Roman
Empire during the fourth century had two major effects on Iranian
Christianity. The first was that, despite their ideological differences with
the Roman church, Christians in Iran were now frequently suspected
of foreign loyalties, which was often used as justification for their
persecution. Indeed, most of the major persecutions of Christians in
Iran were directly connected to the political situation between the two
empires. The decision by Iranian bishops at a synod in 424 to declare
their church formally independent from Constantinople may thus have
been as much politically as doctrinally motivated.

The other effect was that with Christianity now enjoying state
sponsorship in the West, doctrinal disputes tended to be won by
whichever camp had the emperor's support, which the favored party
could then use to suppress those holding rival interpretations; hence the
steady flight of Nestorians to Iran. Similarly, Roman citizens who chose
not to convert to Christianity were out of favor and often in jeopardy.
As a result of the Byzantine church's state-supported persecutions, many
intellectuals and others fled the Mediterranean world for sanctuary in
the Sasanian Empire. Athenian philosophers, Syrian physicians, and
Sabean astrologers all took this route, to the benefit and enrichment of
Sasanian culture.

Gundeshapur in southwestern Iran became the new seat of classical Greek medicine, philosophy, and astronomy, and the school founded there was staffed by pagans and Eastern Christians alike. For the next five centuries Gundeshapur was one of the greatest scientific centers of the world. When the Muslim Arabs conquered the region in the mid-seventh century, they kept the school intact, and for two centuries more many of the leading minds of the new Islamic faith got their education there from Christian teachers.

Nestorianism among the Sogdians

Sogdiana was, until the Samanid dynasty made it the most dynamic center of the Muslim world in the tenth century, never a region of religious orthodoxy. Settled by Iranian tribes from prehistory, it was at the fringes of both East and West, equally removed from the centers of all the great religious traditions. It had always been middle ground, a transit point, a place where anything could and did pass through sooner or later.

Alexander left Greek influences in Sogdiana in the third century BCE. Iranian nomads such as the Sakas, and Turkic nomads as well, were always a nearby presence. The Parthians left the cultural mix there unmolested, and for the Sasanians, the province was too remote for the standardizing efforts of the Zoroastrian magi to be effective.

Sogdian merchants were the real masters of the Silk Road, whoever the ephemeral powers of the time might be. Under the rule of their fellow Iranian peoples, the Parthians and the Sasanians, Sogdian merchants moved easily in the Iranian lands to the west, where some of them were won over to the Christian message, just as others active in the former Kushan lands had embraced Buddhism.

There do not appear to have been any obstacles preventing Sogdian converts to either tradition from importing their new faith to Sogdiana proper or conveying it further east in the course of their business ventures. By 650 there was a Nestorian archibishopric at Samarkand in the heart of Sogdiana, and another even further east at Kashgar; in all over 20 Nestorian bishops had dioceses east of the Oxus River.[10]

For centuries Sogdian was the lingua franca of the Silk Road. But through their widespread dealings, Sogdian traders knew foreign languages as well, which made them especially well equipped to serve as translators. Among the Nestorian texts that have been discovered in the Tarim basin since the beginning of the twentieth century, a preponderance are in Sogdian or show evidence of having been translated from Sogdian versions. Although Syriac was the liturgical language of the Nestorian church, the language in which Nestorian Christianity was disseminated across Asia was principally Sogdian, as it was for Buddhism and Manichaeism as well.[11]

Most of the Christian texts found in the Tarim region were discovered by four German expeditions to the Turfan oasis from 1902 to 1914. The bulk of these are manuscripts dating to the ninth and tenth centuries from a Nestorian monastery at Buyaliq, north of the oasis. They include hymns, Psalms, prayers, lectionaries from the New Testament, and commentaries.[12] Although most are translations from Syriac, some of the Sogdian versions are older than their known Syriac counterparts, and a few do not have known Syriac versions.[13] The Christian texts in Sogdian, unknown before this century, have substantially rounded out scholars' understanding of Nestorianism.

Nestorianism among the Turks

Nomadic Turks in Central Asia were first taught the art of writing by Persian Nestorian priests in the entourage of the dethroned Sasanian emperor Kavad sometime around 550. A group of these priests stayed among the Turks for seven years, and baptized many of them. The priests learned Turkish and rendered it in writing for the first time, using the Syriac alphabet.[14]

The Sogdians of Central Asia, who traded directly with the Turkic nomads, were a more regular cultural influence on them. A Chinese writer of the Sui period noted that "[t]he Turks themselves are simple-minded and short-sighted and dissension can easily be roused among them. Unfortunately, many Sogdians live among them who are cunning and insidious; they teach and instruct the Turks."[15]

The native religion of the Turkic and Mongol peoples of Inner Asia is generally described as shamanistic. They held the sky god, Tangri (modern Turkish: Tanrı), as supreme, the male principle that was balanced by the female earth. Religious behavior was practical; rituals were connected with basic survival needs such as hunting, healing, and fertility. The spirit world was accessed through a shaman, a medium who communicated with the spirits after working himself into an ecstatic trance.[16] Shamans still exist in Inner Asia today, even among nominally Buddhist or Muslim populations.

Apparently some of the first Christian priests to win followers among the Turks were perceived by them as shamans. Syriac records of the Nestorian church recount that in 644 the metropolitan of Marv, Elias, impressed a Turkish king by using the sign of the cross to stop a severe thunderstorm.[17] The king was thereby enticed to accept Christianity, and his subjects along with him. Scholars of archaic Turkish religion have noted that the stopping of thunderstorms, through use of a stone called a *yat*, was a traditional function of the shamans.[18]

The same sources state that in 781–782 a second major conversion occurred among the Turks, again with the conversion of the king leading to that of his subjects. As a result of this second mass conversion, the Nestorian patriarch Timothy in Baghdad established a Central Asian metropolitan specifically to instruct Christian Turks.[19] A contemporary writer states that information concerning the successes of missionaries among the Turks comes from a "letter which some merchants and secretaries of the kings, who had penetrated as far as there for the sake of commerce and of affairs of State, wrote to Mar Timothy."[20]

A third mass conversion took place in 1007, when according to the sources, 200,000 Turks and Mongols became Christians. The identification of this latter group with the Kerait tribe has been questioned,[21] but the scale of the conversion has been generally defended. The medieval Jacobite writer Bar Hebraeus explicitly credits Christian merchants, presumably Sogdians, with bringing the conversion about.

According to Bar Hebraeus's account, the ruler of this nomadic group had been saved from a snowstorm by following a vision of a Christian saint. "When he reached his tents in safety," Bar Hebraeus relates, "he summoned the Christian merchants who were there, and discussed with them the question of faith, and they answered him that this could not be accomplished except through baptism." On hearing this news, the metropolitan sent a priest and deacon to perform the necessary baptisms and offer instruction.[22]

Under the patronage and protection of the Mongol Qara-khitai in the twelfth century, Nestorian Christianity experienced a new surge in popularity. Sometime around 1180 the Nestorian patriarch Elias III established a new metropoly in Kashgar, with authority extending up into the "Seven Rivers" region in the southern part of modern Kazakhstan.

By the dawn of the Mongol period Christianity was certainly the most visible of the major religions among the steppe peoples. What Christianity meant to them, however, is another question. The sources indicate that the essential test of a Christian was baptism; apart from that initiatory ritual, there is little information available regarding how Christianity among the nomads was practiced. Some tribes apparently had portable tent chapels, but there are numerous accounts that show that many of their rituals were simply Christianized forms of traditional practice, such as the drinking of fermented mare's milk, called *kumiz*.

One may also contemplate what the nomads' interest in Christianity was. Was it merely allegiance transferred to the "shamanistic" power that had demonstrated the greatest capabilities? Or was there some thought of cultivating connections with Christian traders along the Silk Road? Both are likely possibilities.

Nestorianism in China

The Chinese, who have inherited one of the world's oldest and greatest civilizations, have a long history of considering other cultures beneath their interest. Uncharacteristically, some of the early emperors of the Tang dynasty—especially Xuanzong (r. 712–756, not to be confused with the Buddhist traveler Xuanzang)—had a fascination with things foreign that sometimes verged on a mania.[23] In such an atmosphere, the alien traditions of traders from the West were unusually welcome and encouraged.

Sogdian and Iranian merchants and missionaries brought Christianity to China during the first half of the seventh century. In fact, the Chinese originally thought the cradle of Christianity was Iran, and referred to it as "the Iranian religion" for over 100 years before correcting their records in the mid-eighth century. An imperial Tang edict of 638 relates that an Iranian priest named A-lo-pen (Abraham? Rabban?) had arrived at court three years earlier.[24] Alopen had brought with him scriptures, which were translated into Chinese so that the emperor could understand them. The emperor approved, and gave the Nestorians permission to propagate their faith throughout the empire. This event is generally considered to mark the introduction of Christianity into China.

A monument erected near the Tang capital of Chang'an (Xi'an) in 781 contains a wealth of information about the local Nestorian community's first 150 years. Iranian and Central Asian names occur throughout, indicating a continuous influx of Westerners along the Silk Road. One of the monument's most interesting pieces of information concerns a monk by the name of Adam, who assisted in the Chinese translation: he is said to have collaborated on the translation of a Buddhist treatise as well. Adam knew no Indian languages, so the Buddhist text in question must have been in Sogdian, presumably his native language.[25]

A Chinese text found at Dunhuang by Paul Pelliot, the *Eloge of the Holy Trinity*, states that no less than 30 Nestorian works had been translated into Chinese by the late eighth century. It does not appear that the Nestorians won many Chinese converts, however. Like the Buddhists, they found themselves in the position of having to communicate concepts and values entirely alien and even offensive to the Chinese. And, if a Chinese census from the year 845 is any indication, Christianity didn't catch on to anything near the extent Buddhism did: the census lists 260,000 Buddhist monks and nuns as against only 3,000 "Christians and Zoroastrians."[26] Thus, while Buddhism was also a foreign religion, the Nestorians in China appear to have been far less successful than their Buddhist rivals in adapting their message to Chinese tastes.

This does not appear to have been for lack of trying, since they referred to their treatises as *sutra*s, and to Christian saints as "buddhas" or "dharma kings." By the time the Xi'an monument was erected, Nestorianism was known in Chinese as "the Luminous Religion" *(ching chiao)*. On the other hand, the name of the Christian savior himself, which is Yishu in Syriac, sounded in the Chinese pronunciation of the time like the term for "a rat on the move."

Whether the rendering of Christian texts into Chinese during the Tang period should be taken as evidence for the existence of native congregations or just diligent attempts by foreign missionaries is hard to tell. In a book called *The Jesus Sutras*, Martin Palmer colorfully recounts his decades-long search for the earliest traces of what he calls "Taoist Christianity" and provides translations of a curious range of hybrid religious texts from Chinese. In 1998 a team led by Palmer found an eighth-century Christian pagoda south of Xi'an, in a rural area near where Laozi is said to have composed the *Tao Te Ching* more than a millennium earlier. The caretaker of the site, a Buddhist nun, told the team that the pagoda had been part of a monastery founded by "monks from the West who believed in one God" and that during the Tang period it had been "the greatest Christian monastery in all of China."[27]

Nevertheless, it would seem that for the most part the Nestorian community in China consisted of foreigners, as was the case with Judaism and Mazda-worship. All three traditions were brought into China as the faiths of traveling merchants, and their fates were tied to those of the expatriate merchant communities themselves.

The Tang court's enthusiastic taste for foreign people, ideas, and things also allowed for the proliferation of religious quackery. Many religious figures were engaged not for their spiritual teachings but for their more worldly skills. Christians and Manichaeans especially were valued for their knowledge of astrology and medicine, inherited from the traditions of Mesopotamia.

One Chinese source mentions a priest who had the power to "chant people to death and then revive them"—evidently a hypnotist. A Buddhist monk from India named Narayanasvamin claimed to be 200 years old and to possess elixirs of immortality. Daoist alchemists had fantasized about such potions since ancient times, but in this case the Indian's concoctions were found to be ineffective and he was dismissed from court.[28]

Religious buildings often served as "cultural centers" in which foreign adherents as well as interested locals could gather. Mazdaean temples in Lanzhou and Luoyang, for example, regularly hosted magic shows, which drew large crowds. Though Emperor Xuanzong actually encouraged such activities during his reign, this kind of foreign influence could be perceived as threatening by other, more xenophobic Chinese rulers.[29]

In 845 the Tang emperor Wuzong, who was a supporter of Daoism, outlawed all foreign religions (even Buddhism, which was hardly foreign any more), forcing them underground. In 980, a Nestorian monk told a Muslim writer in Baghdad that he had been sent by the church to China seven years earlier in order to "set the affairs of the Christian religion in order" there, but had found no Christians surviving anywhere in the country.[30] Christianity appears to have disappeared from China, to be reintroduced under the Mongols three centuries later.

Mani

Mesopotamia in the third century CE was home to a proliferation of religious sects. Long the buffer zone fought over by successive Greek and Iranian empires, it was a meeting ground of cultures where all were represented. Israelites had lived there for 1,000 years alongside Iranian Mazda worshippers and native Mesopotamians, whose original religious beliefs survived among the Sabeans, renowned for their knowledge of astrology. By this time there were also various Christian denominations, as well as hybrid Jewish-Christian gnostic baptist sects.

It was into one of the latter communities, the Elkesaites, that the prophet Mani was born in the year 216 to parents of royal Parthian ancestry.[31] Mani was raised in an ascetic religious environment, where Christian and Jewish ideas were set against a dualistic gnostic backdrop. He received his first revelation at the age of 12, and another when he was 24. From the time of this second revelation, Mani took up the role of prophet, and set out to preach his message.

Mani's first missionary journey was eastwards to the lands of the lower Indus valley: Turan, Makran, and Sindh in what is now southern Pakistan. This region was a thriving center of Buddhism at that time, and Buddhist influences were significant in the formation of Mani's religious thought. The transmigration of souls became a Manichaean belief, and the quadripartite structure of the Manichaean community, divided between male and female monks (the "Elect") and lay followers (the "Hearers") who supported them, appears to be based on that of the Buddhist sangha.

On his return to Iran, Mani managed to convert at least two princes of the new Sasanian ruling house, and spent several years in the entourage of Emperor Shapur himself. Mani must have aspired to make his new faith the official religion of the new empire; unfortunately his rival at court, the magian priest Kartir, had the same idea.

During Shapur's reign Mani enjoyed official patronage and protection. As a result he was able to send followers to all corners of the Sasanian realm in order to preach his message. The new faith rapidly won converts throughout the land. For nearly 50 years the popularity of Mani's vision posed the greatest threat to the traditional magi led by Kartir.

After Bahram I acceded to the Sasanian throne in 273, Mani's fortunes changed. At the instigation of Kartir, the emperor had Mani arrested in 276, just as the latter was attempting to flee to Parthia. It is interesting that in his final interview with Mani, the emperor reproaches him not on the basis of his religious views, but rather on the accusation that he has neglected his duties as a physician:

> What are you good for, since you go neither fighting nor hunting?
> But perhaps you are needed for this doctoring and this physicking?
> And you don't even do that!

Mani defends himself on the same grounds:

> Many are those whom I have made rise from their illnesses. Many
> are those from whom I have averted the numerous kinds of ague.
> Many were those who were at the point of death, and I have revived
> them.[32]

This exchange suggests that religious leaders were valued more for their skills as doctors than as healers of souls, an interpretation that finds ample corroboration elsewhere throughout premodern history.[33]

Following this conversation, the emperor sentenced Mani to prison. After several months, Mani died in detention—possibly from torture—at the age of 60.

Something from Everyone:
A New Universal Tradition

What made Mani's message so attractive to so many people was that he made every effort to "speak their language" (similar to the Christian apostle Paul's entreaty to "be all things to all men"). Mani did so literally but also figuratively, borrowing ideas, symbols, and religious terminology from every tradition he encountered. As noted earlier in the discussion of Buddhist texts, getting new ideas accepted in traditional societies usually requires camouflaging their "newness." One must tap into the mind-set and worldview of the target audience, making the "new" message seem merely a "perfection" of old truth, compatible with people's traditional understanding. Mani and his disciples were unparalleled masters of this technique.

Having been born and raised in the lands where Asian and Mediterranean civilizations had met through the centuries, Mani was conditioned from childhood by heterodox religious notions drawn from a variety of sources. His system blends Semitic and Iranian traditions so completely that scholars continue to argue over which is its real underlying source.[34]

Manichaeism is generally treated as a gnostic system.[35] Gnosticism's origins are obscure, but probably date to sometime before the Common Era. It posits a radically dualistic view of the universe, in which "good" is equated with spirit and "evil" with matter. Gnostics favored esoteric interpretations leading to salvation through knowledge, a possibility that held special appeal for intellectual elites. It was an approach to truth, rather than a religious tradition per se; Gnostics were found among Christians, Jews, and other groups. Representatives of the mainstream invariably perceived the "hidden" interpretations of the Gnostics as a threat to orthodoxy, and continually declared them heretics.

Mani presents himself as the culminating prophet in human history, following Zoroaster, Buddha, and Jesus. His cosmology takes many Iranian figures, including Zurvan, Ormazd (Ahura Mazda), Ahriman (Angra Mainyu), and various good and evil spirits, and imbues them with gnostic interpretations. The universe is seen as a realm of struggle between good and evil, with the good, represented as particles of light, striving to be liberated from the evil matter in which it is trapped.

The most visible figure in Manichaean mythology is Jesus. Mani refers to himself throughout his life as "the Apostle of Jesus Christ." Mani's Jesus takes three forms, however: Jesus the Man, Jesus the Living Soul, and Jesus the Splendor. The first is the historical Jesus of the Christians, but whose death on the cross Mani considers to have been an illusion. The second is the "suffering Jesus" (Jesus patibilis), the force of goodness in the form of light particles that are trapped in all living things. Jesus the Splendor, a conceptualization borrowed from a gnostic group called the Mandaeans (who still exist today), is the embodiment of Light who visited the First Man and will return as Savior at the end of time.

Mani taught that reproduction is an evil, since with each succeeding generation the light particles trapped in every individual are further divided among one's descendents. The Manichaean Elect therefore were to practice abstinence. The following Manichaean parable about a nobleman whose wife has just died (versions of which are found both in early Christianity and later in Islam) illustrates this abhorrence of carnality, as well as worldly delusion symbolized by drunkenness:

> ...He saw [the corpse] and thought, "This is my wife." He went
> in [to the tomb] and lay down beside the corpse. And because he
> was drunk and foolish, he put his arms around the corpse, behaved
> shamelessly and united with it. Because of his exertions the corpse
> burst open. Blood, pus and foul and evil things in its nauseating body
> oozed and flowed out. And the noble man lay in blood and pus with
> his whole body and all his clothes, and he was covered from head to
> foot. And because of his drunken state, he thought to himself, "I am
> very satisfied."
>
> When morning came and the sun rose, the noble man's
> drunkenness passed. He awoke from his sleep. Raising his head, he
> saw that he was lying in a tomb, a corpse being at his bosom. Pus
> and blood were oozing out and spreading a terrible odor. He looked
> at himself and saw that he was all covered with blood and lying in
> excrement. He was struck by panic and seized by fear; he screamed
> loudly, quickly left in his mourning-dress and ran away. The more
> he ran the more he vomited. Then he quickly tore to bits and to
> shreds the gown that had been so pure, threw it away and then ran
> on. He reached a pond, jumped into it, and washed and cleansed
> himself...[36]

But Mani's highly organized propaganda strategy involved more
than simply adopting existing religious stories and symbols and giving
them new meanings and interpretations. In most religions, scriptures
are handed down orally over long periods before being written down,
leaving them open to accusations of human corruption and falsification.
Mindful of this danger, Mani made a point of writing down his
revelations himself, producing at least seven canonical works, which
formed the scriptural foundation for his religion.

Mani also believed strongly in the power of images to convey religious
truth. (This may have been partly a concession to the fact that literacy
was not widespread.) A talented painter, he illustrated his own scriptures.
His skill as an artist won him a reputation, which, somewhat ironically, is
his most enduring legacy, outlasting the very religion he founded. To this
day, his heretical beliefs long forgotten, he is remembered in the Muslim
world as the greatest painter who ever lived.[37]

It was the Manichaean Elect who bore the responsibility of spreading
the message of the faith as itinerant preachers, following the model of

Christian and Buddhist monks. The Elect were distinguished by the wearing of white robes, and adherence to a vegetarian diet. They had to exercise the utmost care not to engage in any activities that contravened the principles of their religion, even activities necessary for their own survival. Even more than Buddhist monks, the Manichaean Elect were utterly dependent on their lay followers, the Hearers, who supported them. They could not even prepare their own food, since that would damage the light particles that were believed to reside in all living things, including vegetables. Before eating, the Elect were to recite, "Neither have I cast it into the oven; another hath brought me this and I have eaten it without guilt."[38]

Indeed, Jason BeDuhn has recently argued that eating was the central practice of the Manichean Elect, since it was through the process of digestion that they separated light particles from matter and then "released" these particles by singing them out as hymns.[39] Augustine of Hippo ridiculed this practice (which BeDuhn whimsically calls "metabolic salvation"), by saying of the Manichaeans that "[t]hey claim to purify the world through their belches."[40]

Manichaeism on the Silk Road

Mani's religion began to enjoy popularity in the Mediterranean world within his own lifetime, although even before the Roman Empire became officially Christian, it persecuted Manichaeans as adherents of a "foreign," Persian faith. Once Christianity became the state religion, Manichaeism was considered an even greater threat, since it claimed to be an esoteric, and therefore, "truer" form of Christianity itself. Although subject to the most ruthless suppression, dualist and anti-worldly ideas that echoed Manichaeism survived in Europe into the Middle Ages, through the Cathar movement in Provence and the Bogomils in the Balkans.

To the east Manichaeism fared better, at least initially. It enjoyed several decades of protection during Mani's lifetime, during which it had spread into Central Asia along the Silk Road beyond the Oxus River. Once again, it was Sogdians who played a major role in the transmission of the faith. Using their linguistic skills, Sogdians translated Manichaean texts from Syriac, Middle Persian, and Parthian into Sogdian, and thence into Turkish and eventually Chinese. By the end of the sixth century the Sogdian Manichaeans were strong enough to declare their independence from the Archegos, the head of the church in Seleucia-Ctesiphon (near modern Baghdad), giving rise to a schism that was to persist for over a century.[41]

An Iranian Manichaean missionary named Mihr-Ormazd traveled to China sometime in the late seventh century.[42] He was granted an audience with the Zhou empress Wu, and presented her with a text entitled *The Sutra of the Two Principles*, which would become the most popular Manichaean work in China.[43]

The missionary's success brought on the jealousy of the Buddhists at court, who quickly became opposed to the new teaching. Sometime after 820, Chinese Buddhists began circulating the following story:

> Wu K'o-chiu, a man of Yüeh, resided in Ch'ang-an...He began to practice Manichaeism and his wife Wang also followed his example. She died suddenly after more than a year. Three years later she appeared to her husband in a dream, saying, "For my perverse belief I have been condemned to become a snake and I am below the stupa at Huang-tzu p'o. I shall die tomorrow at dawn and I wish you would ask the monks to go there and recite for me the Diamond Sutra so that I could avoid other forms of suffering."[44]

The husband does as he is asked, and afterwards becomes a good Buddhist again.

Manichaeism was considered suspiciously by the restored Tang dynasty after 705, and in 732 the emperor issued an edict to the effect that the religion could only be propagated among non-Chinese. The reasoning given for this restriction shows that Buddhists were behind it:

> The doctrine of Mar Mani is basically a perverse belief and fraudulently assumes to be [a school of] Buddhism and will therefore mislead the masses. It deserves to be strictly prohibited. However, since it is the indigenous religion of the Western Barbarians and other [foreigners], its followers will not be punished if they practice it among themselves.[45]

It is clear that just as the Manichaeans in the West attempted to present their religion as an esoteric form of Christianity, in the East they tried to portray it as a type of Buddhism.

As the Sasanian government became increasingly bound up with the Zoroastrian clergy, Manichaeans in Iran gradually moved eastward beyond the reach of the state and the magi. After the Arab Muslims conquered the Sasanian Empire in the 640s many Manichaeans returned from Central Asia to Iran and Mesopotamia. The Umayyad Arabs, based in Damascus, were generally content to leave the religious matters of their subject populations alone. But in 751 the Abbasid revolution brought a wave of religious reform to the Muslim-controlled lands.

During the second half of the eighth century many Persian bureaucrats in the Abbasid administration began to exert a form of cultural revival vis-à-vis the Arab ruling class. In literature this took the shape of the so-called *shu'biyya* movement, through which many Persian literary classics were translated into Arabic. Within the same class of Persian intellectuals, crypto-Manichaeism became a popular form of cultural self-assertion. Soon Mani's faith acquired the dubious status it had possessed in the Sasanian and Roman worlds, as the official religion's archenemy number one. Even those merely suspected of being Manichaeans were ruthlessly persecuted, and many believers chose to flee eastward once again.[46]

The Uighurs

For a relatively brief period of about 77 years, from 763 to 840, the much-maligned Manichaean faith enjoyed the status of an official, state-sponsored religion. This was thanks to the Uighur Turks, who subdued the former Turkish confederation in 744 and founded a state based in what is now Mongolia.

Chinese relations with the steppe had always been characterized by appeasement through bribes, often in the form of silk, as a result of which some of the steppe peoples were able to become quite rich. By the time the Uighurs came to power the Tang were beset by frequent internal problems and came increasingly to rely on the Uighurs for military support.[47]

Beginning in 755 the Tang emperor was faced with a rebellion led by a general of mixed Sogdian and Turkish origin, Rokhshan ("the bright face"), sinicized to An Lushan. The emperor called upon the Uighurs to assist him in putting down the rebellion. It was after retaking the Tang city of Luoyang in 762 that the Uighur kaghan, or king, known in Chinese sources as Mouyu, made the acquaintance of some Sogdian

Manichaeans living there. These Sogdians made a great impression on the kaghan, and when he returned home to his capital of Qara-Balghasun on the Orkhon River in Mongolia, he took four of them along. Within a few months they had persuaded him to adopt Manichaeism. In 763 the kaghan made it the official religion of the Uighur state, banning the Turkish shamanistic tradition.

Why the kaghan did this is something of a mystery. The chief Manichaean monk, known by his Chinese name Jui-hsi, reportedly possessed great eloquence and persuasive skill. The kaghan, as a military man, may have liked the rigid discipline of the Manichaean lifestyle. Another aspect of the religion's appeal was that the Chinese didn't like it, and the Uighurs were seeking to demonstrate their independence from the Tang. A third reason may have been in order to facilitate commercial contacts with the West through the Sogdians.[48]

Characteristically, the Manichaean missionaries among the Uighurs used the strategy of associating their religious concepts with those of the Turks. For example, the Manichaean gods of the two palaces of light are equated with the sun and the moon, which the Turks revered. The term for the palaces themselves was rendered into Turkish as *ordu*, literally the place where a nomadic king's tent is erected. The Manichaeans attached the Turkish word *bilig* ("knowledge"), a term the nomads had associated with leadership from ancient times, to all five of the cardinal virtues (love-knowledge, faith-knowledge, contentment-knowledge, patience-knowledge, and wisdom-knowledge). For "soul" they used the Turkish *qut*, or "heaven-granted blessing."[49]

With the Uighur state to back them up, Iranian and Turkish Manichaeans living in China were able to obtain increased privileges from the Tang government, including the building of new temples. Between the years 768 and 771, the Tang emperor ordered Manichaean temples to be built in Chang'an, Luoyang, Kinzhou, Nanchang, Shaoxing, and Yangzhou.

In the Uighur lands, the Manichaean priests became one of the most powerful social classes. A large number of the Manichaean texts extant today date from the period of Uighur rule in the Tarim region. One text speaks of the efforts to eliminate the practices of the Turks' traditional religion:

> Let all sculpted or painted images of the demons be entirely destroyed by fire; let those who pray to genies or prostrate themselves before

demons all be [?] and let the people accept the Religion of Light. Let [the country] with barbarous customs and smoking blood change into one where the people eat vegetables; and let the state where men kill be transformed into a kingdom where good works are encouraged.[50]

Manichaeans seem to have enjoyed Uighur protection even after Manichaeism ceased to be a state religion. The Muslim writer Ibn Nadim relates that in the ninth century the governor of Khurasan heard there was a community of 500 Manichaeans practicing in Samarkand and wished to kill them. The Uighur khagan sent word to the Khurasan governor that if the Samarkand Manichaeans were harmed, he would kill all the Muslims living under his authority.[51]

The Uighurs used their leverage as supporters of the Tang following An Lushan's rebellion to protect Manichaean communities in China as well, but after the Uighur kingdom was overrun by another Turkic group in 840 there was a backlash. Three years later the Tang government closed all but three Manichaean temples in China, informing the Uighur kaghan that they would be reopened if and when the Uighurs reestablished their kingdom.

Within a few months, however, the Tang government went further and closed the remaining temples, seizing their property and executing the Manichaean priests. The Japanese pilgrim Ennin describes the event:

> An imperial edict was issued, ordering the Manichaean priests of the Empire to be killed. Their heads are to be shaved and they are to be dressed in Buddhist robes and are to be killed looking like Buddhist *sramana*s (monks).[52]

It has been suggested that this persecution was at least in part economically motivated, since the Manichaean temples were probably functioning as money-lending institutions run by Uighur merchants.[53] Two years later a similar pattern would play itself out against the most successful of the foreign religions in China, Buddhism. Christianity and Zoroastrianism likewise lost their protection within the empire at that time, and disappear from the Chinese historical record.

After their defeat in 840 the Uighurs moved southwards into the Tarim basin and established a new capital at Qocho. Although the majority of the new Uighur kingdom's population was Buddhist or

Christian, Manichaeans retained official favor and their monasteries, like those of the Buddhists, prospered from the administration of farmlands. A surviving document from this period describes the activities of these monasteries, including detailed instructions on where and how to distribute and trade their agricultural production (including wine).[54] As of the late tenth century the Uighur khans were still sending Manichaean monks as emissaries to the Chinese court.[55]

Panegyrics addressed to the Uighur kings of Qocho indicate that both Buddhists and Manichaeans saw him as a protector.[56] Texts and art from this period, mostly discovered hidden in monasteries, show markedly syncretistic trends.[57] Manichaeism seems slowly to have lost its adherents to Buddhism and Christianity over the following centuries, and by the time of the Mongol conquest may have become extinct among the Uighurs.

In China, however, the religion continued to succeed in winning native converts. Buddhist writers in the thirteenth century were still producing polemics against Manichaeism, disparaging it along with two Buddhist sects, those of the "White Lotus" and the "White Cloud," as deviant interpretations of Buddhism. The Ming Code of the following century outlawed the three altogether.[58] This continued animosity from Buddhists in China drove Manichaeans underground, but the community survived.

Blurring Distinctions:
Shared Ideas, Symbols, Vocabularies

From the earliest times, Manichaeism attempted to portray itself as an all-inclusive, universal religion. Its missionaries consciously drew on the symbols and vocabulary of their target audience, attempting to render the new teaching more familiar and acceptable.

Mani's disciple Mar Ammo, a Parthian, had great success propagating the new teaching in the eastern lands where Buddhism was prevalent. A Sogdian text states that Mar Ammo "fully exposed the Buddhahood of the Prophet of Light."[59] Another hymn, in Parthian, uses Islamic terminology, such as *dhu'l-fiqar*, the sword of Muhammad, perhaps to disguise its content from persecution by Muslims.[60] Another important early missionary, Mar Zaku, was eulogized by Manichaeans living along the Silk Road as "the Great Caravan-Leader," an epithet that Central Asian Buddhists applied to Avalokitesvara.[61] In another obvious attempt to appeal to Buddhists, an apocryphal letter from Central Asia has Mani write to Mar Ammo that the faithful should practice meditation and strive to acquire merit.[62]

Although the Uighur court in eastern Turkestan championed Manichaeism for nearly five centuries, probably only a minority of their subject population became Manichaeans. Some remained Nestorian, and many more eventually embraced Mahayana Buddhism. The texts and paintings from the Turfan oasis, especially, show a mixing of the three traditions to an extent that often verges on the bizarre. The "Great Hymn to Mani," which has been preserved in Turkish, is a good example:

> We have prepared ourselves with hearts full of praise to praise you,
> My praiseworthy, honorable father, my Mani Buddha...
> You have taken nescience from the living beings in the five forms of existence,
> You have brought them wisdom.
> You have let them partake of parinirvana.
> Hate and many other passions had perturbed their senses and their minds
> When you, our holy father, came down from the Firmament...
> You have erected the ladder of wisdom,
> And overcoming the five forms of existence you have saved us...
> We, the miserable sentient beings... came to see the Buddha-like
>   Sun-God [Jesus], equal to thee.
> Bound in fetters, enduring pain, we remain in this samsara.
> [But] you have preached the true, incomparable doctrine to those bound
>   to transient joys and you have led them to good Nirvana...
> You have shown them the way leading to the Buddha-realms.
> You have heaped up a Sumeru mountain of good deeds...
> When you found the unredeemed sentient beings, you saved them all
>   without exception.
> Awakened beings like us you have thoroughly taught the gem of the
>   gospel-teaching.[63]

A Sogdian hymn mentions "the five assemblies of the five Buddhas of Mahayana,"[64] clearly another conscious attempt on the part of the Manichaeans to speak the language of the eastern Silk Road. A Parthian text from Turfan includes the exhortation, "Awake, brethren, chosen ones, on this day of spiritual salvation the fourteenth of the month of Mihr, when Jesus, the Son of God, entered into *parinirvana*."[65] The

Christian term "crucifixion" and the Buddhist term "parinirvana" were interchangeable to the eastern Manichaeans; both referred to the liberation of Jesus's soul from the body of matter and its return to the Realm of Light.[66]

The increasing influence of Buddhism on the Uighur Manichaeans is markedly visible in a Buddhist-style *pothi* (palm-leaf) book from Bezeklik in the Turfan oasis probably dating to the eleventh century, which includes a colophon on the transfer of merit. Also included is the story of a merchant named Arazan, reflecting the identification of Manichaeism with Silk Road businessmen.[67]

In at least one significant case this mixing up of religious ideas was carried back westwards along the Silk Road to Europe. One of the most popular medieval European tales was the story of Barlaam and Ioasaph, a much recolored account of the life of the Buddha. Through a series of translations, the name of the hero was transformed from the Sanskrit *bodhisattva* to the Sogdian Budasaf to the Uighur Bodhisaf, and back again through Iudasaf to Ioasaf.[68]

In China, too, evidence of conceptual syncretism is abundant. The famous ten-foot high eighth-century Nestorian monument in Xi'an is adorned by a Maltese cross topped by a flaming pearl—a Daoist symbol for yang—and resting on a cloud—symbolizing yin—with a Buddhist lotus flower beneath it, with dragons on either side.[69] The text inscribed below summarizes the essence of Christianity in heavily Buddhist-flavored terms and images (e.g., "the Eight Cardinal Virtues," echoing the Noble Eightfold Path, "hanging up the bright sun," and "an oar of the vessel of mercy," a reference to Amitabha ferrying souls to paradise), along with a sprinkling of Confucianism ("how to rule both families and kingdoms") and Daoism (the "New Teaching of Non-assertion"):

> Fulfilling the old Law as it was declared by the twenty-four Sages, He (the Messiah) taught how to rule both families and kingdoms according to His own great Plan. Establishing His New Teaching of Non-assertion which operates silently through the Holy Spirit, another person of the Trinity, He formed in man the capacity for well-doing through the Right Faith. Setting up the standard of the Eight Cardinal Virtues, He purged away the dust from human nature and perfected a true character. Widely opening the Three Constant Gates, He brought Life to light and abolished Death. Hanging up the bright Sun, He swept away the abodes of darkness. All the evil devices

of the devil were thereupon defeated and destroyed. He then took an oar in the Vessel of Mercy and ascended to the Palace of Light. Thereby all rational beings were conveyed across the Gulf. His mighty work being thus completed, He returned at noon to His original position (in Heaven). The twenty-seven standard works of His Sutras were preserved. The Great means of Conversion (or leavening, i.e., transformation) were widely extended, and the sealed Gate of the Blessed Life was unlocked. His Law is to bathe with water and with the Spirit, and thus to cleanse from all vain delusions and to purify men until they regain the whiteness of their nature.

A few lines further down the imagery becomes more pronouncedly Daoist:

But, at any rate, The Way would not have spread so widely if it had not been for the Sage, and the Sage would not have been so great if it were not for The Way. Ever since the Sage and The Way were united together as the two halves of an indentured deed would agree, then the world became refined and enlightened.[70]

An earlier (641?) Christian text in Chinese bears the very Indian-sounding title *The Shastra on One Deva* (i.e., "Discourse on the Oneness of God").[71] In another early text (638—written by Alopen?), known as the *Jesus-Messiah Sutra*, is found the following passage, very much expressed in Chinese imagery:

Jehovah, who is Lord of Heaven...is like the wind in His countenance. And, who could possibly see the wind?...The Lord of Heaven is incessantly going all over the world, is constantly present everywhere...On account of this, every man existing in this world only obtains life and continues his existence by the strength of the Lord of Heaven...[72]

The *Jesus-Messiah Sutra* also mentions "Buddhas, Kinnaras, and Superintending Devas," perhaps an attempt to translate the concept of "angels, archangels, and hosts of heaven."[73]

A well-known early ninth-century Manichaean text in Chinese begins and ends like a Buddhist sutra. In fact, its conclusion is virtually identical with that of the Diamond Sutra. The Manichaean version reads: "Then, all the members of the great assembly, having heard the

Sutra accepted it with faith and rejoicing, and proceeded to put it into practice." The Diamond Sutra likewise concludes: "...all the monks and nuns, lay-brothers and lay-sisters...having heard the Buddha's words rejoiced with one accord, and accepting them with faith, proceeded to put them into practice."[74]

To ordinary people, unequipped to sift through doctrinal subtleties, this religious mish-mash must have often been quite confusing. One Chinese text offers the following advice:

> Talking about accepting Buddha, one should think of converting to *which* Buddha; not Mani Buddha, not to Nestorian Buddha, nor Zoroastrian Buddha, but Sakyamuni Buddha...[75]

Chapter Five

The Islamization of
the Silk Road

No religious tradition in history favored trade to the extent Islam did. The religion's founder, Muhammad b. Abdallah of Mecca in west-central Arabia, was himself a businessman by profession. While in his 20s he became employed by a wealthy widow by the name of Khadija, and made his reputation by successfully carrying out a trade mission to Syria on her behalf; Khadija married him soon after.

Sometime around 610 CE, Muhammad, who liked to spend time alone meditating in the mountains outside Mecca, began hearing voices during the course of these retreats. At first he began to doubt his own sanity, but his wife Khadija persuaded him that these voices might be divine in nature and should be listened to. Gradually Muhammad came to believe he was receiving revelations from God, calling upon him to "rise and warn" his fellow Meccans that the time had come to mend their ways.

Mecca was a desert town with little to subsist on apart from its trade. Successful merchants must have been its wealthiest inhabitants.[1] Many of the revelations Muhammad received dealt with social injustice, which seems to have been a growing problem in Mecca at that time. Muhammad's message found a growing audience of sympathetic ears among the poor and dispossessed, while it increasingly alienated the upper classes who were the main targets of his criticism. Before long certain powerful residents of Mecca were making life difficult for Muhammad and his followers.

In 622 the citizens of Yathrib, an agricultural oasis some 300 km to the north, were involved in factional disputes they could not resolve. Hearing of Muhammad's reputation for fairness and piety, they invited him to come and arbitrate. He accepted. Sending most of his followers ahead of him, Muhammad put his affairs in order and finally left his hometown, an event known to Muslims as the *hijra*, or migration, which marks the beginning of the Islamic calendar.

Once in Yathrib, the Muslims were not only no longer persecuted, they enjoyed special status. From their new power base they launched raids (Ar. *razzia*) on Meccan-bound caravans, enriching their own treasury while inflicting damage on their former persecutors. After several battles with the Meccans, the Muslims were able to negotiate the right to return to Mecca for the traditional Arabian pilgrimage to circumambulate the sacred *ka'ba* stone; by 628 Mecca was under Muslim control.

As with the Aryans of prehistoric Central Asia, raiding was an established part of the economic life of Arabia. Among the Arabs the only restriction was that one couldn't attack clan members or groups with whom one had made a nonaggression pact. With the successes of the Muslims growing from year to year, eventually all the tribes of the Arabian Peninsula sent emissaries to Muhammad in order to seek such pacts. Their professions of loyalty were described by later Muslim writers as "submission," which in Arabic is *islām*. Small wonder that these sources, and the non-Muslim histories based on them, interpret this as meaning all the Arabian tribes had accepted the new religion.

Understanding this term "submission" in its more restricted literal sense, however, more easily explains what happened upon the Muhammad's death in 632: most of the Arabian tribes rebelled. Later Muslim sources refer to these as rebellions of "apostasy." A simpler interpretation would be that the rebel parties simply saw their nonaggression pacts as having been rendered null and void by Muhammad's passing.

The Muslims immediately chose a successor, or caliph (Ar. *khalīfa*), Abu Bakr, under whose leadership the various Arab tribes were forced to resubmit. Since the Arabian economy required the component of raiding, and since according to the nonaggression pacts no one in Arabia could legitimately be raided, the Muslims were forced to launch forays beyond the Arabian Peninsula into Byzantine and Persian territory. Their successes in defeating the armies of both empires probably surprised many of the Muslims as much as it did their imperial enemies.

It is important to recognize the economic aspect of Muslim expansion, driven by the ancient Arabian tradition of raiding. While in hindsight both Muslims and non-Muslims have read into this early expansion a large element of religious zeal, the Arab armies of the time were simply doing what they were naturally acculturated to do, what the economic conditions of their homeland had always constrained them to do. What had changed was that, for the first time, all the Arab groups of the peninsula had excluded for themselves the possibility of raiding other Arab groups. They were forced, therefore, to raid elsewhere. Their new religious self-concept may indeed have inspired them as well by giving divine meaning to their increasing successes, but other factors were at work as well.

Iranians, in the form of Medes, Achemenians, Parthians, and Sasanians, had been vying with Athenian, Seleucid, and Roman Greeks for hegemony in Western Asia for over a millennium. By the seventh century both the Sasanian Persian and Byzantine Greek empires were exhausted. Moreover, neither treated their subject peoples in Mesopotamia, Syria, or Egypt very well. In many locations townspeople threw open the gates to the Arabs and welcomed them as liberators. The Muslims were, in fact, no more foreign in most of the lands they conquered than had been the previous rulers, and at first they were less exploitative. In Iran the case was somewhat different, and the reasons for the spectacularly rapid collapse of the Sasanian Empire there continue to be debated.[2]

By the 660s, however, the ruling Arab family, the Umayyads, had set themselves up in Damascus in very much the mold of the Byzantine governors they had recently dislodged. Throughout the subsequent decades non-Muslims came to chafe under the new regime. Many Arab Muslims, furthermore, resented the imperial manner of the Umayyads and their "un-Islamic" lifestyles, which frequently featured drinking and debauchery in the mode of their Byzantine Roman predecessors. But the coalition that was to bring about the Umayyads' downfall, and in doing so, forever change the very nature of Islam as a cultural tradition, drew its main support from the non-Arab converts of eastern Iran.

Initially and throughout the Umayyad period, the Arabs had seen Islam as a religion belonging to them; their subjects, likewise, referred to Islam as "the Arab religion" (al-dīn al-'arab). The Qur'an enjoined Muslims to fight the polytheists of the Arabian Peninsula, the original impulse of holy war (jihād) being that Muslims should not have to live under the rule of infidels. Once the Arabs began to expand their reach beyond Arabia this principle took on a broader meaning. But if a given locality agreed to submit to Arab authority and pay the poll tax *(jizya)* levied on protected communities *(dhimmīs,* qualified as "peoples of the Book," i.e., Christians, Jews, and ultimately Zoroastrians), there was no further need for coercion on either side.

In fact Arab Muslims had strong reasons not to want non-Arabs to join the faith, since conversion directly affected both their sources of income and the spread of its distribution among Muslims. There were conversely numerous reasons why non-Muslims might wish to join the ruling group, which could most obviously be symbolized by adopting their faith (Bentley's "conversion by voluntary association" model). Despite some apparent resistance from the Arab elite, by the early eighth century non-Arab converts were probably beginning to outnumber Arab Muslims.

The Qur'an speaks against class and racial distinctions, but even during the Prophet's lifetime this ideal was never met. Early converts and their descendents often felt entitled to greater status and privilege than later converts, and members of aristocratic families never forgot who came from humble ones. Tribal and clan loyalties affected government appointments and led to rivalries.

Often these rivalries developed power bases in garrison towns where particular clan-based factions were dominant. Local governors, therefore, usually had more or less personal armies at their ready disposal. In areas where the Arabs were quartered among non-Arab majority populations, there was increasing pressure from converts to be treated on equal footing with Arab Muslims.

The problem was that a non-Arab, even after converting to Islam, had no tribal affiliation that could provide him an identity within Arab society. A solution to this was devised whereby an Arab Muslim could take a non-Arab convert under his wing as a "client" *(mawlā),* making the convert a sort of honorary tribal member. Of course, such clients were at the mercy of the individual who sponsored them.

Over time this inequality between Arab and non-Arab Muslims became a major complaint for various parties disaffected with Umayyad rule. Not surprisingly it was in eastern Iran, at the fringes of Umayyad power, that a rebel movement emerged which proved capable of overthrowing the central government and completely reshaping Muslim society.

In addition to complaints about the un-Islamic character of the Umayyad elite and the inequalities between Arab and non-Arab Muslims, the anti-Umayyad movement could draw on the issue of the very legitimacy of Umayyad rule. The first Umayyad caliph, Mu'awiya, had assumed power by refusing to recognize the selection of the Prophet's cousin and son-in-law, Ali, as fourth caliph. A significant minority of Muslims felt that leadership should be sought in charismatic authority passed down through the Prophet's line. For the "partisans of Ali" (*shi'at 'Ali;* later, Shi'ites), the Umayyads (and indeed the first three caliphs) had been usurpers from the outset.

All of these antigovernment impulses came together in the so-called Abbasid Revolution of 749–751, in which a Khurasan-based Muslim army rallied behind an Iranian general, Abu Muslim, in the name of an Arab descendant of the Prophet's uncle Abbas. The rebels succeeded in wresting power from the Umayyads, moved the capital to Mesopotamia, and began setting up a new Islamic administration on the Sasanian imperial model. The Arab Abbasids in whose name the rebellion had been carried out quickly turned on their champion Abu Muslim and killed him, fearing his popularity. Even so, the ministers and functionaries of their new government were overwhelmingly Iranian, often recent converts from Zoroastrianism or Christianity—or even, as in the case of the influential Barmak family from Balkh, from Buddhism. In 762 the caliph Mansur built a new capital at Baghdad (meaning "given by God" in Persian), commenting that this would put Muslims in touch "with lands as far off as China."[3]

"Religious" Rebellions in Iran and Central Asia

During the first half of the eighth century Muslim armies repeatedly attempted to assert and maintain their authority over the easternmost parts of the Iranian world, Sogdiana and Bactria. Following the pattern of the Arab tribes at the time of Muhammad, local rulers would "submit" when overwhelmed and then "apostasize" again as soon as they thought they could get away with it. Some, like the Sogdian king Tughshada, did this several times in succession.

Iranians, like the Chinese, have long considered theirs to be the greatest and most ancient of civilizations. For many Iranians, being conquered by the Arabs, a people they had always considered barbaric, was and remains the greatest single trauma in the history of their nation. The Iranian national epic, the *Shāh-nāmeh* ("Book of Kings"), though compiled in the tenth century by an Iranian Muslim poet for a Turkish Muslim patron, portrays the Arab conquest of Iran as a sort of final and ultimate tragedy.

Because the Zoroastrian priesthood, the magi, was so directly identified with the ruling house throughout most of the Sasanian period, the fall of the dynasty inevitably meant the fall of the priestly class. This did not mean, however, that Iranian religion in other forms could not provide a rallying focus for resistance to Arab rule.

In Sogdiana a resistance movement took shape in 777 around a figure known as Muqanna', or "the Veiled One," a self-declared prophet whose followers, like the Manichaeans, wore white robes. According to Narshakhi, a Sogdian Muslim writing a century later, Muqanna' said of himself:

> Do you know who I am? I am your lord and lord of all the world...I am the one who showed myself to people as Adam, then in the form of Noah, also in the form of Abraham, Moses, then in the guise of Jesus, Muhammad the prophet, in the guise of Abu Muslim, and now in this guise which you see...I have the power to be in any guise I wish to show.[4]

His missionaries distributed letters that read:

> Verily al-Muqanna' has strength, power, glory, and proof. Accept me and realize that I have dominion. Glory and omnipotence are mine. There is no other God but me. He who follows me will go to Paradise, but he who does not accept me will rest in Hell.[5]

Narshakhi writes that in Sogdiana "most of the villages accepted the faith of Muqanna'," and that the Muslims were "impotent" before them. The movement was so successful in Central Asia, he writes, that the caliph in Baghdad "feared that there was a danger that Islam would be lost and the religion of Muqanna' would spread throughout the entire world."[6]

Like many successful religious figures, Muqanna' may have been a master illusionist. When begged by a crowd to reveal himself, he had his assistants direct sunlight into the mob by use of mirrors, in order to dazzle them. Many present claimed afterwards that they had seen God. When after nine years of struggle the Muslim armies finally cornered Muqanna' in his fortress stronghold, he told his followers that he would go up to heaven and bring down angels to help them, then threw himself into a fire. Narshakhi states that in his time Muqanna's followers still followed their faith in secret. "Their religion is such," he says, "that they neither pray nor fast, nor do they wash after sexual intercourse." He goes on to accuse them of promiscuity: "They say that a woman is like a flower; [no matter] who smells it, nothing is detracted from it."[7]

The single most effective anti-Muslim resistance movement in Iran proper, which began around 816 and lasted more than 20 years, was waged in Azerbaijan by a sect practicing the *Khurram-dīn,* or "Happy Religion." Led by a prophetic figure named Babak, the *Khurram-dīniyya* were a group descended from a sixth-century social reform movement led by an individual named Mazdak who advocated the redistribution of private property, including wives. Widely popular with the impoverished masses, Mazdakism enjoyed a period of official favor under the Sasanian emperor Kavad from 488 to 531 but was brutally crushed under his son and successor, Khusrow I, with the support of the magi.

While not much is known of the *Khurram-dīniyya* doctrine, apparently they had a joyous approach to life and were generally peaceful except when faced with persecution. Following the public execution of their leader, Babak, in 837, which was particularly drawn out and grisly, the movement ceased to be a political force, but many of its followers continued a secret existence while outwardly professing Islam, and the sect may still survive today.[8]

Islam and Trade in the Eastern Lands

As with any case of mass cultural conversion, the Islamization of Central Asia was a complex process that occurred on more than one level. The first, and most visible, was the spread of political power. It is worth noting that the expansion of a particular religion's rule is not identical with the spread of faith, although historians often write as if it were.

Muslim dominance of the western half of the Silk Road came fairly early and was established, albeit through a period of false starts and occasional reversals, by the mid-eighth century. Muslims thereafter controlled much of trans-Asian trade, which became the second major factor in the Islamization of Central Asian culture. Gradually a third factor, the influence of charismatic Sufi preachers, entered into the process.

The reality of Muslim rule could no longer be reasonably ignored once the numerous eighth-century attempts to rally behind local, non-Islamic religious figures had all failed. Politics was therefore an initial influence encouraging Central Asians to abandon their native cultural traditions and join the growing world culture of Islamic civilization. It appears, however, that for the most part only local rulers, especially those who had raised arms against the Muslims, were ever subjected to the "convert or die" alternative that has so long been the stereotype characterizing the spread of Islam. Other people, at least at first, would have embraced the faith of their new rulers for other reasons, spiritual or otherwise.

One of the most commonly cited incentives to religio-cultural conversion is the pursuit of patronage. Anyone directly dependent on the government for his livelihood might sense advantages in joining the cultural group of his patrons, and accepting the norms and values of that ruling group. To a large extent, converts to Islam do appear to have held onto their preconquest positions, and being a Muslim increased one's chances of attaining a new or better one.

A second, and probably greater factor driving Islamization was the Muslim dominance of commercial activity. A businessman might well feel that becoming a Muslim would facilitate contacts and cooperation with other Muslim businessmen both at home and abroad; he would also benefit from favorable conditions extended by Muslim officials, and from the Islamic laws governing commerce.

The presence of Muslim rule and the increasing Muslim dominance of trade meant that Islamization came first in the urban areas along the Silk Road, and only in later centuries spread to the countryside. The gradual Islamization of the nomadic Turkic peoples of Central and Inner Asia was at first directly tied to their increasing participation in the oasis-based Silk Road trade in the tenth century,[9] accelerated by the political activities of three Turkic Muslim dynasties—the Qara-khanids, the Ghaznavids, and the Seljuks—and supplemented by the proselytizing efforts of Sufi missionaries.[10]

The third major factor accounting for the Islamization of the Silk Road, which follows those of politics and economics, is assimilation.

Whatever the reasons for one's converting to Islam, Islamization occurs most profoundly (and irrevocably) among the succeeding generation, since the convert's children in principle will be raised within the father's new community, and not his original one.[11] Furthermore, although a Muslim man may marry a non-Muslim woman, Islamic law requires that the children of a mixed marriage be raised as Muslims. However, in light of our remarks in chapter One on women's roles in religious education, it may be safe to assume that aspects of pre-Islamic local religion survived through transmission by non-Muslim wives of Muslim men.

Central Asians of the countryside, being less directly affected by the factors described above, held onto their Iranian (usually agriculturalist) or Turkic (usually pastoral nomadic) native religious traditions longer than did their urban counterparts. Gradually, though, the same influences were felt throughout the rural areas. An additional, and even more significant Islamicizing influence especially on the pastoral peoples came through the activities of Sufi shaykhs, who took it upon themselves to spread Islam to the remotest areas. Their influence stemmed largely from their personal charisma, which often made them the authoritative sources for the religion even above and beyond the Qur'an, *hadith*s (stories about the Prophet), or Islamic law.

It was the shaykh's own personal interpretations of the Islamic message that formed the basis of the faith as the pastoral folk heard it. These personal interpretations were often accommodating toward preexisting local beliefs and practices, leading to the development of "popular" expressions of Islam that could deviate significantly from the normative tradition emanating from the cities. In some ways local religion in Central Asia, whether of the Iranian or Turkic variety, never really disappeared. Rather, it acquired Islamic meanings, interpretations, and appearances.

The Fate of Zoroastrianism and Buddhism in Central Asia

It appears to be the case that by the time of the Arab conquest in the middle to late seventh century CE, those elements of Sogdian religiosity most noticed and commented on by Muslim writers—such as fire worship and the exposure of corpses—were elements normally associated with Zoroastrianism. This is in contrast to the Muslim accounts of the conquest of Sind, where local religiosity appears to have remained strongly Buddhist-oriented. But even in the Muslim accounts of Central Asia, we see aspects of local culture that do not mesh entirely with the canonical Zoroastrianism of Sasanian Iran.

Narshakhi comments that in his day there were mosque doors in Bukhara that bore images with the faces scratched out. He explains that these doors had been taken by lower-class converts to Islam from the suburban villas of the unconverted rich, each of whose gate bore the image of a patron idol.

In contrast to this example, Narshakhi elsewhere provides evidence of more recognizably "Zoroastrian" practice. He relates that upon the death of the local ruler Tughshada, who had nominally submitted to Islam as a means of retaining his position but repeatedly "apostasized" whenever he thought he could get away with it, his servants "removed his flesh and brought his bones to Bukhara."[12]

Other cases of the Sogdians' use of iconography incompatible with both canonical Zoroastrianism and Islam can be seen in their burial customs. While, like the Sasanians, Central Asian Iranians exposed their dead to have their bones picked clean by vultures, unlike the Zoroastrians of the Iranian plateau they then buried the bones in clay ossuaries decorated with figures.[13]

Accounts of Sogdian merchants and their trading communities along the Silk Road eastward into China variously identify them as having Buddhist or Zoroastrian practices. While Sogdians of both faiths may well have been represented within these expatriate communities, the lines need not be so clearly drawn, for as we have seen, the Sogdians' pool of religious beliefs and practices could include elements of both traditions. In addition, the balance of elements likely differed among various Sogdian communities or even individuals.

As Sogdiana became administratively incorporated into the *dār al-islām*, the Sogdians came to assimilate themselves into the broader Persian cultural sphere, adopting Persian in preference to their original, related tongue and becoming increasingly identified as Persians. The revival of Zoroastrian letters in the ninth century, which came as a reaction to the mass conversions of Zoroastrians to Islam in Iran, probably improved communication of the institutional form of the religion to those Central Asians who had not yet turned to Islam. Zoroastrians were usually classified as a "protected" *(dhimmī)* community in Central Asia as in Iran, and in Samarkand the Zoroastrian community was entrusted with the maintenance of the water piping system in lieu of paying the *jizya*, the poll-tax levied on non-Muslims.[14]

From the seventh century Chinese sources make increasing reference to Zoroastrian communities there. Many Zoroastrians appear to have fled eastward along the Silk Road after the Muslim conquest of Iran, following in the steps of Peroz, son of the last Sasanian emperor, Yazdigerd III, who was welcomed at the Tang court at Chang'an as the "King of Persia" and made a general in the imperial guard. Peroz was accompanied by many refugees, who were allowed to build fire temples and practice their faith.

As late as the Mongol period, Zoroastrian exile communities are mentioned as flourishing in China. Zoroastrianism is not a missionary religion, and these communities do not appear to have included local converts, but they very likely included Mazda-worshippers of Central Asian origin in addition to the refugees and merchants from Iran proper. Numerous Tang period temples at Chang'an, Luoyang, Kaifeng, and elsewhere appear to have been Mazdaean. Popular Chinese tales from the Tang period attest to the familiarity of the Chinese population with the figure of the Mazdaean merchant.[15]

Despite the Muslims' ideological aversion to Buddhism as an "idol-worshipping" religion inferior to the religions "of the Book," there is ample evidence of Buddhist survivals well into the Muslim period. The Barmak family, furthermore, which gave the early Abbasid government many of its most powerful and effective administrators, was originally a family of hereditary caretakers of Balkh's main Buddhist shrine.

The Barmaks controlled a monastery known as Naw Bahar ("new spring" in Persian, a false cognate derived from the Sanskrit *nava vihāra,* or "new temple"), which appears to have been the center of a network of monasteries dispersed throughout Iran.[16] Since Buddhist monasteries controlled enormous wealth, the family was likely among the major economic players in the region. It has been suggested that the Barmaks' conversion to Islam robbed the eastern lands of a major potential anti-Muslim rallying force, thereby facilitating Islamization in those regions.[17] However, the execution by the Abbasids of Abu Muslim, just three years after the Iranian general had led their revolution to success, led to the rise of widespread rumors of his reincarnation, pointing to a survival of Buddhist belief among the general population.[18]

The best-known of the classical Muslim historians, Muhammad b. Jarir Tabari, mentions Buddhist idols being brought from Kabul to Baghdad in the late ninth century.[19] Narshakhi gives some interesting information pertaining to Bukhara. He states that at the bazaar adjoining the Makh mosque—which appears to have been a Buddhist temple that the Sasanians had turned into a fire temple before the Muslims came and transformed it once again—a twice-annual fair was held where 50,000 dirhams worth of Buddhist idols were sold.[20] Another Muslim historian, Ibn Hawkal, writes that in the tenth century wooden animal figures were for sale in Samarkand.[21]

The Samanids, an Iranian Muslim dynasty that took over many formerly Buddhist lands in Central Asia, seem to have borrowed certain influences into their architecture, such as the four-archway plan of the religious schools, the *madrasa*s, that developed during their reign. In fact, the very idea of the madrasas themselves may have been absorbed from the Buddhist schools, since these institutions first appear in this part of the Muslim world.

Further east, where Muslim power took longer to consolidate and Buddhism survived longer as a result, similar patterns can be observed. Aurel Stein in the course of his excavations in the Tarim basin discovered an early Turkish Muslim shrine that was purported to be the tomb of four imams, but which he determined had originally been a Buddhist monument.[22] Another such shrine in the Tarim region is mentioned in the sixteenth-century Muslim hagiography *History of the Uwaysis*, which contains a legend about a Sufi named Muhibb-i Kuhmar ("Lover of the Mountain Snake") and a holy snake, apparently modeled on a Buddhist snake story connected with the philosopher Nagarjuna.[23]

The Later Development of Jewish Trade Networks

Jews certainly participated in the Silk Road trade networks that linked the Roman Mediterranean with Han China in classical times. During the Muslim period Jewish traders known as Radanites (Ar. al-*radaniyya*, perhaps from Persian *rāh-dān*, "one who knows the way") held a privileged status that allowed them to move freely between the Muslim and Christian worlds, but the origins of the Radanite system must go back several centuries at least prior to the coming of Islam, since the

Radanite networks are highly developed by the time they appear in Muslim writings.[24] Latin sources seem to indicate that already in the preceding centuries, Mediterranean trade was dominated by Jews from the West and Syrians from the Byzantine East.[25]

The original base of the Radanites was in Roman Gaul, centered in Arles and Marseilles.[26] They trafficked particularly in slaves, and controlled a large operation in Verdun for turning them into eunuchs. It was this involvement in the slave trade that brought the Jewish Radanites into contact with the Turkish Khazars of the north Caspian region, a transit point for captured Slavs (from Lat. *sclav*, "slave"; hence Ar. *saqāliba*).

Controlling an important northern offshoot of the Silk Road, the Khazars were ideally situated to serve as middlemen between East and West. They enjoyed a symbiotic relationship with the settled Iranian peoples to the south and the east along the Silk Road, which was well expressed in the Turkish proverb *Tātsiz Türk bolmas; bāşsiz börk bolmas,* meaning "There is no Turk without an Iranian [merchant partner, just as] there is no cap without a head." Perceiving the commercial benefits associated with the Radanites' neutral religious status, the Khazar elite eventually embraced Judaism, although the supreme ruler, the Kaghan, as well as the general population of his subjects, retained their original shamanistic Turkic religion.[27]

The ninth-century Persian geographer Ibn Khurdadbih describes the Radanites thus:

> These merchants speak Arabic, Persian, Roman (i.e., Greek), the language of the Franks, Andalusians, and Slavs. They journey from west to east, partly on land, partly by sea. They transport from the west eunuchs, female and male slaves, silk, castor, marten and other furs, and swords.[28]

Ibn Khurdadbih describes four different trade routes on which the Radanites were active. The first is from Gaul across the Mediterranean and overland to the Red Sea and via the Indian Ocean to the East Asia, the second is via Mesopotamia, and the third across North Africa. The fourth route mentioned by Ibn Khurdadbih went northward through the Khazar lands, from whence it joined the Silk Road:

> Sometimes they likewise take the route behind Rome, and, passing through the country of the Slavs, arrive at Khamlif (Etil), the capital

of the Khazars. They embark upon the Jorjan Sea (the Caspian), arrive at Balkh, betake themselves from there across the Oxus, and continue their journey toward the Yourts of the Toghozghor (the Tüqqüz Oghuz Turks), and from there to China.[29]

Naturally the raising of Judaism to official status within the Khazar dominions would have facilitated and encouraged the northern alternative. In any event Ibn Khurdadbih's account makes it clear that Jews were active along all the world's major trade routes at that time, which implies the existence of diaspora communities of Jews living all along the various stages of those routes. The widespread extent of these diaspora communities and the fact that they remained in communication with each other is borne out by the many locations referred to in the Gaonic responsa literature (rabbinic instruction on questions of Jewish life), which began in the eighth century.[30]

The Assassins

Frankish Crusaders in the eleventh and twelfth centuries brought to Europe stories of a secretive extremist sect led by "The Old Man of the Mountain," a group that came to be known as the Assassins. The derivation of this term continues to be debated; popular tales derive it from the Arabic word *hashīshiyūn,* claiming that members of the sect would drug themselves before carrying out their spectacular and usually public murders of well-known Muslim politicians and other figures. A more sober etymology traces back to *assasiyūn,* "the people of the foundation."[31]

The sect in question was an offshoot of the "partisans of Ali," known variously as the Sevener Shi'ites, since their lineage of spiritual leaders (imams) diverges from the Shi'ite majority after the sixth imam; as the Isma'ilis, after their seventh imam, Isma'il; or in earlier Muslim sources, as the Batinites (from the Arabic *bātin,* "esoteric"), because of their secretive doctrines and practices.

A Sevener dynasty, the Fatimids, ruled from Egypt throughout the eleventh century, drawing much of their prosperity from trade linking the Mediterranean with the Red Sea. The Fatimids provided Sevener Shi'ism with state sponsorship, fostering an active and often quite successful missionary program. The most famous Sevener missionary of this period was the poet-philosopher Nasir-i Khusrow, who traveled the Silk Road westward from his home in eastern Khurasan to Cairo, the Fatimid capital, apparently making a tour of Sevener centers along the way.[32]

The Sunni state based in Baghdad found the Seveners' missionary successes threatening, and often persecuted Sevener communities wherever they could. It was in response to this persecution that Sevener devotees began their campaign of political killings, designed to strike terror into the hearts of their enemies. The Assassins, as these defenders of their faith have come to be known, were eminently successful in carrying out their missions.[33] Perhaps their most famous victim was Nizam al-Mulk, the Persian prime minister of the staunchly Sunni Seljuk Turks, who was stabbed to death in his litter in 1092.

Two years later the Sevener community split over the issue of succession. The minority faction came to be known as the Nizaris, after a martyred leader. The Nizari cause was taken up by Hasan-i Sabah, a Persian trained in Cairo who had ordered Nizam al-Mulk's killing.[34] Hasan's community operated out of a mountain fortress at Alamut in northern Iran. This region, which had always resisted incorporation into the caliphate and had been home to many heterodox movements, provided a safe haven for the Nizaris for over 120 years, until a concerted effort by the Mongols finally dislodged them in 1226.

The Islamization of Turkic Dynasties

When the first Muslim merchants and missionaries came to the Tarim basin they found one of the most religiously diverse cultures in the world. By that time the majority of inhabitants were probably Buddhists, but there were Manichaean and Nestorian Christian communities as well. Various local cults and traditional religions must also have been represented.

According to local accounts, the Islamization of Kashgar began in the first half of the tenth century when Satoq Bughra, a local Turkish boy from the clan later known as the Qara-khanids, was converted by one Nasr b. Mansur of the Samanid family, which was ruling Transoxiana and eastern Iran.[35] Nasr may have been sent to negotiate trade agreements, since according to the story caravans from Bukhara followed him in large numbers.

Eventually Satoq Bughra became khan of Kashgar and gave Islam official status there. Although aspects of this account may belong to legend, it does fit in with the Samanids' well-known policy of sending missions to the various Turkish tribes throughout Inner Asia in hopes of transforming them from raiders into traders.

With the conversion of Satoq Bughra Khan, who died around 955, the Qara-khanids became the first Turkish dynasty officially to espouse Islam.[36] The Muslim historians Ibn Athir and Ibn Miskawayh state that in 960 an immense number of Turks—200,000 tents—converted to Islam.[37] The group in question has commonly been identified as the Qara-khanids. Throughout the first half of the eleventh century Islam gained in importance across the eastern part of the Central Asian Silk Road that was under their control.

Other Turkic ruling groups, the Ghaznavids and the Seljuks, also converted to Islam before coming to control large areas from Anatolia to India in the eleventh century. The Ghaznavids originally became Islamicized in the service of the Iranian Samanids of Bukhara, before challenging and eventually taking much of the southern territory of their former employers.

The Oghuz Turkish chieftain Seljuk embraced Islam around 985, apparently for political reasons. His descendents took control of the Ghaznavid lands in 1040. From 1055 the Seljuks established hegemony over Baghdad, and with the somewhat reluctant acquiescence of the caliph, assumed the role of champions of Sunni Islam. Islamization was therefore central to their legitimizing ideology. At the same time, the Seljuks were a major force in the Turkicization of the Muslim world, especially with their conquest of much of Byzantine Anatolia by the late eleventh century and the establishment of the Sultanate of Rūm (i.e., eastern "Rome").[38]

Along the northwestern spur of the Silk Road, which included the Volga basin, the Turkic Bulgars became Islamized during the tenth century. This seems to have been largely an effect of their trade connections with the Muslim world. An eleventh-century Muslim Bulgar historian, Ya'qub b. Nu'man al-Bulgari, writes that the Bulgar king had accepted Islam after a Muslim merchant healed him and his wife from some disease.[39]

Among the eastern Turks, Islam was still very much tied to the merchant class by the eve of the Mongol conquest. Buddhism remained strong in the towns of the Tarim basin, as did Nestorianism and traditional shamanistic religion among the steppe nomads.

The *pax mongolica* established through the thirteenth-century conquests of Chinggis Khan and his successors was a boon to overland trade. Thus, no doubt at first unintentionally, the Mongols strengthened the position of the Silk Road Muslims by creating conditions under which their business could prosper as never before. Although many of the Mongol elite held onto their native traditions for several more generations, those most concerned with trade sooner or later tended to throw their support behind the Muslims, and many themselves adopted Islam.

The Further Islamization of the Tarim

With the support of a converted ruler, Sufi missionaries could more freely travel and preach among the Turkish and Mongol general populations. Most of the later Turkic tribal groups developed origin legends that attributed their Islamization to a particular charismatic individual from the Muslim West, a class that came to be known as *khoja*s (from the Persian *khwāja*, or "master").

Many of the earliest Sufi missionaries who came from Transoxiana to the Tarim basin (or *altı şahr*, "Six Cities," as the region is known in Muslim sources) were members of the popular and predominantly Turkish Yasavi order. By the late fourteenth century, however, the more Sharia-minded and politically involved Naqshbandiyya began to displace them.[40] Hagiographies and histories from the sixteenth and seventeenth centuries portray the subsequent Islamization of the Tarim region as very much the story of these Naqshbandi shaykhs and their inspiring, pious deeds, which often included taking up arms against non-Muslim Turks, Mongols, and Chinese to support candidates for power who were pro-Muslim.

Chinese Muslims

Today there are about ten million ethnically Chinese Muslims, known as Hui, living in China. Just exactly who the Hui are and where they came from continues to be a matter of debate.

Persian and Arab Muslim traders traveled to China from the very beginnings of Islamic expansion. Modern legends have the Muhammad's uncle, Sa'ad Waqqas, bringing Islam to China during the his lifetime, but this story lacks evidence.[41] The earliest written reference to Muslims traveling the Silk Road to China is in the New Tang History, which states that a delegation sent by the caliph 'Uthman arrived at Chang'an (Xi'an) in 651.[42]

In 757 the Tang emperor requested the aid of various mercenary groups to help him put down the rebellion of An Lushan; in addition to the then-pagan Uighurs, Muslims are mentioned as being among those who helped restore Tang power. In reward for their services the Muslim soldiers were given lands in Central China. A number of them settled and took Chinese wives. In 801 another continegent of Arab and Sogdian Muslims were hired by the Tibetans who were attacking Yunnan in the southwest of China. Although the Tibetans and Muslims were defeated, the Tang allowed the Muslims to settle there and marry Chinese women.[43] The Hui are presumed to have been originally descended from these mercenary groups.

Like other foreign communities, the Muslims in China lived mainly in self-governing enclaves and resisted sinicization. They had their own educational systems, their own community leaders, and their own economy, which was connected by the Silk Road with that of Muslim communities to the west.

There is little evidence that individual Chinese actually chose to convert to Islam. Once Muslim communities were established in China, however, a significant aspect of their growth was the adoption of unwanted Chinese children, who were raised as Muslims. This influx of Chinese blood, combined with the fact that Muslim soldiers and merchants who settled in China married Chinese women, contributed to the eventual creation of a distinct Chinese Muslim ethnicity. Again, the fact that mixed marriages were the rule suggests significant (if unverifiable) women's input into the early development of Chinese Islam.

During the period of the Yuan dynasty (i.e., the Mongols) in the thirteenth and fourteenth centuries, Persian and Arab Muslims were brought to China to serve as administrators. Because of their experience in commerce, Muslims were the favoured candidates for positions in finance, tax collection, and so forth. This trend reinforced existing Chinese stereotypes of Persian and Arab Muslims (whom, incidentally, the Chinese did not distinguish from Jews) as conniving, untrustworthy merchants. An exception to this negative image is seen in the case of Sayyid Ajall of Bukhara, governor of Yunnan province under the

Mongols, whom Chinese sources (such as the later Ming chronicles) treat as a fair and talented administrator and, curiously, as a proponent of Confucian ethics.[44]

The Hui, meanwhile, gradually took shape as an indigenous Chinese Muslim group and have retained that identity up to the present day. The eventual assimilation of Islam into Chinese culture can be seen in the architecture of the Great Mosque at Xi'an, whose pagoda-shaped minaret is adorned with dragons!

A Reversal for Islam

During the first half of the twelfth century, the Islamicized Qara-khanids were displaced in eastern Central Asia by a Mongolian non-Muslim group, the Qara-khitai. (It was from the name of this latter group that Europeans derived the term "Cathay," which they long applied to China). The next two centuries would pose the greatest challenge to Muslim domination of the Silk Road.

The ancestors of the Qara-khitai, known as the Kitans, had conquered China in 947, founding the Liao dynasty, but were overthrown in 1115 by a tribe or confederation called the Jürchens who established the Chin dynasty. They moved westward and conquered many Silk Road towns that had been under Muslim control for several centuries. Various religions were represented among the Qara-khitai. The Muslim writer Ibn al-Athir states that their first leader, called the Gür-khan, was a Manichaean. Other references suggest he may have been a Nestorian Christian.[45] Most likely, in keeping with steppe tradition, he saw potential value in all religions.

In any event under the Qara-khitai Muslims lost their preeminent position along central part of the Silk Road, to the benefit of the followers of other traditions. In some places the Qara-khitai had mosques turned into Buddhist temples or Christian churches. Whether this indicates merely the preferences of the Qara-khitai themselves or an attempt by them to win the support of non-Muslim populations that had been living under Muslim rule, unfortunately cannot be known from the historical evidence. We simply do not know what proportion of the population in any given locality adhered to any particular religious tradition. Clearly, however, Central Asian Christianity, Manichaeism, and Buddhism had fallen into a defensive phase of their respective histories. The activities of first the Qara-khitai and then the Mongols reversed that trend and put Muslims on the defensive, at least temporarily.

The most significant conquests in the westward movement of the religiously mixed Qara-khitai were the Silk Road cities of Samarkand and Bukhara, which they wrested from the Muslim Sultan Sanjar in 1141.[46] This reverse in the supremacy of Islam in Central Asia inaugurated two centuries of exacerbated tensions and competitive intrigue between exponents of Christianity, Buddhism, and Islam, which crested under Mongol rule in the thirteenth century. Muslims would emerge dominant once again by the end of the Mongol period, but throughout this time such an outcome was far from being a given.

Chapter Six

Ecumenical Mischief

Echoes and rumors of the Qara-khitai exploits reached the Frankish Crusaders in the Levant, who, through a bit of creative phonetics, interpreted the ruler's title, Gür-khan, as "Prester John" (Syriac: Yuhanan) and developed the myth of a Christian king from the East who would come to join forces with them in the Holy Land and help to crush Islam there.[1] This myth was to persist for nearly two centuries, as the persona of Prester John came optimistically to be associated with a succession of Turkish or Mongolian steppe figures having Christian connections.

It was at least partly in hopes of contacting this nonexistent ally that a series of embassies was sent from Western Europe into the far-off depths of Inner Asia. The ambassadors themselves often joined in the struggle for supremacy that took place at the Mongol courts between representatives of the major world religions of the time.

Prester John stories circulated vigorously during the early thirteenth century. First, there were the successes of the mostly Christian Naiman Mongols against the Khwarazm-shah Sultan Muhammad, perhaps the most powerful figure in the Muslim world at that time. Then as details filtered westward regarding the new scourge of the steppes, Temujin, who would become known as Chinggis Khan, information regarding Christian members of his household (particularly women) gave rise to yet further hopes. This, of course, was at a time when the Mongol army under Temujin's grandson Batu had not yet laid waste to Eastern Europe, and the Mongols' westward advances could still be interpreted as directed specifically at Muslim centers of power.

In fact, the Naimans' appearance in western Central Asia was due to the fact that they were fleeing Temujin's attempts to consolidate the various Mongol and Turkic tribes under his solitary command. The Naiman leader, Küchlük, is referred to as a Buddhist, while his wife was a Christian, or possibly the other way around.[2] In any event, he was no friend of Muslims, and when his ally the ruler of Kashgar was killed in a local uprising, he intervened to put down the rebellion and subsequently launched a full-scale persecution of the local Muslim community, forbidding the ritual prayer (salāt) and commanding Muslims to convert to Christianity or Buddhism.[3]

The Muslim population of Kashgar by that time must have been significant, since when Temujin sent an army against Küchlük and promised to give Kashgar religious freedom, a large number of the inhabitants allied themselves with Temujin's forces. Following Küchlük's expulsion, Temujin's general Jäbä issued a proclamation that "everyone should follow the religion of his ancestors and leave others alone."[4] The Persian historian Juvaini later reported that the Kashgarians told him Chinggis Khan's army had come as an act of "divine mercy."[5]

Sometimes, however, the Muslims were their own worst enemies. According to a later Persian writer, Khwand Amir, when Jäbä and another Mongol general, Sübödei, turned their attentions to the city of Rayy in northern Iran, the local jurists of the Shafite school of law "went out to greet them and encouraged Jäbä and Sübödäi to slaughter the half of the city that was Hanafite." The Mongols did so, but then, saying to themselves, "What good can be expected of men who plot to have their own countrymen's blood shed?" they killed the Shafites too. Likewise, when they proceeded southward to the city of Qom, it was on the urging of some Sunnis that the Mongols put the local population, which was mostly Shi'ite, to death.[6]

Religion among the Mongols

The religiosity of the Mongols and related steppe peoples is generally considered to fall under the rubric of shamanism, and featured a somewhat vague notion of a supreme sky god, Tangri. However, their interest in spiritual matters centered largely on applications to real-life issues, such as the acquisition of food, victory in battle, and personal health. Thus, they were open to any sort of religious practice or ritual that might help them to find success in realizing their immediate aims.

This led to a kind of general openness in which any religion tended to be seen as being potentially effective, at least until proven otherwise. Successive Mongol khans repeatedly asked representatives of every religion—Christianity, Islam, Buddhism, Daoism—to pray for them, and the Mongol elite frequently patronized all of these religions by constructing places of worship and by giving gifts to religious figures. They drew the line on foreign religious practice only when it infringed on their own, such as the Muslim method of slaughtering animals for meat, or bathing in running water.[7] Edicts against these practices were promulgated by Chinggis Khan, and enforced sporadically by his successors.[8]

Like previous steppe conquerors, the Mongols aimed to reap the benefits of controlling the trans-Asian trade routes, and among all those groups fitting this historical pattern they were the most successful in bringing the greater part of Eurasia under their rule. This meant that once Mongol power was firmly established, travel across Asia, though still difficult, was facilitated as never before. This led to a surge in long-distance trade and attendant cultural exchanges. The Polos have left the best-known legacy of these times, but Roman Catholic monks such as William of Rubruck, John of Plano Carpini, and others made the trip before and after them, often combining proselytization with diplomacy. Coming the other direction from the Turkish Nestorian town of Kosheng (Marco Polo's Tenduc) north of China, the monks known as Rabban Sauma and Markos (who later became the patriarch Mar Yaballaha III) traveled to the West, with Rabban Sauma going on to Italy and France. They were preceded on the westward road by a Taoist monk named Chang Chun, whom Chinggis Khan had summoned while on campaign in what is now Afghanistan.[9]

In more worldly matters Chinggis was aided by information gained from merchants whom he enlisted to accompany him. This meant especially Muslims, since by that time Silk Road commerce was largely dominated by them.[10] As the Mongol victories expanded the territories under their control, they required both advisors and administrators experienced in matters of rule. For this they engaged the services of individuals native to or familiar with the cultures of the conquered regions. Often, especially in Central and Western Asia, this meant relying on Muslims, but Christians, Buddhists, and others were not excluded from positions of influence. Muslim merchants, valued for their financial acumen, were appointed as fiscal advisors and tax collectors[11] (although this led to their being stereotyped by the subject populations as greedy and corrupt). Finally, during their bloody campaigns, the Mongols made a point of sparing craftsmen and other talented people of whatever race or religion and sending them off to work in Mongolia or wherever their services were needed.

Another aspect of the Mongols' attitude toward religions is that they tended to perceive them as being identified with a particular community.[12] The Mongols recognized the need to earn legitimacy in the eyes of their subjects, and Chinggis Khan "cultivated the religious leaders of the conquered areas, believing that good relations with the clergy would translate into good relations with the people whom they led."[13] In particular, he issued an edict that exempted Christian, Muslim, and Buddhist priests and scholars from taxation.[14] In general, Mongol attitudes were based on practical considerations, which helps to explain the eventual conversion of the western Mongols to Islam and those of the East to Buddhism.

Steppe Christianity

The European Christians cannot be too severely faulted for what appears in hindsight to have been an unrealistic assessment of the Mongols' attachment to Christianity. It is true that overall perhaps only a small percentage of the steppe population adhered to this faith, and even their knowledge of it may have been fairly superficial. Still, of the major religions, Christianity seems to have been initially the best represented within steppe society.

Apart from the ostensibly Christian Kerait and Öngöt tribes, Christian names appear among the central Mongolian Merkits, and even further east among the Tatars.[15] As a result of such christianization, whatever its depth or actual meaning in terms of the religious life of the steppe, we have a definite Christian presence in Inner Asia by Chinggis Khan's time, reflected in the loyalties of Küchlük the Naiman and several members of the Mongol royal family as well. Sorghaghtani Begi, the mother of two future Great Khans, Möngke and Khubilai, as well as of Hülegü, the founder of the Il-Khan dynasty of Iran, was a Nestorian Christian, although she patronized other religions as well.[16] Rumors of this Christian presence at the Mongol court, together with several forged "letters from Prester John" that were circulating in the Mediterranean world at the time, fed European hopes of gaining a powerful ally in their struggle against their Muslim neighbors.[17]

Favor to Muslims

Like the Christians, the Muslims writers often tried to portray the early Mongol conquerors as supporters and therefore potential converts to their religion. Unlike the Christian sources, however, the major Muslim accounts of the period were written under Mongol patronage and therefore demonstrate a clear tendency toward revisionism. The Persian historian Rashid al-din, writing as an Il-Khan official, portrays Chinggis's successor Ögödei as a defender of the expatriate Muslim community in China from the bigotry of locals, by having him say:

> The poorest Tazik Muslim has several Khitayan slaves standing before him, while not one of the great amirs of Khitai has a single Muslim captive. And the reason for this can only be the wisdom of God, who knows the rank and station of all the peoples of the world; it is also in conformity with the auspicious *yasa* [law] of Chinghiz-Khan, for he made the blood-money for a Muslim 40 *balish* and that for a Khitayan a donkey. In view of such clear proofs and testimonies how can you make a laughing stock of the people of Islam?[18]

It may be noted that a defensive tone seems to underlie this passage— apparently the Chinese *were* "making a laughing stock of the people of Islam."

Rashid al-din likewise has Ögödei rescue a Muslim who, unable to repay a loan from an Uighur, had been told to embrace idolatry (presumably Buddhism) or be publicly humiliated and beaten; the khan is said to have given over the Uighur's house and wife to the Muslim and ordered the Uighur to be beaten instead.[19] Juzjani, writing in India in the late thirteenth century, cites another example of Buddhist intrigue against the Muslims: at the instigation of Chaghatai Khan (who was known for his antipathy toward Muslims), one of the Buddhist monks claimed to have heard from Chinggis Khan in a dream that the Muslims would bring about the end of Mongol rule, and that to prevent this they should all be killed. Ögödei, according to Juzjani, "perceived that this statement was false ... and that it appeared to have been hatched by his brother, Chaghatai," and had the monk executed.[20]

Rashid al-din states that the Mongols credited Muslims with "great sexual powers,"[21] and later claims of Möngke Khan that "... of all the peoples and religious communities he showed most honor and respect to the Muslims and bestowed the largest amount of gifts and alms upon them."[22]

Thus, while Christian and Muslim accounts each made certain claims of Mongol sympathy, the reasoning was different. The Christian accounts were wishful thinking and propaganda aimed at a remote Christian audience; Muslim accounts, such as those of Juvaini and Rashid al-din, were written to satisfy and flatter their Mongol patrons. On the other hand, the Central Asian Muslim exile Juzjani, writing from India, and post-Mongol writers such as the early sixteenth-century historian Khwand Amir are more circumspect.

Early European Embassies to the Mongol Court

By 1238 news of Mongol devastations in the Ukraine and Russia was beginning to reach Europe. The Mongol invasions of Poland in 1240 and Hungary in 1241 made it disappointingly clear to Europeans that the hordes from the East were not aiming exclusively at the conquest of Muslim-held lands. A full-scale Mongol attack on Europe was fortuitously avoided, however, by the Great Khan Ögödei's death, which necessitated the recall of all the royal generals to Mongolia in order to choose a successor.

Encouraged by this reprieve, and no doubt misunderstanding its nature, Pope Innocent IV sent an embassy led by the Franciscan monk John of Plano Carpini to the Mongol court in 1245. This mission, which called upon the Mongols to be baptized and submit to the pope's authority, was also intended as a means for gathering intelligence regarding possible future Mongol plans to invade Europe. Thus, John and subsequent ambassadors represented what the twentieth-century explorer Owen Lattimore cleverly termed "the C.I.A., or Christian Intelligence Agency of its time."[23]

John's account of his sojourn at the Mongol court, during which he was privileged to witness the coronation of Güyük as Great Khan in 1246, bears witness to the sectarian intrigues already taking place there. Güyük appears to have looked favorably on Christianity. According to Rashid al-din, he had had a Christian attendant, Qadaq, since childhood, and

> [t]o this was afterward added the influence of (his secretary) Chinqai. He therefore always went to great lengths in honoring priests and Christians, and when this was noised abroad, priests set their faces toward his court from the lands of Syria and Rum (Byzantium) and the As (Ossetia) and the Oros (Russia). And because of the attendance of Qadaq and Chinqai he was prone to denounce the faith of Islam, and the cause of the Christians flourished during his reign, and no Muslim dared to raise his voice to them.[24]

At his accession, Güyük quickly did away with several Muslims who had become very powerful during the regency of his mother, Töregene, including her financial advisor, Abd al-Rahman, and her confidante, a Persian woman by the name of Fatima.[25] Conversely, he reinstated Ögödei's chief secretary, the Nestorian Chinqai mentioned earlier, whom Töregene had forced out.[26]

Chinqai oversaw the rendering into Latin of Güyük's reply to Pope Innocent, and was probably responsible for the passage in which the Mongol emperor rebukes the pontiff for his "arrogance" in claiming Catholicism to be the only true form of Christianity.[27] While Güyük's "cabinet reshuffling" may have been more politically than religiously motivated from his own point of view, it must have appeared otherwise to representatives of the competing religious sects.

Juzjani claims that Buddhist priests were constantly inciting Güyük to persecute Muslims. One well-known Buddhist advisor is said to have told the Great Khan, "If thou desirest that the sovereignty and throne of the Mughals should remain unto thee, of two things do one: either massacre the whole of the Musalmans, or put a stop to their generating and propagating." Güyük then issued an order for all Muslim men under his rule to be castrated; this disaster was averted only by a "miracle" in which one of the Buddhist conspirators had his genitals ripped off by the khan's dog, which was taken as a sign to leave the Muslims alone.[28] Elsewhere, however, Juzjani confirms Güyük's partiality to Christians.[29]

One of the earliest and most cynical examples of the Mongols courting Christian hopes for political ends is seen in a letter sent in 1248 to King Louis, then in Cyprus about to launch the Seventh Crusade, by a Mongol official named Eljigidei in Tabriz. In this letter, Eljigidei "prays God for the success of the Christian forces against the enemies of the Cross." He claims to have been sent by Güyük to protect the Christians and rebuild their churches, and affirms that "Latins, Greeks, Armenians, Nestorians, Jacobites and all worshippers of the Cross are one in the eyes of God and the Mongol emperor."[30]

Actually Eljigidei, recently appointed commander of the western Mongol forces, was planning an attack on Baghdad and hoped to entice Louis to carry out a diversionary invasion of Egypt. The two Persian Nestorians who brought the letter furthermore told the French king that Güyük was Prester John's grandson and that both he and Eljigidei had embraced Christianity and wished to help the Crusaders recapture Jerusalem.[31] Louis's response, carried by the Dominican monk Andrew of Longjumeau, eventually reached the Mongol court in 1250 some time after Güyük's death, and the empress dowager, Oghul Qaimish, sent a reply that simply demanded annual tribute, echoing nothing of Eljigidei's promises.[32]

The report that Andrew brought back included mention of German slaves languishing in Central Asia. This notice sparked the imagination of a Franciscan friar named William of Rubruck, who was attached to King Louis's court at the time. Word was also circulating that Chinggis Khan's great-grandson Sartaq, head of the Juchid Golden Horde, which ruled Russia, was a Christian. William resolved to travel via Sartaq's court to Inner Asia and preach Christianity to the Mongols, and if possible minister to Christians living there.[33]

William's trip was a mixed success. He never found the German slaves, and Möngke Khan, Güyük's successor, did not allow him to stay on permanently in Mongolia to carry out his intended missionary effort. Furthermore, William's interpreter was an uncooperative drunkard, who constantly frustrated what opportunities the friar might have had to spread his view of the gospel. On the other hand, William's account of his journey, which lasted from 1253 to 1255, is one of the most detailed and informative travelogues of its time.

Among other things, William is the first medieval European to encounter and describe Buddhism. His first impression was that the Buddhists were simply wayward Christians:

> In the town of Cailac (Qayaliq, in present-day Kazakhstan) they possessed three idol temples, two of which I entered in order to see their stupid practices. In the first one, I encountered a man who had on his hand a little cross in black ink, which led me to believe he was a Christian, since he answered like a Christian all the questions I put to him. So I asked him: "And why do you not have here a cross and an effigy of Jesus Christ?" "It is not our custom," he replied. From this I concluded that they were Christians, and that the omission was due to faulty doctrine.[34]

William was thwarted in his attempt to learn more about this strange sect from the local Muslims, who refused to talk about them. Subsequently, whenever he asked any Muslims about the Buddhists' religion, "they were scandalized."[35]

According to William, in China the Nestorians and Muslims lived with alien status. His impression of his fellow Christians in the East was not positive:

> The Nestorians there are ignorant. They recite their office and have the Holy Scriptures in Syriac, a language they do not know, so that they chant like the monks among us who know no grammar; and for this reason they are completely corrupt. Above all they are usurers and drunkards, and some of them, furthermore, who live among the Tartars, have several wives just as the Tartars have. On entering the church they wash their lower members, in the Saracen manner (i.e., the Muslim "lesser ablution"); they eat meat on Friday and follow the Saracens in having their feasts on that day...The result is that when any of them rear the sons of aristocratic Mo'als (i.e., Mongols), even though they instruct them in the Gospels and the Faith, nevertheless by their immorality and their greed they rather alienate them from the Christian religion.[36]

William also states that the Nestorians would not allow members of other Christian sects, such as the many Hungarian, Alan, Russian, Georgian, and Armenian slaves, into their churches unless they would be re-baptized as Nestorians.[37] In addition, they practiced divination, and even resorted to the services of Muslim diviners.[38] The Nestorians shunned the symbol of the Cross, and when the captive French craftsman Guillaume Boucher fashioned one as a gift for Möngke's chief secretary, Bulghai, Nestorian priests stole it and the object was never found.[39]

During his stay at Möngke's court, William was hosted by an Armenian monk named Sargis (Sergius) who was constantly at odds with the Muslims at court. Once, during a court ceremony, Möngke's younger brother Arigh Böke indicated a pair of Muslims and asked Sargis whether he knew them. "I know that they are dogs," he answered. In response the Muslims said, "Why do you insult us when we do not insult you?" The ensuing argument was broken up by Arigh Böke, but the next day Sargis started a brawl with some Muslims in the street. As a result of this the troublemaker was ordered to move his tent away from the center of the encampment, and William, as his guest, had to go with him.[40]

William had earlier been exposed to the anti-Muslim intrigues of Armenians while en route, when he discovered that Armenian translators had taken liberties in transforming his letter of introduction from King Louis into a call for a joint war against the Muslims.[41] Likewise, he discovered that Sargis "had told Mangu Chan that if he were prepared to become a Christian the whole world would enter into subjection to him, and that the Franks and the Great Pope would obey him…"[42]

One factor demonstrating Möngke's respect for Christianity was his appointment of Bulghai, a Nestorian Christian, as his chief secretary.[43] However, soon after his accession his predecessor's Christian minister Chinqai was accused of conspiracy and handed over to the Muslim courtier Danishmand Hajib for execution; likewise, a Buddhist plot in the town of Beshbaliq that aimed to massacre the Muslim population during their Friday prayer was discovered by Möngke, who ordered the local Uighur governor publicly executed instead.[44]

It is clear that in typical Mongol fashion, Möngke's policy was to support each religion equally in view of what powers they might provide.[45] William mentions that on feast days the clergy of each religion in turn came before the khan to pray for him and bless his cup. In William's somewhat cynical view, the khan "believes in none of them… and yet they [the clerics] all follow his court as flies do honey, and he makes them all gifts and all of them believe they are on intimate terms with him…"[46]

Nowhere is the failure of the Christian, Muslim, and Buddhist leaders to understand the Mongol attitude toward religion clearer than in the preceding passage; William alone seems to have assessed the situation with any accuracy. Later, he tried to explain to the Mongols that his purpose in coming to Möngke was not for any diplomatic reason but simply "to utter the words of God, if he were willing to hear them." The reaction of the Mongols was that "[t]hey seized on this and asked what were the words of God that I wanted to say, thinking that I intended to foretell some success for him as many others do."[47]

Möngke, like Güyük before him, enjoyed setting the competing clerics against each other in formal debates.[48] As a prelude to holding such a debate between William and others at court, Möngke declared, "Here you are, Christians, Saracens, and tuins (Buddhist monks), and each of you claims that his religion is superior and that his writings or books contain more truth."[49] The only account we have of the ensuing debate is William's, in which he portrays himself as putting the Buddhists, the Muslims, and the Nestorians to shame. "But for all that," he admits, "no one said, 'I believe, and wish to become a Christian.'"[50]

In William's final interview with the khan, Möngke explains to him that "[w]e Mo'als believe that there is only one God, through whom we have life and through whom we die, and towards him we direct our hearts… But just as God has given the hand several fingers, so he has given mankind several paths. To you God has given the Scriptures and you Christians do not observe them." Möngke then criticizes the Christians for their divisiveness and greed, although tactfully explaining that he is not referring to William.[51]

In 1258 Möngke convened a debate similar to the one in which William had participated, but this time limited to Taoists and Buddhists whose rivalry in China went back to the Tang period. The khan appointed his younger brother Khubilai to preside, and following the debate Möngke expressed his preference for Buddhism, saying that it was like the palm of the hand and the other religions like fingers.[52]

Meanwhile, back in the West, Mongol ambitions were leading to the revived possibility of a Christian-Mongol alliance against the Muslims. The presence of Christians close to the Mongol ruler of Iran, Hülegü, including his wife Doquz Khatun and his general Kitbuqa, lent weight to these renewed hopes. In 1254 Hethum, the king of Armenia, agreed to provide troops for the Mongol army in return for protection of Anatolia's Christian communities, and once again, the promise that Jerusalem would revert to the Christians. Following the Mongol conquest of Baghdad in 1258, during which Muslims were slaughtered while Christians were spared, Hülegü gave over the royal palace to the Nestorian Catholicus Mar Makikha, and had a new cathedral built for him.[53]

Kitbuqa's conquest of Aleppo and Damascus in early 1260 made it appear that Jerusalem would soon be in Mongol hands. This hope was quashed, however, by the Mongols' unexpected defeat by Mamluk forces from Egypt at Ain Jalut later in the year. The Mamluk victory ended Mongol expansion to the southwest, and may have caused at least some of the Mongols to begin to doubt the power of Christianity and to wonder if Islam might be the more powerful religion. The stability of Mamluk power was further ensured by an alliance with the Mongol Golden Horde under Juchi's son Berke, who had either converted to Islam or perhaps been raised as a Muslim and was hostile to Hülegü.[54]

An interesting anecdote is related by Juzjani to illustrate Berke's defense of Islam. A young Christian of Samarkand had converted to Islam; an unnamed visiting Mongol official, "the inclinations of which accursed one were towards the Christian faith," failing to persuade the youth to renounce Islam and return to Christianity, executed him. On hearing of this, Berke sanctioned the slaughter of Samarkand's Christians while they were assembled in church.[55] Juzjani also claims that Sartaq died as a result of Berke's praying for his death.[56]

Berke's conversion did not lead to the complete Islamization of the Golden Horde at that point, however. Christian missionaries—mainly Latin but also Russian Orthodox—continued to compete for influence there well into the fourteenth century. Their major rivals appear to have been individual Sufi shaykhs. Sometime around 1320 a Dominican missionary by the name of William Adam wrote a treatise calling for increased missionary activity in the Volga region in order to meet the challenge of growing Muslim influence there. The conversion of the Juchid ruler Özbek Khan, whom Central Asian Muslims credit with Islamizing the Golden Horde, is attributed by William to the activity of Sufi faqirs sent by the Mamluk sultan. He also claims that because of the Sufis, the ruler of the Golden Horde "has lately, along with many other Tartars, become a most evil Saracen, an enemy and persecutor of Christians."[57]

Mongol rule reached its greatest sophistication under Khubilai Khan, who became Great Khan following Möngke's death in 1259. Khubilai's initial attitude toward the great religious traditions was a typical Mongol openness to anything that could be of use. Marco Polo quotes him as saying:

There are four prophets who are worshipped and to whom all the world does reverence. The Christians say their God was Jesus Christ; the Saracens Mahomet; the Jews Moses; and the idolaters Sakyamuni Burkhan, who was the first to be represented as God in the form of an idol; and I do honour and reverence to all four, so that I may be sure of doing it to him who is greatest in heaven and truest, and to him I pray for aid.[58]

Likewise, the Muslim historian Khwand Amir states that

Khubilai Khan used to tend to administrative affairs from sunup until midmorning, and then he used to gather the ulema of Islam, the learned of the Jews, Christian monks, and the wise men of China and hold deliberations, for he enjoyed listening to philosophical and religious debates. During his reign he ordered the Qur'an, the Torah, the Gospel, and Sakyamuni's book translated into Mongolian.[59]

Khubilai took pains to avoid religious rivalries at court. Rashid al-din states that the Great Divan included four ministers (Pers. *finjān*, Ch. *pingchang*) "from among the great amirs of the various peoples, Taziks, Khitayans, Uighurs, and Christians."[60] Further, according to Khwand Amir,

[i]t was Khubilai Khan's practice to appoint to the post of vizier four men who were of the same religion in order that disputes and disagreements on religion would not arise and so that the ministry's funds would be safe from embezzlement.[61]

This policy does not seem to have been particularly effective, however, as the following case illustrates. Rashid al-din records that at one point Khubilai appointed a presumably Christian Uighur by the name of Sanga, who was hostile to Muslims, to a ministerial position.

After a Muslim at court accused Sanga of lying to the khan about his wealth, Khubilai had the Uighur executed.[62]

Tibetan Buddhists, meanwhile, maintained their rivalry with native Chinese Daoists, and eventually used their influence (through Phags-Pa) to persuade Khubilai to suppress the latter and destroy their books in 1281; the only Daoist text to survive this purge was the Dao De Jing.[63] A notable aspect of Khubilai's administrative policy was his distrust of the native Chinese in his service. Although he had shifted his court to China and built a new capital, Khanbaliq (present-day Beijing), several early betrayals by Chinese advisors led him to turn increasingly to foreigners, particularly Muslims.[64] Since the foreigners had no support base in China apart from their Mongol patrons, Khubilai saw them as being more reliable.[65] Likewise, perhaps, Khubilai's suppression of Daoists and Confucians was "intended to deprive of their spiritual support the Chinese who were subject to the Mongol dynasty."[66]

The most well-known Muslim figure at Khubilai's court was his infamous finance minister, Ahmad, whose 20-year campaign of extortion earned him the hatred of Khubilai's Chinese subjects and foreigners alike. His relations with the Great Khan's Buddhist and Confucian officials were particularly bitter. The Chinese advisors would accuse Ahmad of profiteering, and he would respond by charging them with embezzlement. Eventually, Ahmad's Chinese opponents were either dismissed or executed at his instigation, died of natural causes, or resigned their posts in disgust, with the result that by 1280 Ahmad's power was almost unchallenged.[67] Two years later, however, he was assassinated by a Chinese general named Chien-hu. Khubilai put many Chinese to death whom he suspected of having a part in this conspiracy, but when Ahmad's house was searched and it was discovered how much treasure he had accumulated, the khan had his body exhumed and flung to the dogs, in Marco Polo's account, or wagons driven over it, according to Rashid al-din.[68]

Following Ahmad's posthumous disgrace, Khubilai took a more restrictive attitude toward his subject Muslim population, such as reinstating the ban on halal slaughter.[69] Rashid al-din asserts that the anti-Muslim policies, which also banned circumcision, were implemented at the instigation of a Christian official by the name of Isa Tarsah Kelemechi (Ch. Aixueh), whom Rashid further accuses of inciting slaves of Muslims to denounce their masters. As a result, he claims, "most Muslims left the country of Khitai."[70]

Isa Kelemechi appears to have nearly sealed the Muslims' fate for good by pointing out to Khubilai the Qur'anic verse that commands, "Kill the polytheists, all of them!"[71] The khan then somewhat sarcastically asked the Muslims at his court why they didn't carry out this directive and kill their Mongol overlords. None of the Muslims could reply, until one finally volunteered, "Thou art not a polytheist since thou writest the name of the Great God at the head of thy yarlighs (edicts)."[72] This response saved the Muslims for the time being, but the restrictions against them remained in place for several more years. During that time revenues from Muslim trade declined severely, so that in 1287 Khubilai lifted the ban on halal slaughter.[73]

This was the same year that in the West, the Il-Khan ruler Arghun sent his second embassy to the Vatican, this time led by the Nestorian Turk Rabban Sauma. In his letter to the pope, Arghun repeats an earlier request for European assistance in attacking the Levant and Egypt, and states that if he succeeds in capturing Jerusalem, he will become a Christian.[74]

Intrigue and Mayhem in the Il-Khan Lands

Arghun was a son of Abaqa, who is presented in Christian sources as a patron of Christianity.[75] In 1281 Abaqa gave his blessing to the ordination of Yaballaha III, whom the Nestorians had elected as Catholicus. An Öngöt Turk from China who had traveled to the West with Rabban Sauma in hopes of making a pilgrimage to Jerusalem, Mar Yaballaha had been chosen by the Nestorians to head their church because of his cultural affinities with the new Mongol rulers. The following year Abaqa is said to have attended Easter mass in Baghdad.[76] Shortly thereafter, however, Abaqa died and was succeeded by his brother Tägüdar, who had converted to Islam and taken the name Sultan Ahmad. One of the new ruler's first acts was to dismiss the Christian and Jewish astrologers and physicians at the Il-Khan court. In addition, "[i]dol temples, churches and synagogues were destroyed, and in their place rose mosques."[77]

A pair of high-ranking Syrian clergy, who were jealous of the foreigner Mar Yaballaha's appointment as Catholicus and Rabban Sauma's as Visitor General, passed to Sultan Ahmad the accusation that the two Turks favored the succession of another of Abaqa's sons,

Arghun. The evidence condemning Mar Yaballaha and Rabban Sauma was found to be inadequate, but their position was clearly precarious until Arghun's victory over Sultan Ahmad in 1284. When Arghun heard of the conspiracy of the two Syrians, he ordered their executions; they were saved, however, through the intervention of Mar Yaballaha, who asked that they only be stripped of their ranks.[78]

During Arghun's reign a Jewish physician by the name of Sa'ad al-dawla rose to the position of chief tax collector and later prime minister. According to Muslim sources, "Sa'ad al-dawla gave the governorships of most of Arghun Khan's realm to his relatives." The same sources state that "in all fairness, it must be said that during the time of Sa'ad al-dawla's vizierate all of the realm flourished, and none of Arghun Khan's amirs or retinue was able to transgress the rights of the subjects and peasants in any way."[79]

Sa'ad al-dawla appears to have nominally converted to Islam, although he is said to have urged the khan to claim prophethood and found a new religion "that would wipe out all traces of former religions." As a result of this advice, Arghun barred Muslims from the court, and at Sa'ad al-dawla's suggestion decided "that the Kaaba should be turned into an idol temple and that the Muslims and all others should be made to worship images instead of God." Finally, while Arghun had fallen ill, a group of courtiers captured Sa'ad al-dawla and executed him, and "the friends of Islam were given a new lease on life."[80]

In 1291 Arghun died and was succeeded by his younger brother Gaykhatu, who in typical Mongol fashion "confirmed all the religious sectaries each in his status and honored all the chief dogmas, whether of Christians or Arabs or Jews or Pagans, and showed partiality to none."[81] He did, however, bestow gifts upon the Nestorian Catholicus, to the order of 20,000 dinars. He also commissioned the construction of a new cathedral at the Il-Khan capital of Maragha, which he visited twice during the following year. Finally, Gaykhatu commissioned the building of a new monastery north of the capital; in short, "anything that the Mar Catholicus opened his mouth about and desired he did not refuse."[82] The effects of this apparent favoritism on relations with the Muslims of the realm would soon manifest themselves.

In 1295 Gaykhatu was overthrown and put to death by his nobles. A cousin, Baidu, seized power, but his accession was challenged by Ghazan, Gaykhatu's brother. Ghazan had been baptized and raised a Christian. His chief general, however, a man by the name of Amir Nawruz, was a

Muslim,[83] and offered the support of a Muslim army if Ghazan would promise to embrace Islam in the event of his victory over Baidu. This was soon accomplished, and Ghazan accordingly converted.

The Muslim accounts of this event make it clear that part of the religious struggle in the Il-Khan territories was between Mongols who had converted to Islam and those who hadn't:

> Also accepting to obey Islamic law, [Ghazan] abandoned polytheism and the despicable nation of the Turks. That very day nearly a hundred thousand obstinate polytheists became believing monotheists and were delivered from the darkness of infidelity and idolatry.[84]

Within a few months, however,

> ...a group of princes and noyans...who had been opposed to the adoption of Islam, conspired to do away with Ghazan Khan and Amir Nawroz by any means possible and then turn Muslim mosques into churches and temples.[85]

In the East, meanwhile, Khubilai's successor Temür Khan had appointed a cousin, Ananda (presumably a Buddhist), to govern the Tungut province. The urban population there had become largely Chinese Muslim, while the countryside remained pagan. Ananda converted to Islam as a result of falling in love with a Muslim woman, and coerced most of his 150,000 soldiers into converting as well. This caused some friction with Temür Khan, who tried to force him to renounce Islam, but when Ananda heard of Ghazan's conversion in Iran "and that all the Mongols in Persia had become Muslims, breaking all the idols and destroying idol-temples (presumably, mainly churches)," he took heart and "in imitation of him (Ghazan), strove to strengthen the faith of Islam"[86]—one imagines, by equally forceful means.

It is against this backdrop of tension among the Mongols themselves that we should see the persecutions of Nestorians in the West described in Christian sources. Mar Yaballaha's history states it was Nawruz who issued the following edict:

> The Churches shall be uprooted, and the altars overturned, and the celebrations of the Eucharist shall cease, and the hymns of praise, and

the sounds of calls to prayer shall be abolished; and the heads (chiefs?) of the Christians, and the heads of the congregations (i.e., synagogues) of the Jews, and the great men among them shall be killed.

Immediately the Muslims broke into and looted the Maragha cathedral and took the priests hostage. Some they tied up naked; Mar Yaballaha himself was hung upside down and beaten while his captors urged him to renounce his faith in favor of Islam. In the end he was ransomed by local Christians for 5,000 dinars. King Hethum of Armenia finally intervened with his private armed retinue to stop the looting of Maragha's churches and bought off the Muslim mob.[87] Nawruz continued to harass Mar Yaballaha, however, and sent orders that the Catholicus return the cash gifts Gaykhatu had bestowed upon him.[88] In addition, Nawruz ordered the destruction of the churches of Tabriz and Hamadan. Those of Mosul and Baghdad ransomed themselves, while the caliphal palace given to the patriarch by Hülegü was taken back by the Muslims, who also converted the Nestorian cathedral into a mosque and had the bones of the patriarchs Mar Makikha and Mar Denha exhumed and taken away.[89]

When Ghazan heard of the tribulations being inflicted upon the Christians, he issued an edict exempting them from the *jizya* (the poll tax on non-Muslims), and stated further that "none of them shall abandon his faith, that the Catholicus shall live in the state to which he hath been accustomed, that he shall be treated with the respect due his rank, that he shall rule over his throne, and shall hold the staff of strength over his dominion." In addition, the new khan sent Mar Yaballaha 5,000 dinars by way of reparation.[90] Yet not surprisingly, "in proportion as the king [Ghazan], little [by little], was increasing the honour which he paid to the Catholicus, the hatred which was in the hearts of the enemies [of the Catholicus] increased, and they forged evil plots, and they sent information about everything which took place to ... Nawruz."[91]

The following year "a certain man, who was called by the name of Shenâkh êl-Tâmûr, came into Maraghah, and he cast about a report that he had with him an Edict ordering that every one who did not abandon Christianity and deny his faith be killed."[92] This news, though false, inspired the Muslims to indulge in a fresh round of looting at the cathedral. Among the items they carried off were a gold seal given to the patriarch by Möngke Khan and a silver one from Arghun.

An attempt by local officials to bring the perpetrators to justice sparked off a general uprising, during which the cathedral was severely damaged and many of the monks killed. Mar Yaballaha himself escaped with some companions and took refuge in the house of one of Ghazan's Christian wives, a woman by the name of Burgesin Argi.[93] When Ghazan, who was traveling at the time, heard of the incident, he ordered the Muslims of Maragha rounded up and tortured until they returned what they had looted, but they returned only "a very small part of what they had stolen, and the rest remained with them."[94]

Some time later in Arbil, local Kurds began circulating a story that some of Ghazan's Christian soldiers had attacked them and killed one of their elders. According to Yaballaha's history, "fighting and hatred followed, and revolt increased, and evil grew, and fury and bitter hatred flourished in both parties, namely, in both Christians and the Arabs [i.e., the Muslims]. And they laid ambushes each party for the other, and they fought pitched battles..."[95] During this time Ghazan was occupied in putting down a rebellion that Nawruz had launched in Khurasan. The Christians of Arbil, meanwhile, had fled to the citadel, where they were besieged by Muslims, who greatly outnumbered them. Ghazan's Muslim advisors characterized the situation as a Christian revolt. In response to this Mar Yaballaha came to court to present the case of the besieged Christians. The khan ordered a reconciliation between the Christians and the Muslims of Arbil, which cost the Christians 20,000 dinars in indemnities. They were, however, allowed to keep control of the citadel.[96]

Later Papal Missions

The first genuine successes of the Latin Church in the Mongol east were due to the efforts of John of Montecorvino, a Franciscan monk sent to the Mongol court at Khanbaliq in 1290. Over the next four decades, until his death in 1328, John tirelessly propagated Catholicism among the various Christians of the realm, who were by then quite numerous. In addition to the local Turkic and Mongol Nestorian communities, large numbers of Armenians, Slavs, Greeks, and other Christians had been brought forcibly from Europe and the eastern Mediterranean following the Mongol victories earlier in the century.

John's first great coup was to win over the Nestorian Öngöt ruler Körgüz Küregen ("Prince George") for the pope, and his subjects along with him, although following George's death the local Nestorian priests turned the people back to their original faith. John also had great influence with the Caucasian Alans, who followed the Greek Orthodox rite, and with the Armenians, whose language he had learned during a previous mission in their country. In 1307 news of John's efforts in China reached the pope, who responded by making him the first archbishop of Khanbaliq and Patriarch of the Orient.

John's efforts were constantly hampered by the Nestorian priests, however, who quite naturally saw him as a competitor trying to muscle in in their turf. Eventually, they went so far as to accuse him of being an impostor, and nearly succeeded in bringing about his ruin, as he describes in the following passage from the second of three letters he hoped would reach the pope:

> ...the Nestorians, who call themselves Christians, but behave in a very unchristian manner, have grown so strong in these parts that they did not allow any Christian of another rite to have any place of worship, however small, nor preach any doctrine but their own. For these lands have never been reached by any apostle or disciple of the apostles and so the aforesaid Nestorians both directly and by the bribery of others have brought most grievous persecutions upon me, declaring that I was not sent by the Lord Pope, but that I was a spy, a magician and a deceiver of men. And after some time they produced more false witnesses, saying that another messenger had been sent with a great treasure to the Emperor and that I had murdered him in India and made away with his gifts. And this intrigue lasted about five years, so that I was often brought to judgement, and in danger of a shameful death. But at last, by God's ordering, the Emperor came to know my innocence and the nature of my accusers, by the confession of some of them, and he sent them into exile with their wives and children.[97]

John's battle for the Catholic faith in Mongol China was a most lonely one, and he claims in his letter that if he had had only two or three other Catholic priests to buttress his position against the Nestorians, he might have succeeded in converting the khan himself.[98] Indeed, it appears that John lacked even the support of his fellow Italian Franciscan and theoretical subordinate, Andrew of Perugia, perhaps having to do with the rift between the Spirituals and the Community that existed within the order at that time.[99]

It is clear that the Mongol emperor continued to exercise a tolerance unknown among the clerics of various sects who operated within his realm. Andrew unwittingly sums up this difference in his remark that "[i]n this vast empire there are verily men of every nation under heaven and of every sect; and each and all are allowed to live according to their sect. For this is their opinion, or I should say their error, that every man is saved in his own sect."[100]

Likewise Peregrine, whom the pope had sent together with Andrew in order to consecrate John as archbishop, reports that under the Mongols the Catholic monks were allowed to preach to the Buddhists and even in Muslim mosques,[101] though Andrew admits that "of the Jews and the Saracens none is converted" and that "of the idolators [Buddhists] exceedingly many are baptized, but when they are baptized they do not adhere strictly to Christian ways."[102] Nevertheless, it has been estimated that John may have made as many as 10,000 converts to Catholicism during his years in China, mainly of individuals from various Christian sects.[103] There were apparently a few European merchants living in China at that time as well who had even brought their families along, as attested by the gravestone of an Italian girl who died in Yangzhou in 1342.[104]

In 1336 the Alans of Khanbaliq wrote to the pope requesting he send a successor to replace John, who had been dead for eight years. It has been suggested that the Alans needed someone who could stand up to the Nestorian clergy as John had done.[105] Although the pope's appointee never reached China, a papal embassy led by John of Marignolli did, traveling via the Central Asian Silk Road. Along the way they witnessed the effects Muslim persecutions were having on Central Asia's Christian communities following the Islamization of the western Mongols.

At Almaliq they found that the local Chaghatayid Muslim ruler, Ali Sultan, had wiped out the Franciscan mission there during the previous year.[106] Marignolli and his entourage proceeded to Khanbaliq, where they stayed for three years. During this time he claims to have held "many glorious disputations with the Jews and other sects."[107] It seems the Jews, like the Nestorians and the Muslims, found the sculptures and paintings of the Catholics' saints to be particularly offensive and verging on idol worship.

Choosing the sea route for his return journey to Europe, Marignolli stopped in the port city of Zaytun long enough to commission the casting of two church bells, which, as a parting insult, he had placed within the Muslim quarter. Upon his arrival at Avignon in 1353 Marignolli conveyed a letter from the Great Khan requesting that the pope send more Franciscans to China. This was at a time when the plague had begun to sweep Europe, however, and no further Catholic missions were sent to East Asia until the sixteenth century.

A Miscarried Policy

Although individual Mongol rulers occasionally favored one or another of the religions of their domains, their general policy was to attempt to balance the various traditions so that each might serve them to the extent it could. This policy, by variously allowing representatives of each tradition to believe they were gaining the upper hand vis-à-vis their rivals and could act against them with impunity, led to an enormous amount of destruction and bloodshed. The situation was perhaps analogous to the Qur'anic observation with regard to the fair treatment of multiple wives: "Ye will not be able to deal equally between (your) wives, however much ye wish (to do so)"(Qur'an 4: 129). In practice the Mongols could not hope to treat the adherents of diverse faiths equally, since any favor shown to one group tended to inflate their sense of importance while incensing the others.

In fact, the tolerance and favor shown by the Mongols to each of the major religions of their realm had the undesired effect of exacerbating existent tensions and rivalries between them, and the Christians, whose status within steppe society at the outset of Mongol rule exceeded that of Islam and Buddhism, were the ultimate victims of this intensified rivalry. But while in hindsight it appears inevitable that the Mongols had eventually to embrace the faith of the majority in each sphere of their disintegrating empire—Buddhism in the East and Islam in the West—the sources of the time show how much was actually due to chance and individual personalities.[108] Khubilai Khan's advisor Phags-Pa seems to have been singularly instrumental in winning support for the Tibetan form of Buddhism, which otherwise might never have made such a mark in the eastern realm of the empire. At least as late as the early fourteenth century, the direction of events in the West was every bit as uncertain.

Chapter Seven
A Melting Pot No More

By the time the Portuguese, Dutch, English, and French began their sea-borne encounters with Asian civilization, the Silk Road's 2,000-year-long role in transmitting cultural traditions was ending. A popular form of Islam, linked to Sufi orders such as the Yasaviyya and the Naqshbandiyya, was the main religious presence throughout Central Asia, reaching even the last holdouts of steppe paganism among the Turkic nomads. By the sixteenth century the religious melting pot into which the Silk Road had continuously poured its various influences, was no more.

The End of Christianity in Medieval Central Asia

Historians have tended to breeze over the question of exactly how and when Christianity was extinguished in Central Asia. Modern accounts, echoing the portrayal in Marlowe's sixteenth-century poem *Tamburlaine the Great*, often offer no more than a curt comment to the effect that Timur himself was the cause, waging holy war to extirpate all religious rivals. René Grousset's interpretation is typical: according to this twentieth-century French historian, Timur "killed from piety. He represents a synthesis, probably unprecedented in history, of Mongol barbarity and Muslim fanaticism, and symbolizes that advanced form of primitive slaughter which is murder committed for the sake of abstract ideology, as a duty and a sacred mission."[1]

But although Timur's biographers do mention his victories over Christian rulers in the Caucasus, such as the "infidels" of Georgia, they make no reference to anti-Christian crusades by Timur in Central Asia.[2] Indeed a contemporary Christian source, the Dominican archbishop of Sultaniyya in Iran, commented that Timur "does not harm Christians—especially Latins—and receives them well; merchants in particular are allowed to go about their business and worship as if they were in Christiandom."[3]

It is true that Timur's historians dubbed him a *ghāzī*, a fighter for the faith, but the context of this title is struggles with either competing Muslim sects or "heathens" such as uncooperative groups of steppe nomads who posed a serious obstacle to his empire-building activities.[4] Christianity, having lost its last Mongol patrons decades earlier, no longer posed any political threat and is not likely to have concerned Timur. On the other hand, for Timur, a political upstart from the recently converted Barlas tribe, orthodox Sunnism was a propaganda tool to be used against his genuine rivals, whether Muslim or shamanistic.[5]

It may be that by Timur's time there were no Christians left in Central Asia. Nestorian tombstone inscriptions indicate that the communities of the "Seven Rivers" (southern Kazakhstan and Kyrgyzstan) were devastated by plague in 1338 and 1339.[6] At that same time the Chaghatayid ruler Jenkshi, who had allowed Roman Catholic missionaries to come from Europe and proselytize within his realm, was murdered as a result of family intrigues. He was succeeded by a descendant of Ögödei, a convert to Islam named Ali Sultan, who encouraged Muslim pogroms in which all the Catholic missionaries were killed. One assumes local Nestorians were targeted as well, especially since many had enjoyed government positions under Jenkshi.[7]

One effect that Timur's policies definitely did have was to solidify the status of the Muslim elite classes, such as religious scholars and Sufi masters. He did this by granting them lands and tax-exempt financial bases through the administration of pious endowments, known as *waqfs,* which could be in the form of buildings—including not only mosques and religious schools but also bazaars—land, or utilities such as water for irrigation.

The trusteeships for these pious endowments could be stipulated to remain within families, guaranteeing their income and status over generations. Under Timur's successors several such families of religious leaders became the economic masters of numerous Silk Road towns including Samarkand and Bukhara. Some of these families have remained powerful in Central Asia right up to the present day.

In China, after the end of Mongol rule in 1368, it appears that Christianity suffered from its association with the expelled dynasty. Christians of the Öngöt, Kerait, and other Turkish and Mongol tribes were cut off once and for all from the support of any political power sympathetic to their tradition. It appears that over time the Christians of the steppes turned increasingly to Buddhist lamas for the fulfillment of their spiritual needs. Early in the twentieth century, European Catholic missionaries felt they detected echoes of a forgotten Christian tradition (baptism, confession, extreme unction) among some Mongol groups, such as the Erküts of the Ordos in Inner Mongolia.[8] The faint traces of long-gone Inner Asian Christianity have continued to inspire contemporary Christian travel writers such as Martin Palmer and Sébastien de Courtois, filling their works with wistful romanticism.[9]

The "Failure" of Christianity along the Silk Road

Christianity was a part of the religious culture of the Silk Road for over a millennium, but ultimately left strangely little mark. Apart from the remote and politically insignificant Öngöt kingdom north of China, there were no Nestorian-ruled lands to compare even with the brief state sponsorship that Manichaeism enjoyed in the eighth and ninth centuries. By the late fourteenth century the tradition had essentially vanished, leaving only the scantest traces. Ironically, even in the West Asian and North African heartlands of Islam, substantial Christian communities have survived to the present day, including Nestorians in northern Iraq and Iran. One may well ask why their fate in Central Asia was different.

This is a question that has preoccupied and often vexed Christian historians, by whom the history of Asian Christianity has almost exclusively been written. Their tone is one of tragedy, of promise unfulfilled. Many of their explanations focus on the "defectiveness" of Asian Christianity, which is seen as either simply heretical (from the viewpoint of Western Christians) or at best superficial. The Nestorians have been accused of accepting "converts without making sure that Christianity was a spiritual reality in their lives."[10] Nestorianism was more successful among the steppe peoples on the fringes of Silk

Road civilization than it was in the urban centers, which has led to its characterization as a religion of "low civilization."[11]

These arguments are found already in the medieval accounts of William of Rubruck and John of Montecorvino, which in many ways set the tone for Western perceptions of the Nestorians in the East. The Western Christians constantly accused the Nestorians of sectarian bias as well, as if the medieval Roman Catholics were somehow more open to ecumenical cooperation (and as the accounts of Rubruck and Montecorvino amply demonstrate, they weren't).

More recent, circumspect accounts have pointed out the complexity of Christian doctrine, which the steppe peoples do not appear ever to have fully mastered, and the alien nature of many Christian concepts in a Central Asian setting.[12] Buddhism, however, was neither less complex nor more inherently compatible with either the Central Asian or the Chinese mind-sets, at least initially; it had to be transformed. Christianity too was transformed in the East; yet, it failed to take hold.

One aspect that has not been emphasized is the lack of a powerful Nestorian entity sponsoring trade. Even where Nestorianism was officially tolerated and protected, as in the Sasanian Empire, Nestorian merchants never enjoyed the kind of preferential advantages accorded by Buddhist or Muslim rulers along the Silk Road to members of their traditions. The only exception to this is under the rule of some of the Mongols, when policies favoring Nestorians backfired by provoking anti-Christian reaction from Muslims.

The major successes of Nestorian missionaries in converting Central Asians were among the steppe peoples, who were after all peripheral participants in the Silk Road commercial system. Given the dramatic change in lifestyle and values that the adoption of a new culturo-religious tradition often entails, one should perhaps marvel at the "success" of Christianity in Asia, which thrived for over 1,000 years despite the factors indicated, rather than bemoaning its ultimate "failure."[13]

The Last Manichaean Community

Manichaeism, known in Chinese as the "Religion of Light" *(Ming chiao)*, survived in China by going underground following the persecutions of 841–846. Manichaeans met in secret, and outwardly resembled Daoists or Buddhists. At that time, a Manichaean teacher by the name of Hulu (perhaps Turk. *Ulugh,* "great") traveled from the capital at Chang'an to Fuzhou in the southeastern province of Fujian, where he developed a following. Marco Polo seems to have encountered this Manichaean community during the course of his travels in the thirteenth century, although he mistook them for Christians.[14]

A Chinese tradition developed whereby Laozi, the putative founder of Daoism, traveled to the West and was transformed into a pomegranate; centuries later the fruit was eaten by an Iranian queen, who became pregnant by it and gave birth to the prophet Mani. According to this tradition, Mani united the teachings of Laozi and the Buddha.[15] This appropriation of Daoism enabled Chinese Manichaeans to represent their temples as Daoist and their religion as a school of Daoism, a strategy that proved useful in enabling Manichaeism to persist under the Song rulers who viewed the foreign religion with suspicion and outlawed Manichaean temples.[16] Even so Manichaeans were often vilified during the Song period, referred to as "vegetarian demon-worshippers"—it was unfortunate that the initial character in the Chinese transcription of Mani's name, *mo,* meant "demon."[17]

Like the Christians in pagan Rome, the sect was seen as a threat not because of its beliefs so much as because of its secretive nature.[18] This persecution was eased under the Mongols, who placed the Manichaeans under the jurisdiction of the Nestorian bishop.[19] The Ming dynasty, however, which expelled the Mongols during the fourteenth century, forced the Manichaeans of China underground once again.

Despite this renewed assault, the religion survived in Fujian as late as the seventeenth century,[20] and traces of it remain there today. A Manichaean temple has been identified at Cao'an, about 20 km south of the modern city of Quanzhou, the great medieval port known to Westerners as Zaytun. The shrine contains a stone statue that appears at first glance to represent the Buddha; on closer inspection, however, numerous features indicate that it is the prophet Mani. An inscription in the courtyard, moreover, mentions "Mani, the Buddha of Light."[21] Eating vessels with Manichaean inscriptions have recently been unearthed nearby.[22] According to one report, "The Cao'an temple is still in use today. It is inhabited by pious old women who worship and take care of the Mani relief, considering [it] to be a picture of Buddha Sakyamuni."[23]

Further Islamization in the East

As noted in chapter Five, the Islamic presence along the Silk Road came initially through the military efforts of the Arabs to bring trading centers under their control, leading to the eventual conversion of merchant and other urban classes. Even so, for centuries in most of the urban centers, Muslim businessmen continued to face competition from Buddhist and other commercial networks. The nomadic, mostly Turkic, peoples became Islamicized in stages, a process that lasted well into the seventeenth century. Nomadic groups wishing to gain control over the Silk Road cities often embraced Islam, usually of the Sunni variety, as a way of claiming legitimacy. Infused with the convert's zeal but often lacking a deep understanding of the tradition, they did not always observe the Qur'anic principle that there should be "no compulsion in matters of faith" (2:256).

Tribal politics was never far from the center of shifts in religious alliances among the peoples of the steppe. The army of Chinggis Khan was a confederation of Turkic and Mongol tribes that he succeeded briefly in bringing under his authority. After Chinggis's death the vast empire he had established slowly began its long process of disintegration. Throughout the subsequent years, decades, and centuries these tribal groups would band together and disband again to meet the needs of the time and place, whether it be to defend themselves against intertribal raiding or to launch an attack on oasis states.[24]

While individual aspirants to power might attempt to impose Islam in an effort to consolidate their authority among merchants and other town dwellers, this sometimes backfired as many of the steppe nomads reacted to forced conversions with hostility.[25] According the the *Tārīkh-i rashīdī*, during the mid-fifteenth century one such convert, the Chaghatayid Tughluq Temür, executed any of his entourage who refused to convert with him: "[Tughluq and his spiritual master] then decided that for the propagation of Islam, they should interview the princes one by one, and it should be well for those who accepted the faith, but those who refused should be slain as heathens and idolaters."[26] Later, after a frail Sufi missionary miraculously defeated a well-known warrior in single combat, "[t]he people raised loud shouts of applause, and on that day 160,000 persons cut off the hair of their heads and became Musulmans."[27]

In the last decade of the fourteenth century Tughluq Temür's youngest son and eventual successor, Khizr Khwaja, "undertook a holy war *(ghazāt)* against Khitai" (here, apparently meaning the Tarim region). He conquered the Silk Road towns of Qara Khoja and Turfan, "and forced their inhabitants to become Musulmans, so that at the present time it is called *dār al-islām*."[28]

Khizr Khwaja's son Muhammad Khan in turn continued the policy of pressuring his subjects to become Muslim. He is said to have pursued this policy so vigorously "that during his blessed reign most of the tribes of the Moghuls became Musulmans." These efforts were apparently met with some resistance, for "[i]t is well known what severe measures he had recourse to, in bringing the Moghuls to be believers in Islam. If, for instance, a Moghul did not wear a turban, a horseshoe nail was driven into his head: and treatment of this kind was common."[29]

The groups known today as Kazakh and Kyrgyz, who have given their names to two present-day republics in Central Asia, were the last of these ever-reshuffling tribal alliances to be Islamicized. Another component group, the Mongol Qalmaqs, never were, but instead embraced Buddhism.

The designation "Qyrgyz" (by which name the modern Kazakhs were known prior to the twentieth century; the modern Kyrgyz were called "Qara-Qyrgyz") first appears in Muslim sources of the tenth century in reference to the conquerors of the town of Aq Su (Whitewater) in the "Seven Rivers" region, now southern Kazakhstan.[30]

Chinese records state that Muslim caravans brought silk from Kucha to this tribe every three years. Most of the Qyrgyz-Qazaqs must have remained apart from this sedentarizing group, however, since Muslim sources refer to them as infidels as late as the mid-sixteenth century.[31] One such source calls the Qyrgyz "the originators of all the revolts in Moghulistan," and explains that "they were still infidels, and hence their hostility to Islam."[32]

Another Muslim, writing in 1582, offers the qualification that "they are neither infidels, nor Muslims."[33] A seventeenth-century writer says that the Qyrgyz worship idols and are not "true" Muslims.[34] By the latter statements we can understand that the people in question had accepted certain Islamic practices, symbols, and vocabularies, while retaining or "Islamicizing" much of their traditional religious heritage. This is, in fact, the type of blend of traditions that one finds among these peoples today.

The Islamic content absorbed by these steppe tribes during the centuries immediately before and after the Mongol period can be attributed largely to the work of Sufi missionaries, such as Ahmad Yasavi (1103–1167), Najm al-din Kubra (d.1221), and their followers, who were often perceived to have magical powers, and like Christians and others before them, often assumed a role traditionally filled by shamans. Like shamans, they were sometimes believed to be able to fly.[35] To this day among the Kazakhs one can find shamans who perform traditional shamanistic rituals using the Qur'an, Arabic letters, and such.[36]

Miracle working *(karamāt)* had always been a successful strategy for missionaries among the steppe peoples, and few are the famous Sufi masters who don't at least posthumously acquire miraculous or healing powers in their hagiographies.[37] According to the fourteenth-century Moroccan traveler Ibn Battuta, even before becoming Muslims the nomads around Samarkand used to visit the tomb of Qusam ibn Abbas (a cousin of the Prophet who was killed there in 676), in order "to gain blessing as the result of the miraculous signs which they witnessed on its behalf."[38]

It seems some Sufi shaykhs were not above verbal deception either as a way of securing influence. Ibn Battuta relates that a preacher by the name of Badr al-din Maydani was once asked by Kebek, ruler of the Chaghatayid White Horde in Transoxiana from 1309–1326, whether the Qur'an, which Muslims claimed to contain everything, mentioned his name. "Yes," the preacher replied. "It is in His word (most High is He), 'In whatsoever form He would He hath composed thee (Ar. *rakkabak*).'" As a result of this flattery, Kebek "showed great favour to him and increased respect for Muslims."[39]

Sufi preachers, like Nestorians and Manichaeans before them, usually traveled to the steppes as part of trade missions. In conjunction with the charismatic appeal of these Muslim missionaries, therefore, the more commercially minded among the nomads must have perceived the advantages that could accrue from adopting at least enough of the religio-cultural tradition of the town-based merchants to foster good business relations.

Conclusions

European historians, the conceptualizers of the Silk Road, generally agree that the concept loses its meaning by the sixteenth century. Lack of a unifying political authority in Central Asia made long-distance overland trade in expensive goods less and less viable,[40] although regional commerce in essential commodities remained active.[41]

Instead, long-distance trade realigned itself along a new axis connecting India in the southeast with the emerging power of Russia in the northwest.[42] Western Central Asians, at least, were able to maintain their role as middlemen between the tsarist and Mughal empires throughout the seventeenth and eighteenth centuries. Increasingly, an even more important role, however, was played by Hindus, who established trading communities throughout Iran and Central Asia and whose networks extended as far as Moscow and Amsterdam.[43]

During the nineteenth century, however, British and Russian empires converged on Central Asia, turning it into a mere buffer zone and shutting off the flow of trade altogether but for a smugglers' trickle. The Chinese began consolidating their hold on East Turkestan, turning Asia into a colonial pie split three ways. For most of the twentieth century the peoples of Central Asia lived separated and under the rule of foreign regimes; only in the past two decades have the imperial borders slowly started to open again and the commercial and cultural contacts of the Silk Road begun to resume.

In terms of religious culture, sixteenth-century Central Asia was one of the most thoroughly Islamicized areas of the Muslim world, more so than the Arab and Iranian heartlands of Western Asia and Egypt, which retain significant non-Muslim minorities even to the present day. Only North Africa, also relatively peripheral to the heartland of Islamic civilization, matched Central Asia's nearly total degree of Islamization.

It has been suggested that this apparent paradox can be accounted for by the fact that Central Asia was removed from the centers of rival religions such as Christianity, that preexisting religious institutions were weak, and that communication with central religious authority was difficult or nonexistent.[44] This explanation begs certain questions, however. Why, for example, did Christianity survive in southern India, and how did Manichaeism in Fujian maintain for so long a distinct identity within the sea of popular Chinese religion?

An alternative explanation, which does not preclude accommodation with the one preceding, is that the peoples of Central Asia were almost entirely dependent, either directly or indirectly, on trade that was dominated by Muslims. This is true even for the Qazaq and Qyrgyz nomads, who were the last to be Islamicized. Islamization was likewise most complete in other areas of the world most directly plugged into the Muslim-controlled trade routes, such as the coasts of Africa and Southeast Asia. Conversely in India and Spain, which retained non-Muslim majorities, the dependence of local economies on long-distance trade was nowhere near as generalized.

Despite occasional pogroms waged by the steppe peoples among themselves, direct coercion was at most a minor aspect of the Islamization of the Silk Road. The major factor, from which others derived, was the early and lasting involvement of Muslims in long-distance trade.

The story of the religions of the Silk Road is a part of the broader history of the conversation of cultures, a conversation that was made possible by the network-building activities of individuals possessing sufficient commercial skills and sense of adventure to overcome profitably the immense difficulties and dangers of travel across the center of the vast Eurasian continent.

Epilogue:
The Religion of the Market

The Jewish and Christian bibles foretell one outcome of history. If economics foresees another, it is in effect offering a competing religious vision. The prophecies of economics would then be a substitute for the traditional messages of the Bible. Perhaps the biblical God has reconsidered. Perhaps, instead of Jesus, he has now chosen economists to be a new bearer of his message, replacing the word of the Old and New Testaments that has now become outdated for the modern age—as Islam advertised the Koran as a later and more accurate statement of God's real plans for the world. Perhaps God has decided that the underlying ordering forces of the world, the ultimate reality that will shape the future outcome of history, will be truly economic.

Robert Nelson, Economics as Religion[1]

As noted in chapter One, the patterns underlying contemporary globalization are nothing new. Historians such as Fernand Braudel, Immanuel Wallerstein, André Gunder Frank, Jerry Bentley, and others have demonstrated that the Eurocentric view—according to which world systems supposedly first emerged with the European "discoveries" of the fifteenth century—is excessively narrow. And this book has sought to make the case that for as long as global networks have been in existence—that is, for at least 3,000 years—religion and trade have gone hand in hand. As a concluding note we would like to suggest that the same is true today.

But isn't modern-day globalization driven by so-called free-market capitalism? Indeed, it is, and that proves the point: global networks today are underpinned by an all-encompassing economistic worldview that is fundamentally religious in nature. As a growing number of religion scholars are now conceding, the dominant faith system in the contemporary world is neither Christianity nor Islam, nor indeed any of the traditionally recognized religions, but rather a new hybrid faith that some have begun to call the Religion of the Market.[2]

The Religion of the Market possesses, in the words of theologian Jay McDaniel, "the complete ecclesiastical apparatus": its priests are the economists, its missionaries the advertising agencies, and its church the shopping mall.[3] It promotes a simple but uncompromising ethical system, in which the highest value is to spend money and consume goods and services. Harvey Cox, a professor at Harvard Divinity School, has noted the Market is referred to today in terms previously reserved for God.[4] One might add that the IMF and the World Bank have been functioning as a kind of Vatican, sending down infallible decrees that national leaders must put into action or risk excommunication from the global community.

Indeed, even in the wake of the current world financial crisis, anyone who questions the basic foundations of this new global religion is dismissed as a heretic. And just as a Silk Road merchant 15 centuries ago had to do business within a network dominated by Buddhists, and a few centuries later by Muslims, anyone seeking to enter the global marketplace today must jump on the bandwagon of corporate capitalism or die. Inevitably, doing so requires adjusting one's principles and beliefs to accord with the dogmas of the dominant system. And as has always been the case with proselytizing religions in the past, the Religion of the Market has proved adept at preaching in terms familiar to its diverse target audiences, so that we now have such concepts as "Jesus, C.E.O." and trendy Islamic "Dawahwear" fashions. From upmarket Buddhist retreats in California to condo developments in India advertising "luxury living in the sacred playground of Krishna," theologies of prosperity have emerged from every corner of the world.

The lands of the former Silk Road are no exception. From "Islamic" Iran to "communist" China, official ideologies have been adapted to accommodate the Religion of the Market. Iranian banks offer returns of 12–24 percent on savings accounts, despite an ostensible Islamic ban on interest. And China has proven willing to sacrifice everything— from human rights to the environment—in the interest of maximizing economic growth. The Silk Road idea is being revived and marketed as a commodity, as government tourist offices across Central Asia seek to bring in hard currency. The spirit of fourteenth-century writer Francesco Pegolotti has seemingly returned, with the recent publication of books such as *The New Silk Road: Secrets of Business Success in China Today* and *The Silk Road to International Marketing: Profit and Passion in Global Business.*[5]

All these observations offer a double benefit: we can perhaps better understand the nature of our present situation by seeing it as part of an ongoing historical pattern, and at the same time, by reflecting on current realities we can better make sense of the past. Historians often get the sense from their work that *plus ça change, plus c'est la même chose,* and there is perhaps some comfort in seeing that we are no more or less human than our ancestors. Conversely, those who feel disturbed or marginalized by the dominant ideology of the day can take heart from the certainty that, despite Fukuyaman prophecies that civilization has attained its ultimate realization in the form of Western "democracies," in reality history is never completed and no system remains permanently on top. For better or worse something new will always rise to take its place, and the cycle will go on.

Notes

Chapter One

1. See Morris Rossabi, "The 'Decline' of the Central Asian Caravan Trade," in James Tracy, ed., *The Rise of Merchant Empires: Long-Distance Trade in the Early Modern World 1350-1750*, Cambridge: Cambridge University Press, 1990, pp. 351–370; also Niels Steensgard, *The Asian Trade Revolution of the Seventeenth Century: The East India Company and the Decline of the Caravan Trade*, Chicago: University of Chicago Press, 1974. Some scholars, however, have recently sought to revise the conventional view of decline in overland trade during this period; see, for example, Muzaffar Alam, "Trade, State Policy and Regional Change: Aspects of Mughal-Uzbek Relations, c.1550-1750," *Journal of the Economic and Social History of the Orient* 37 (1994), pp. 202–227, and Robert McChesney, *Central Asia: Foundations of Change*, Princeton, NJ: Darwin Press, 1996, pp. 53–54, note 3.
2. See Peter Hopkirk, *The Great Game*, Tokyo: Kodansha International, 1992.
3. See Elena Kuzmina, *The Prehistory of the Silk Road*, Philadelphia: University of Pennsylvania Press, 2008. A more general history is David Christian, *A History of Russia, Central Asia and Mongolia, Volume 1: Inner Eurasia from Prehistory to the Mongol Empire*, Oxford: Blackwell, 1998. For a collection of studies on specific aspects of this movement see Victor Mair, ed., *The Bronze Age and Early Iron Age Peoples of Eastern Central Asia*, 2 vols., Washington, D.C.: Institute for the Study of Man, 1998.
4. The earliest evidence of horse domestication, including bit-worn teeth and vessels bearing traces of horse milk, dates to 3500 BCE in northern Kazakhstan. See Alan K. Outram, et al., "The Earliest Horse Harnessing and Milking," *Science* (March 6, 2009), pp. 1332–1335.
5. Laszlo Torday, *Mounted Archers: The Beginnings of Central Asian History*, Durham: Durham Academic Press, 1997, p. 91.
6. This appearance was likely due to parasites infesting the horses' skin.
7. John Noble Wilford, "New Finds Suggest Even Earlier Trade on Fabled Silk Road," *New York Times*, March 16, 1993, pp. C1, C8.

8. *La Pratica della Mercatura,* in Henry Yule and H. Cordier, eds. and trs., *Cathay and the Way Thither,* 4 vols., London: Hakluyt Society, 1937 [1913–1916].

9. By the fifth century even silk was not making the complete trip from China, as it was being produced in Iran, India, and eventually the Byzantine Empire (Xinru Liu, *Religion and Silk,* Delhi: Oxford University Press, 1996, p. 9).

10. See Andre Gunder Frank and Barry Gills, eds., *The World System: From Five Hundred Years to Five Thousand,* London: Routledge, 1992.

11. See Peter Hopkirk, *Foreign Devils on the Silk Road,* Amherst, MA: University of Massachusetts Press, 1984 [1980].

12. A point emphasized by Jason BeDuhn in his review of the first edition of this book (*Journal of Chinese Religions* 29 (2001), pp. 295–296.

13. Sir Aurel Stein, *The Ruins of Desert Cathay,* 2 vols., New York: Dover, 1987 [1912], vol. 2, p. 194.

14. Albert von le Coq, *Die buddhistische Spätantike in Mittelasien:* vol. 2, *Die manichäischen Miniaturen,* Graz, 1973 [1923].

15. D.S. Margoliouth, "An Early Judeo-Persian Document from Khotan in the Stein Collection, with Other Early Persian Documents," *Journal of the Royal Asiatic Society,* 1903, pp. 735–761; Bo Utas, "The Jewish-Persian Fragment from Dandan-Uiliq," *Orientalia Suecana* 17 (1968), pp. 123–126.

16. A.V.W. Jackson, H.W. Bailey, W.B. Henning, I. Gershevitch, and Mary Boyce in England and W. Bang, A. von Gebain, W. Sundermann, P. Zieme, and H.-J. Klimkeit in Germany were among the major contributors to this effort.

17. See, for example, Jerry Bentley, *Old World Encounters,* New York: Oxford University Press, 1993, and Philip Curtin, *Cross-Cultural Trade in World History,* Cambridge: Cambridge University Press, 1984.

18. See Xinru Liu, *Ancient India and Ancient China: Trade and Religious Exchanges, AD 1-600,* Delhi: Oxford University Press, 1988, especially pp. 68–69.

19. Gavin Hambly, *Central Asia,* London: Weidenfeld and Nicolson, 1967, p. 7.

20. The travels of the Japanese pilgrim Ennin (793–864) have been translated by Edwin O. Reischauer as *Ennin's Diary: The Record of a Pilgrimage to China in Search of the Law,* New York: Ronald Press, 1955.

21. Bentley, *Old World Encounters.*

22. On Africa see Mervyn Hiskett, *The Course of Islam in Africa,* Edinburgh: Edinburgh University Press, 1994, pp. 100, 108, and J.S. Trimingham, *The Influence of Islam upon Africa,* New York and Washington, D.C.: Praeger, 1968, pp. 38–40. On Indian Ocean trade see André Wink, *Al-Hind: The Making of the Indo-Islamic World,* vol. 1, Leiden: Brill, 1990, especially pp. 25–85, and K.N. Chaudhuri, *Asia before Europe: Economy and Civilisation of the Indian Ocean from the Rise of Islam to 1750,* Cambridge: Cambridge University Press, 1990.

23. Thomas Allsen, review of Richard C. Foltz, *Religions of the Silk Road,* in *Iranian Studies* 32/4 (1999), p. 575.

24. For a fictionalized portrait of a Sogdian merchant's world in the eighth century, see Susan Whitfield, *Life along the Silk Road,* London: John Murray, 1999, pp. 27–54.

25. See the recent study by Étienne de la Vaissiére, *Sogdian Traders: A History*, tr., James Ward, Leiden: Brill, 2005.
26. Stein, *Ruins;* vol. 2, pp. 114–115; F. Grenet and N. Sims-Williams, "The Historical Context of the Sogdian Ancient Letters," *Transition Periods in Iranian History, Studia Iranica, Cahier 5*, Paris, 1987, pp. 101–122.
27. Stein, *Ruins*, vol. 2, p. 186.
28. See Richard Frye, *The Golden Age of Persia*, London: Weidenfeld and Nicolson, 1975, pp. 150–174.
29. See Richard Frye, *Bukhara: the Medieval Achievement*, Costa Mesa, CA: Mazda Publishers, 1997 [1965].
30. See Donald Leslie, *The Survival of the Chinese Jews*, Leiden: Brill, 1972, pp. 18 ff.
31. Abu Nasr Ahmad Qubawi, preface to Abu Bakr Muhammad Narshakhi, *Tārīkh-i Bukhārā*, tr. R.N. Frye, Cambridge, MA: Mediaeval Academy of America, 1954, p. 1.
32. Sergei P. Poliakov, *Everyday Islam: Religion and Tradition in Rural Central Asia*, Armonk, NY: M.E. Sharpe, 1992, especially pp. 59–75.
33. Richard Eaton, *The Sufis of Bijapur, 1300-1700*, Princeton, NJ: Princeton University Press, 1978, pp. 155–174.
34. Susan Whitfield, using a range of mostly Chinese sources, has attempted to convey something of women's experiences along the Silk Road through several composite, semi-fictionalized portraits in her book *Life along the Silk Road*.
35. Translation by Nicholas Sims-Williams in Susan Whitfield and Ursula Sims-Williams, eds., *The Silk Road: Trade, Travel, War and Faith*, Chicago: Serindia, 2004, p. 249. These letters were most likely dictated to a professional letter writer, since women at the time were mostly illiterate.Since the letters were found in Dunhuang, presumably they were never delivered.
36. Peter Bryder, "Cao'an Revisited," *Research into China Overseas Communication History* 16/2 (1989), pp. 35–42, and "...Where the Faint Traces of Manichaeism Disappear," *Altorientalische Forschungen* 15/1 (1988), pp. 201–208.

Chapter Two

1. Harold Peake and Herbert John Fleure, *The Steppe and the Sown*, New Haven: Yale University Press, 1928. See the studies by Thomas Barfield, *The Perilous Frontier*, Oxford: Blackwell, 1989, and Anatoly Khazanov, *Nomads and the Outside World*, Cambridge: Cambridge University Press, 1984. For a revisionist view see Christopher Beckwith, *Empires of the Silk Road: A History of Central Eurasia from the Bronze Age to the Present*, Princeton: Princeton University Press, 2009.
2. René Grousset, *Empire of the Steppes*, tr. Naomi Walford, New Brunswick, NJ: Rutgers University Press, 1970, p. ix.
3. See, for example, Georges Dumézil, *Mythe et Epopée*, 3 vols., Paris: Gallimard, 1968–1973; also J.P. Mallory, *In Search of the Indo-Europeans: Language, Archaeology, and Myth*, London: Thames and Hudson, 1989, and J.P. Mallory

and D.Q. Adams, *The Oxford Introduction to Proto-Indo-European and the Proto-Indo-European World*, New York: Oxford University Press, 2006.

4. Joseph Fletcher, "The Mongols: Ecological and Social Perspectives," *Harvard Journal of Asiatic Studies* 46/1 (1986), p. 31.

5. B.A. Litvinskii, "Prehistoric Religions: The Eurasian Steppes and Inner Asia," in Mircea Eliade, ed., *Encyclopedia of Religion*, New York: Macmillan, 1987, vol. 11, p. 517.

6. Ibid., pp. 517–518.

7. See the extensive treatment in David W. Anthony, *The Horse, the Wheel, and Language*, Princeton: Princeton University Press, 2007.

8. Old Iranian Saka, Greek *Scythai* (Scythian), and Sogdian *Sughde*, as well as the biblical Hebrew *Ashkenaz* (via Assyrian *Askuzai*) appear all to derive from *skudo*, an ancient Indo-European word for archer; cf. English "shoot". For a discussion of the term in its various forms see Beckwith, *Empires of the Silk Road*, pp. 377–380.

9. Herodotus, *The Histories*, tr. Aubrey de Sélincourt, rev. A.R. Burn, New York: Penguin, 1972, pp. 291–295 (Book 4: 71–72, 75, 65); Peter Golden, *An Introduction to the History of the Turkic Peoples*, Wiesbaden: Otto Harrassowitz, 1992, p. 49.

10. Herodotus, *Histories*, pp. 127–128 (2: 215–216).

11. Ibid., p. 289 (4: 59). Herodotus treats the Massagatae and the Scythians as separate peoples, but they were both Saka groups.

12. Ruth Meserve, "Inner Asian Religions," in Mircea Eliade, ed., *Encyclopedia of Religion*, New York: Macmillan, 1987, vol. 7, p. 241.

13. Herodotus, *Histories*, pp. 278–279 (4: 24). See also E.D. Phillips, "The Argippaei of Herodotus," *Artibus Asiae* 23 (1960), pp. 124–128.

14. A large number of Indo-European mummies have recently been discovered in Western China, some as much as 3,000 years old. See J.P. Mallory and Victor H. Mair, *The Tarim Mummies: Ancient China and the Mystery of the Earliest Peoples from the West*, London: Thames and Hudson, 2000; also E.J.W. Barber, *The Mummies of Urumchi*, New York: Norton, 1999.

15. Meserve, "Inner Asian Religions," p. 241.

16. On the persistence of horse sacrifice see J.A. Boyle, "A Form of Horse Sacrifice amongst the 13th- and 14th-century Mongols," *Central Asiatic Journal* 10 (1965), pp. 145–150.

17. For an overview of these ongoing disagreements see Mary Boyce, *Zoroastrianism: Its Antiquity and Constant Vigour*, Costa Mesa, CA: Mazda Publishers, 1992, pp. 1–26.

18. The hallucinatory substance from which this beverage was concocted, a mystery for over 2,000 years, has recently been identified as the plant known as harmel *(Peganum harmala)*. See David S. Flattery and Martin Schwartz, *Haoma and Harmaline: The Botanical Identity of the Indo-Iranian Sacred Hallucinogen "Soma" and Its Legacy in Religion, Language, and Middle Eastern Folklore*, Berkeley: University of California Press, 1989.

19. Although in modern Persian *dīv* means "demon," the original positive character of the *daēva*s survives in later Iranian names, such as the Sogdian Devashtic and the Persian Divdad.

20. Shahin Bekhradnia, "The Tajik Case for a Zoroastrian Identity," *Religion, State and Society* 22/1 (1994), p. 109.

21. For example, Jamsheed Choksy, *Conflict and Cooperation: Muslim Elites and Zoroastrian Subalterns in Medieval Iranian Society,* New York: Columbia University Press, 1997, p. 4.

22. On Achæmenid religion see Martin Schwartz, "The Religion of Achæmenian Iran," in Ilya Gershevitch, ed., *Cambridge History of Iran,* vol. 2, *The Median and Achæmenian Periods,* Cambridge: Cambridge University Press, 1985, pp. 664–697.

23. Janos Harmatta, "Religions in the Kushan Empire," in *History of the Civilizations of Central Asia,* vol. 2, Paris: UNESCO, 1994, p. 315.

24. K. Maurer Trinkhaus, "Mortuary Ritual and Mortuary Remains," *Current Anthropology* 25/5 (1984), p. 677.

25. Arthur Christensen, "Die Moschee Makh in Buhara," *Orientalische Litteraturzeitung* 7 (1904), pp. 49–51.

26. Behistun inscription, column 5; cf. Richard Frye, *The Heritage of Central Asia,* Princeton, NJ: Markus Wiener, 1996, p. 83.

27. W.B. Henning, "A Sogdian God," *Bulletin of the School of Oriental and African Studies* 28/2 (1965), p. 251.

28. Nicholas Sims-Williams, "Some Reflections on Zoroastrianism in Sogdiana and Bactria," in David Christian and Craig Benjamin, eds., *Realms of the Silk Roads: Ancient and Modern,* Turnhout: Brepols, 2000, p. 7. Despite this observation, Sims-Williams, like his colleague Frantz Grenet, tends to interpret any relic of old Iranian religion in Central Asia as "evidence for Zoroastrianism."

29. Henning, "A Sogdian God," p. 247.

30. Ibid., p. 251; cf. Grenet and Sims-Williams, "The Historical Context of the Sogdian Ancient Letters."

31. Schwartz, "Religion of Achæmenian Iran," p. 681; cf. Geo Widengren, *Les réligions de l'Iran,* Paris: Payot, 1968, p. 357.

32. Allen H. Godbey, "From Persia to China," in William C. White, ed., *Chinese Jews,* 2nd edition, New York: Paragon, 1966, pp. 136–137.

33. Irene Franck, *The Silk Road,* New York: Facts on File, 1986, p. 63.

34. Itzhak Ben-Zvi, *The Exiled and the Redeemed,* Philadelphia: Jewish Publication Society of America, 1957, p. 67; Julius Brutzkus, "Bukhara," *Encyclopaedia Judaica,* Berlin: L. Schneider,1929, vol. 4, p. 1126. Interestingly, the Muslim Pukhtuns of Afghanistan also have a tradition that claims descent from the Lost Tribes.

35. L. Rabinowitz, *Jewish Merchant Adventurers: A Study of the Radanites,* London: Goldston, 1948, p. 51.

36. V.A. Livshits and Z.I. Usmanova, "New Parthian Inscriptions from Old Merv," in *Irano-Judaica* III, pp. 99–105.

37. Jacob Neusner, "Jews in Iran," in Ehsan Yarshater, ed., *Cambridge History of Iran*, vol. 3, *The Seleucid, Parthian, and Sasanian Periods*, Cambridge: Cambridge University Press, 1983, p. 912.

38. See Shaul Shaked, "Iranian Influence on Judaism: First Century B.C.E. to Second Century C.E.," in W.D. Davies and Louis Finkelstein, eds., *The Cambridge History of Judaism*, vol. 1, Cambridge: Cambridge University Press, 1984, pp. 308-325; David Winston, "The Iranian Component in the Bible, Apocrypha, and Qumran: A Review of the Evidence," *History of Religions* 6 (1966), pp. 183-216. For an opposing view see James Barr, "The Question of Religious Influence: The Case of Zoroastrianism, Judaism, and Christianity," *Journal of the American Academy of Religion* 53 (1985), pp. 201–235.

39. See, for example, Gedaliahu G. Stroumsa, "A Zoroastrian Origin to the *Sefirot?*" in Shaul Shaked and Amnon Metzer, eds., *Irano Judaica* III, Jerusalem: Ben-Zvi, 1994, pp. 17–33.

40. Shaul Shaked, "Iranian Functions in Esther," *Irano-Judaica*, Jerusalem: Ben-Zvi, 1982, pp. 292–303.

41. James Russell, "Zoroastrian Elements in the Book of Esther," in Shaul Shaked and Amnon Metzer, eds., *Irano-Judaica* II, Jerusalem: Ben-Zvi, 1990, pp. 33–40.

42. Almut Hintze, "The Greek and Hebrew Versions of the Book of Esther and its Iranian Background," in *Irano Judaica* III, pp. 34–39.

43. David Flusser, "Hystaspes and John of Patmos," in *Irano-Judaica*, pp. 12–75.

44. Carsten Colpe, "Development of Religious Thought," in Ehsan Yarshater, ed., *Cambridge History of Iran*, vol. 3, *The Seleucid, Parthian, and Sasanian Periods*, Cambridge: Cambridge University Press, 1983, pp. 831–833.

45. Shaked, "Iranian Influence," p. 324.

46. Quoted in Leslie, *Survival of the Chinese Jews*, p. 3.

47. Michael Pollock, *Mandarins, Jews and Missionaries*, Philadelphia: Jewish Publication Society, 1980, pp. 255–256.

48. Pollock, *Mandarins*, p. 257.

49. Wilford, "New Finds."

50. Leslie, *Survival*, p. 4.

51. Rudolf Loewenthal, "The Jews of Bukhara," *Central Asian Collectanea*, no. 8, Washington, D.C., 1961, p. 6.

52. Victor Mair, "Old Sinitic *Myag, Old Persian Magus, and English 'Magician,'" *Early China* 15 (1990), pp. 27–47.

53. Homer H. Dubs, "Taoism," in H.F. MacNair, ed., *Philosophy and Religion*, Berkeley and Los Angeles: University of California Press, 1946, pp. 286–287.

54. Iwamoto Yutaka, *Bukkyo setsuwa kenkyu*, vol. 4: *Jigoku meguri no bungaku*, Tokyo: Kaimei shoten, 1979, pp. 184–199; cited in Stephen F. Teiser, *The Ghost Festival in Medieval China*, Princeton, NJ: Princeton University Press, 1988, p. 24.

55. See, for example, Ts'un-yan Liu, "Traces of Zoroastrian and Manichaean Activities in pre-T'ang China," in *Selected Papers from the Hall of Harmonious Winds*, Leiden: Brill, 1976, pp. 2–55.

Chapter Three

1. His dates have been posited variously as 624–544, 563–483, or 448–368 BCE; current consensus is that at least part of his life was in the fifth century BCE. He is also known in many texts as Sakyamuni, "the Sage of the Sakyas."
2. As Johan Elverskog explains in his book *Buddhism and Islam on the Silk Road: A History of Cross-Cultural Exchange* (Philadelphia: University of Pennsylvania Press, 2010), the economy of the Maurya Empire, like that of the Kushans who followed, depended on urban merchants and rural landowners who had Buddhist sympathies.
3. Peter Harvey, *An Introduction to Buddhism: Teachings, History and Practices*, Cambridge: Cambridge University Press, 1990, p. 74.
4. The Theravada tradition has been questioned on this point; see Richard Gombrich, *Theravada Buddhism*, London: Routledge, 1988, p. 133.
5. On various traditional accounts of the schism see Etienne Lamotte, *History of Indian Buddhism*, Louvain and Paris: Peters Press, 1988, pp. 274–292.
6. Harvey, *Introduction to Buddhism*, pp. 74–75. Early Mahasanghika texts from Bamiyan, Afghanistan, can be found in Jens Braarvig, ed., *Manuscripts in the Shøyen Collection: Buddhist Manuscripts I*, Oslo: Hermes, 2000.
7. Ge Ling Shang, personal communication.
8. Gregory Schopen, "Notes on the Cult of the Book in Mahāyāna," *Indo-Iranian Journal* 17/3–4 (1975), pp. 147–181. See also Paul Harrison, "Searching for the Origins of the Mahayana: What Are We Looking For?" *The Eastern Buddhist* 28/1 (1995), pp. 56, 67, and Aramaki Noritoshi, "Towards a New Working Hypothesis on the Origin of Mahāyāna Buddhism," *The Eastern Buddhist* 35/1–2 (2003), pp. 203–218.
9. Sasaki Shizuka, "A Study on the Origin of Mahayana Buddhism," *The Eastern Buddhist* 30/1 (1997), pp. 79–113.
10. Paul Williams, *Mahayana Buddhism: The Doctrinal Foundations*, London: Routledge, 1989, pp. 277–278, note 7.
11. Ibid., p. 49.
12. Paul Harrison, "Who Gets to Ride in the Great Vehicle? Self-Image and Identity among the Followers of the Early Mahayana," *Journal of the International Association of Buddhist Studies* 10/1 (1987), p. 80.
13. Williams, *Mahayana Buddhism*, p. 5.
14. Hsüan-tsang [Xuanzang], *Records of the Western Countries (Ta T'ang Si Yu Ki)*, in Samuel Beal, tr., *Buddhist Records of the Western World*, New Delhi: Oriental Reprints, 1969 [1884], vol. 1, pp. 47–48.

15. See J. Harmatta, "Sino-Indica," *Acta Asiatica* 12/1–2 (1964), p. 4. The inscriptions speak of spreading the *dharma*, however, not Buddhism per se.

16. Janos Harmatta, "Religions in the Kushan Empire," in *History of the Civilizations of Central Asia,* vol. 2, Paris: UNESCO, 1994, p. 314.

17. On the interaction between Iranian and Greek religious ideas see Colpe, "Development of Religious Thought."

18. Hsüan-tsang, *Records,* vol. 1, p. 139.

19. Sally Hovey Wriggins, *Xuanzang: A Buddhist Pilgrim on the Silk Road,* Boulder, CO: Westview Press, 1996, p. 68.

20. B.A. Litvinskii and I.R. Pichikian, "The Hellenistic Architecture and Art of the Temple of the Oxus," *Bulletin of the Asia Institute,* new series, 8 (1994), pp. 47–66; Harmatta, "Religions in the Kushan Empire," p. 314.

21. I.B. Horner, tr., *Milinda's Questions,* 2 vols., London: Luzac & Co., 1969; Lamotte, *History of Indian Buddhism,* pp. 419–426. See also A.K. Narain, *The Indo-Greeks,* Oxford, 1957.

22. Guitty Azarpay, "A Jataka Tale on a Sasanian Silver Plate," *Bulletin of the Asia Institute,* new series, 9 (1995), pp. 99–125.

23. See Craig Benjamin, *The Yuezhi: Origin, Migration and the Conquest of Northern Bactria,* Turnhout: Brepols, 2007.

24. Ronald E. Emmerick, "Buddhism in Central Asia," in Mircea Eliade, ed., *Encyclopedia of Religion,* New York: Macmillan, 1987, vol. 2, p. 401.

25. Bivar, in Hambly, *Central Asia*, p. 47; cf. Stein, *Ruins,* vol. 2, p. 414.

26. Harmatta, "Religions in the Kushan Empire," pp. 317–318.

27. Oskar von Hinüber, "Expansion to the North: Afghanistan and Central Asia," in Heinz Bechent and Richard Gombrich, *The World of Buddhism,* London: Thames and Hudson, 1984, p. 104.

28. Jan Nattier, "The Meanings of the Maitreya Myth: A Typological Analysis," in Alan Sponberg and Helen Hardacre, eds., *Maitreya, the Future Buddha,* Princeton, NJ: Princeton University Press, 1988, p. 46, note 60, citing Przyluski.

29. Ronald E. Emmerick, "Buddhism among Iranian Peoples," in Yarshater, ed., *Cambridge History of Iran,* vol. 3, pp. 955–956; Lamotte, *History of Indian Buddhism,* pp. 498–499.

30. Lamotte, *op. cit.*, pp. 668–675.

31. Ibid., pp. 677–678.

32. Litvinsky, "Buddhism in Central Asia," p. 25.

33. Ibid. It has been suggested that the name "Bukhara" is originally derived from "vihara," which could indicate that a Buddhist temple once stood there.

34. Emmerick, "Buddhism among Iranians," p. 960.

35. See G. Koshelenko, "The Beginning of Buddhism in Margiana," *Acta Asiatica* 14/1–2 (1966), p. 182.

36. David Utz, "Arshak, Parthian Buddhists, and 'Iranian' Buddhism," in *Buddhism Across Boundaries: Chinese Buddhism and the Western Regions,* John McRae and

Jan Nattier, eds., *Sanchung: Fo Guang Shan Foundation for Buddhist and Culture Education*, 1999, pp. 446–470, and Takayasu Higuchi, "Buddhist Ruins of West Turkestan," *Bukkyoshigaku Kenkyu* 27/1 (1984), pp. 119–141.

37. Mariko Namba Walter, "Buddhism in Western Central Asia," paper presented at the American Historical Association annual conference, Seattle, WA, January 1998, pp. 1, 3.

38. Litvinsky, "Buddhism in Central Asia," p. 25.

39. Walter, "Buddhism in Western Central Asia," p. 7.

40. Ibid., p. 8.

41. The Caucasoid mummies described in Mallory and Mair, *The Tarim Mummies*, were likely the Tocharians' ancestors. Tocharian loanwords in Chinese suggest that chariots and town building were among the Western inventions the Tocharians brought to China (Alexander Lubotsky, "Tocharian Loanwords in Old Chinese," in Mair, ed., *Broze Age and Early Iron Age Peoples*, pp. 379–390). Tocharian B—one of two or three related languages—was apparently spoken in the region up to the tenth century when it was gradually replaced by Uighur Turkish.

42. Mariko Walter, "Mahayana and Hinayana in Central Asian Buddhist History: The Nature of Buddhism in Chinese Turkestan," paper presented at the Association for Asian Studies annual conference, January 1997, pp. 5–6.

43. Erik Zürcher, *The Buddhist Conquest of China*, Leiden: Brill, 1959, p. 26.

44. Ibid., p. 27.

45. Harrison, "Who Gets to Ride in the Great Vehicle?" p. 68; Idem., "The Earliest Chinese Translations of Mahayana Sutras: Some Notes on the Works of Lokaksema," *Buddhist Studies Review* 10/2 (1993), pp. 135–177, and "Searching for the Origins of the Mahayana," p. 55.

46. Zürcher, *Buddhist Conquest*, p. 35.

47. Walter, "Buddhism in Western Central Asia," p. 4. On the continuing role of Parthian families into the Sasanian period see Parvaneh Pourshariati, *Decline and Fall of the Sasanian Empire: The Sasanian-Parthian Confederacy and the Arab Conquest of Iran*, London: I.B. Tauris, 2008.

48. Takayasu Higuchi, "Buddhist Ruins of West Turkestan," *Bukkyoshigaku Kenkyu* 27/1 (1984), pp. 119–136 (in Japanese). I thank Mariko Walter for this reference.

49. Walter, "Buddhism in Western Central Asia," p. 6.

50. Emmerick, "Buddhism among Iranians," p. 960–961.

51. Jan Nattier, "Church Language and Vernacular Language in Central Asian Buddhism," *Numen* 37/2 (1990), pp. 195–219.

52. He may have been the one responsible for introducing into India the popular Heart Sutra as well. (Jan Nattier, "The Heart Sutra: A Chinese Apocryphal Text?" *International Journal of Buddhist Studies* 15/2 [1992], p. 180.)

53. Antonino Forte, "An Ancient Chinese Monastery Excavated in Kirgiziya," *Central Asiatic Journal* 38/1 (1994), pp. 41–57.

54. Chou Yi-liang, "Tantrism in China," *Harvard Journal of Asiatic Studies* 8 (1945): 241–272.

55. Bentley, *Old World Encounters,* p. 97.

56. Faxian, *Buddhist Country Records (Fo Kwo Ki),* in Beal, tr., *Buddhist Records,* vol. 1, pp. xxiii–lxxxiii.

57. Sung Yün, *Buddhist Books in the Western Countries,* in Beal, tr., *Buddhist Records,* vol. 1, p. xciii.

58. For an engaging book-length treatment see Sally Hovey Wriggins, *Xuanzang: A Buddhist Pilgrim on the Silk Road,* Boulder, CO: Westview Press, 1996.

59. Chang Yueh, "Preface," in Beal, tr., *Buddhist Records,* v.1, p. 6. Chang claims Xuanzang translated all of these texts, but this is unlikely.

60. One of the best challenges to the familiar idea that violent religious fanaticism was particular to Muslim conquerors has come from the work of Richard Eaton. In *Temple Destruction and Muslim States in Medieval India* (Gurgaon: Hope, 2004), for example, Eaton shows that beneath the chroniclers' rhetoric, which portrayed Muslim campaigns as being motivated by a desire to spread Islam and crush idolatry, in fact, since the temples were where Hindu rulers kept their wealth, the pattern of looting and desecrating temples by competing powers long pre-dated the Muslims' arrival in India.

61. For reasons that are not clear, local Muslim governors did occasionally permit Buddhist missions to transit their territories in Central Asia. Often, however, they were robbed or detained (Jan Yün-hua, "Buddhist Relations between India and Sung China," *History of Religions* 6 [1966], pp. 142–143).

62. Huili, *Life of Hsuan-tsang,* tr. Yung-hsi Li, Peking: The Chinese Buddhist Association, 1959, p. 46.

63. Ibid., p. 47.

64. No incontrovertibly Buddhist remains have been unearthed in Sogdiana proper, in contrast to areas to the south of the Hissar Mountains where they abound.

65. Litvinsky, "Buddhism in Central Asia," p. 50.

66. Narshakhi, *Tārīkh-i Bukhārā,* p. 23. This rooster, whom Maria Subtelny refers to as the "Cosmic Cock," appears later in the Muslim *mi'raj* story of the Prophet Muhammad's miraculous night journey to heaven (Maria Subtelny, "The Cosmic Cock: Zoroastrian Mythological Elements in the Islamic Ascension Narrative," paper presented at the 7th International Society for Iranian Studies biennial conference, Toronto, July 31–August 3, 2008).

67. G. Uray, "Tibet's Connections with Nestorianism and Manicheism in the 8th-10th Centuries," *Wiener Studien zur Tibetologie und Buddhismuskunde* 10 (1983), pp. 407, 421. On the Ladakh paintings see Hans-Joachim Klimkeit, *Manichaean Art and Calligraphy,* Leiden: Brill, 1982; on the inscriptions see Nicholas Sims-Williams, *Sogdian and Other Iranian Inscriptions of the Upper Indus,* 2 vols., London, 1989–1992.

68. Marc Des Jardins, personal communication.

69. See Christopher I. Beckwith, *The Tibetan Empire in Central Asia,* Princeton, NJ: Princeton University Press, 1987.

Chapter Four

1. Quoted in S.N.C. Lieu, *Manichaeism in the Later Roman Empire and Medieval China*, 2nd ed., Tübingen: Mohr, 1992, p. 98.

2. Chabot, *Synodicon Orientale*, p. 302, quoted in Samuel H. Moffett, *A History of Christianity in Asia*, vol. 1, San Francisco: Harper, 1992, p. 197.

3. See Moffett, *Christianity in Asia*, pp. 51–53.

4. Alphonse Mingana, *The Early Spread of Christianity in Central Asia and the Far East: A New Document*, Manchester: Manchester University Press, 1925, pp. 7–8.

5. Ibid., p. 4.

6. Neusner, "Jews in Iran," p. 914.

7. For an extended, albeit romanticized narrative of these vicissitudes see Nahal Tajadod, *Les Porteurs de Lumière: l'épopée de l'église perse*, Paris: Albin Michel, 2008 [1993].

8. Bedjan, *Acta Martyrum* 2: 351, quoted in Moffett, *Christianity in Asia*, p. 142. These accusations, while somewhat misrepresenting Christian belief and practice, are helpful in understanding the political use of prejudice.

9. See, for example, Jacob Neusner, *Aphrahat and Judaism: The Christian-Jewish Argument in Fourth-Century Iran*, Leiden: Brill, 1971, and A.V. Williams, "Zoroastrians and Christians in Sasanian Iran," *Bulletin of the John Rylands Library* 78/3 (1996), pp. 37–53.

10. Mingana, *Early Spread of Christianity*, p. 74.

11. Emile Benveniste, "Le Vocabulaire chrétien dans les langues d'Asie centrale," *L'Oriente Cristiano nella Storia della Civiltà*, Rome: Accademia Nazionale dei Lincei, 1964, pp. 85–91.

12. Nicholas Sims-Williams, "Syro-Sogdica I: An Anonymous Homily on the Three Periods of Solitary Life," *Orientalia Christiana Periodica* 47 (1981), p. 441.

13. Ibid., p. 443.

14. Mingana, *Early Spread of Christianity*, p. 9.

15. Lieu, *Manichaeism in the Later Roman Empire*, p. 228.

16. See Mircea Eliade, *Shamanism: Archaic Techniques of Ecstasy*, Princeton, NJ: Princeton University Press, 1964. The term "shaman" comes from the Tungus language; the Turkish word is *qam*, and the Mongolian *bö'e*. Medieval Muslim sources use the Arabic term *kahin* (as in Hebrew).

17. Mingana, *Early Spread of Christianity*, pp. 11–12; Erica C.D. Hunter, "The Conversion of the Kerait to Christianity in A.D. 1007," *Zentralasiatische Studien* 22 (1989–1991), p. 160.

18. J.A. Boyle, "Turkish and Mongol Shamanism in the Middle Ages," *Folklore* 83 (1972), pp. 184–193.

19. Mingana, *Early Spread of Christianity*, p. 12.

20. Ibid., p. 13.

21. Hunter, "The Conversion of the Kerait."

22. Mingana, *op.cit.*, p. 15.

23. See Edward Schafer, *The Golden Peaches of Samarkand: A Study of T'ang Exotics,* Los Angeles: University of California Press, 1962.

24. Kazuo Enoki, "Nestorian Christianism in Medieval Times," *L'Oriente Cristiano,* Rome1964, pp. 72–73.

25. Paul Pelliot, "Les influences iraniennes en Asie Central et en Extrême-Orient," *Revue d'Histoire et de Littérature Réligieuses* (1912), p. 108.

26. Martin Palmer, *The Jesus Sutras: Rediscovering the Lost Scrolls of Taoist Christianity,* New York: Ballantine, 2001, p. 236. The fact that the latter two are lumped into one category suggests that Christianity was still identified with Iran.

27. Ibid., p. 23.

28. Schafer, *Golden Peaches,* p. 50.

29. Ibid., pp. 53–54.

30. Ibn Nadim, *Fihrist of al-Nadim: A Tenth Century Survey of Muslim Culture (Fihrist al-'ulūm),* tr. Bayard Dodge, 2 vols., New York: Columbia University Press, 1970, pp. 836–837.

31. The Mandaeans survive to this day in small communities throughout southern Iraq and Iran; see Jorunn Jacobsen Buckley, *The Mandaeans,* New York: Oxford University Press, 2002.

32. W.B. Henning, "Mani's Last Journey," *Bulletin of the School of Oriental and African Studies* 10 (1939–1942), pp. 941–953.

33. Jacob Neusner, "Rabbi and Magus in Third-century Sasanian Babylonia," *History of Religions* 6 (1966), p. 173.

34. Geo Widengren and Gherardo Gnoli have argued that Manichaeism is in essence Iranian, while Samuel Lieu has argued in favor of its more Semitic character.

35. Jason BeDuhn has suggested that rather than being gnostic in its essence, Manichaeism used gnostic ideas to win converts in regions where gnosticism was popular, but turned to other vocabularies (e.g., Buddhist) further east (Jason David BeDuhn, review of Hans-Joachim Klimkeit, *Gnosis on the Silk Road, Journal of the American Oriental Society* 115/2 (1995), pp. 344–346).

36. Hans-Joachim Klimkeit, *Gnosis on the Silk Road,* San Francisco: Harper, 1993, p. 314. This story is similar to one in the apocryphal Acts of John, and reappears in Islamic guise in a tenth-century work by Ibn Babai.

37. See, for example, the sixteenth-century treatise by Qazi Ahmad Qumi, *Gulistān-i hunar,* tr. V. Minorsky, *Calligraphers and Painters,* Washington, D.C.: Smithsonian, 1959, pp. 177–180.

38. Samuel N.C. Lieu, *Manichaeism in Central Asia and China,* Leiden: Brill, 1998, p. 138.

39. Jason David BeDuhn, *The Manichaean Body: In Discipline and Ritual,* Baltimore: Johns Hopkins University Press, 2000.

40. *Contra Faustum,* cited in Philip Schaff, ed., *Nicene and Post-Nicene Fathers,* Grand Rapids: Eerdman's, 1983, v. 4, 5: 10.

41. Lieu, *Manichaeism in the Later Roman Empire,* pp. 112–113, 220.

42. Some evidence has been derived from Daoist sources, however, of even earlier Manichaean activity in China; see Liu, "Traces of Zoroastrian and Manichaean Activities in pre-T'ang China."

43. Lieu, *Manichaeism in the Later Roman Empire*, p. 230.

44. Ibid., p. 236.

45. E. Chavannes and P. Pelliot, *Un traité Manichéen retrouvé en Chine*, Paris: Imprimérie Nationale, 1913, p. 154.

46. The Arabic sources use the Persian loanword *zindiq* to refer to Manichaeans but also to dualistic heretics in general. Originally meaning "one who engages in commentary *(zand)*," the word was first used by the magi against rivals seeking to interpret the Avesta for themselves.

47. See Barfield, *The Perilous Frontier*, pp. 150–157.

48. Colin Mackerras, "The Uighurs," in Denis Sinor, ed., *Cambridge History of Early Inner Asia*, Cambridge: Cambridge University Press, 1990, p. 331.

49. Xijuan Zhou, "The Transformations of Manichaeism under the Khocho Uyghurs," *Journal of Central Asian Studies* 5/2 (2001), pp. 2–15.

50. Mackerras, "The Uighurs," p. 335; Chavannes and Pelliot, *Un Traité Manichéen*, pp. 193–194, 198.

51. Ibn Nadim, *Fihrist*, p. 803.

52. *Ennin's Diary*, p. 232.

53. Lieu, *Manichaeism in the Later Roman Empire*, p. 238.

54. Xijuan Zhou, "Manichaean Monasteries under the Khocho Uyghurs," *International Journal of Central Asian Studies* 8/1 (2003), pp. 129–146. Zhou points out that in engaging in such economic activity, not to mention possessing livestock, horses, and servants, the Manichaeans of Qocho "seem to have broken almost all the rules" for monks laid down in Mani's *Compendium* (p. 143).

55. Ibid., p. 129.

56. Zhou, "Transformations," p. 3.

57. Klimkeit, *Gnosis*, p. 273.

58. Pelliot, "Influences iraniennes," p. 114. This law remained on the books in China and also in Vietnam into the twentieth century, leading Pelliot to remark that the French colonial government of Indochina in his time was continuing to proscribe a religion that had long ceased to be practiced!

59. Lieu, *Manichaeism in the Later Roman Empire*, p. 107.

60. Klimkeit, *Gnosis*, p. 52.

61. Mary Boyce, *A Reader in Manichaean Middle Persian and Parthian*, Leiden: Brill, 1975, p. 139; cf. *Lotus Sutra*, Chapter 24.

62. Boyce, *Reader*, p. 51.

63. Hans-Joachim Klimkeit, "Christians, Buddhists and Manichaeans in Medieval Central Asia," *Buddhist-Christian Studies* 1 (1981), p. 49.

64. Klimkeit, *Gnosis*, p. 151.

65. Hans-Joachim Klimkeit, "Jesus' Entry into Parinirvana: Manichaean Identity in Buddhist Central Asia," *Numen* 33 (1986), p. 225.

66. Klimkeit, *Gnosis,* p. 69.
67. Larry Clark, "The Manichaean Turkic Pothi-Book," *Altorientalische Forschungen* 9 (1982), pp. 189–190; cf. Lieu, *Manichaeism in Central Asia and China,* pp. 46–47.
68. D.M. Lang, "St. Euthymius the Georgian and the Barlaam and Ioasaph Romance," *Bulletin of the School of Oriental and African Studies* 17 (1977), pp. 306–325; Widengren, "Mani," p. 91.
69. P.Y. Saeki, *The Nestorian Documents and Relics in China,* 2nd ed., Tokyo: Academy of Oriental Culture, 1951, p. 26.
70. Ibid., p. 55.
71. Ibid., p. 6.
72. Ibid., p. 125.
73. Moffett, *Christianity in Asia,* p. 310.
74. Lieu, *Manichaeism in Central Asia and China,* pp. 67–68.
75. Cited in Zhou, "Manichaean Monasteries," p. 145.

Chapter Five

1. Traditional accounts of its size and importance may be exaggerated; see Patricia Crone, *Meccan Trade and the Rise of Islam,* Princeton: Princeton University Press, 1987.
2. The recent study by Pourshariati, *Decline of the Sasanian Empire,* presents an interesting revisionist view according to which influential Parthian families in northeastern Iran switched their support—on which Sasanian power had relied—from the Persians to the Arabs.
3. Abu Ja'far Muhammad b. Jarir al-Tabari, *Ta'rikh al-rusul w'al-muluk,* 3 vols., ed. M.J. DeGoeje, Leiden: Brill, 1879–1901, vol. 3, p. 272.
4. Narshakhi, *History of Bukhara,* p. 66.
5. Ibid.
6. Ibid., p. 67–68.
7. Ibid., pp. 74–75.
8. Ehsan Yarshater, "Mazdakism," in *Cambridge History of Iran,* vol. 3, pp. 1005–1006.
9. Jiger Janabel, "The Islamization of Southern Qazaqstan in the Ninth and Tenth Centuries," paper presented at the American Historical Association annual conference, Seattle, WA, January 9, 1998.
10. A detailed case study of one such figure, Baba Tükles, is given by Devin DeWeese in *Islamization and Native Religion in the Golden Horde,* State College, PA: Penn State University Press, 1994.
11. See Richard Bulliet, "Conversion to Islam and the Emergence of a Muslim Society in Iran," in Nehemia Levtzion, ed., *Conversion to Islam,* New York: Holmes and Meier, 1979, pp. 30–51.

12. Ibid., 62.
13. Trinkhaus, "Mortuary Ritual," p. 676. French scholar Frantz Grenet has published extensively on Central Asian burial practices.
14. V.V. Bartold, *Four Studies on the History of Central Asia*, 3 vols., Leiden: Brill, 1959–1961, vol. 1, p. 16.
15. Edward H. Schafer, "Iranian Merchants in T'ang Dynasty Tales," *Semitic and Oriental Studies Presented to William Popper*, Berkeley: University of California Press, 1951, pp. 403–422.
16. Richard Bulliet, "Naw Bahar and the Survival of Iranian Buddhism," *Iran* 14 (1976), pp. 140–145.
17. Ibid., p. 144.
18. Ibid., p. 145.
19. Tabari, *Ta'rīkh*, vol. 3, p. 1841.
20. Narshakhi, *History of Bukhara*, pp. 20–21.
21. Ibn Hawkal, in M.J. DeGoeje, ed., *Bibliotheca Geographorum Arabicorum*, Leiden, 1889, vol. 2, p. 365.
22. Stein, *Ruins*, v. 2, pp. 440–441.
23. Julian Baldick, *Imaginary Muslims: the Uwaysi Sufis of Central Asia*, London and New York: I.B. Tauris, 1993, pp. 163–165.
24. See Ibn Khurdadbih, *Kitāb al-masālik wa'l-mamālik*, DeGoeje, ed., *Bibliotheca Geographorum Arabicorum*, vol. 6, p. 114.
25. Rabinowitz, *Jewish Merchant Adventurers*, p. 15.
26. Omeljan Pritsak, *The Origin of Rus*, vol. 1, Cambridge, MA: Harvard University Press, 1981, p. 25.
27. See Golden, *Introduction*, pp. 241–242.
28. Quoted in Rabinowitz, *Jewish Merchant Adventurers*, p. 9.
29. Ibid., p. 10.
30. Ibid., pp. 41–42, 86.
31. See Farhad Daftary, *The Assassin Legends*, London: I.B. Tauris, 1994.
32. Wheeler M. Thackston, Jr., tr., *Naser-e Khosraw's Book of Travels*, Albany: SUNY Press, 1986, p. xi.
33. See Bernard Lewis, *The Assassins: A Radical Sect in Islam*, New York: Oxford University Press, 1967.
34. Stories of a childhood friendship between Hasan, Nizam al-Mulk, and the astronomer-poet Omar Khayyam most likely belong to legend. See Lewis, *The Assassins*, p. 40.
35. Nasr appears in some accounts as Abu'l Nasr Samani. For a legendary account of Satoq Bughra in the sixteenth-century hagiographical *History of the Uwaysis*, see Baldick, *Imaginary Muslims*, pp. 77–81.
36. On the Qara-khanids see Peter Golden, "The Karakhanids and Early Islam," in Denis Sinor, ed., *Cambridge History of Early Inner Asia*, Cambridge: Cambridge University Press, 1990, pp. 343–370, and Idem., Introduction, pp. 214–19.

37. Ibn al-Athir, *Al-Kāmil fi'l-ta'rīkh*, in DeGoeje, ed., *Bibliotheca Geographorum Arabicorum*, vol. 8, p. 396; Ibn Miskawayh, *Tajārub al-Umam*, tr. D.S. Margoliouth, Oxford: Oxford University Press, 1920–1921, p. 181.
38. See Golden, *Introduction*, pp. 217–18.
39. Ibid., p. 258. The modern Bulgarians are descended from a western branch of the Bulgars who became slavicized.
40. See Joseph Fletcher, "The Naqshbandiyya in Northwest China," in B.F. Manz and Jonathan Lipman, eds., *Studies on Chinese and Islamic Inner Asia*, London: Variorum, 1995, p. 5.
41. Donald Leslie, *Islam in Traditional China: A Short History*, Canberra: Canberra College of Advanced Education, 1986, pp. 72–74.
42. Ou-yang Hsiu, *New T'ang History*, Shanghai: Commercial Press, 1936, 221b/11b–12, cited in Hajji Yusuf Chang, "The Hui (Muslim) Minority in China: An Historical Overview," *Journal of the Institute of Muslim Minority Affairs* 8/1 (1987), p. 63. On apocryphal stories of the introduction of Islam into China, see Isaac Mason, "The Mohammadans of China: When, and How, They First Came," *Journal of the North China Branch of the Royal Asiatic Society*, pp. 42–78.
43. Chang, "The Hui Minority in China," p. 63.
44. See Jacqueline Armijo-Hussein, "Sayyid 'Ajall Shams al-Din: A Muslim from Bukhara, Serving the Mongols in China, and Bringing 'Civilization' to Yunnan," unpublished Ph.D. dissertation, Harvard University, 1997.
45. Barthold, *Four Studies*, vol.1, p. 103.
46. The anti-Muslim character of Qara-khita'i rule is glossed over by the thirteenth-century Muslim writer Juzjani, who suggests that the Gür-khan "had secretly become a Muslim" and states that the Qara Khita'i "were just sovereigns, and were adorned with equity, and ability, and used to treat Muhammadans with great reverence..." (Minhaj al-din Juzjani, *Tabaqāt-i Nāsirī*, tr. H.G. Raverty, 2 vols., New Delhi, 1970 [1881], vol. 2, p. 912).

Chapter Six

1. See Igor de Rachewiltz, *Papal Envoys to the Great Khans*, London: Faber and Faber, 1971, pp. 29–40.
2. Ghiyas al-din Muhammad Khwand Amir, *Habīb al-siyār*, tr. W.M. Thackston, Cambridge, MA: Dept. of Near Eastern Languages and Civilizations, 1994, vol. 1, p. 14. According to de Rachewiltz, Küchlük was born a Christian but converted to Buddhism at the instigation of his wife (de Rachewiltz, *op. cit.*, pp. 49–50).
3. Barthold, *Four Studies*, vol. 1, p. 35.
4. Khwand Amir, *op. cit.*, p. 15.
5. Barthold, *op. cit.*, p. 37.
6. Khwand Amir, *op. cit.*, p. 18.

7. See, for example, the anecdotes in Juzjani (*op. cit.*, vol. 2, pp. 1107–1115) and Rashid al-din Fazlullah, *Jāmiʿ al-tawārīkh*, tr. J.A. Boyle, *The Successors of Genghis Khan*, New York and London: Columbia University Press, 1971, pp. 77–78.

8. Morris Rossabi, "The Muslims in the Early Yüan Dynasty," in John Langlois, ed., *China under Mongol Rule*, Princeton, NJ: Princeton University Press, 1981, p. 261.

9. Accounts of the journeys of Chang Chun and other Chinese are found in Emilii Bretschneider, *Medieval Researches from Asiatic Sources*, Osnabruck: Biblio Verlag, 1987 [1910].

10. Barthold, *Four Studies*, vol. 1, p. 39.

11. See, for example, Boyle, *Successors*, p. 94.

12. Devin DeWeese suggests that "what is at work in Mongol attitudes towards religions such as Christianity and Islam is hardly 'tolerance' or ecumenism, and certainly not religious indifference, but an assumption that religion is above all a matter of practice and communal affiliation, not of 'belief'" (DeWeese, *Islamization and Native Religion*, pp. 100–101, note 73). DeWeese somewhat overstates the case, since his argument overlooks the Mongols' instrumentalist interest in religions, as described earlier.

13. Morris Rossabi, *Khubilai Khan*, Berkeley and Los Angeles: UC Press, 1988, p. 7.

14. Boyle, *Successors*, pp. 219–220. Jews, however, were not granted this exemption.

15. de Rachewiltz, *Papal Envoys*, p. 46.

16. Rashid al-din, who calls her "the most intelligent woman in the world," states that "though she was a follower and devotee of the religion of Jesus she made great efforts to declare the rites of the law of Mustafa and would bestow alms and presents upon imams and sheikhs" (Boyle, *Successors*, pp. 199–200).

17. See de Rachewiltz, *Papal Envoys*, 34–35, 39.

18. Boyle, *Successors*, p. 78.

19. Ibid., p. 87. Juzjani likewise asserts that "[b]y nature, Ögödei was exceedingly beneficent and of excellent disposition, and a great friend to Musalmans. During his reign the Muhammadans in his dominons were tranquil and prosperous in condition, and treated with respect" (Juzjani, *op.cit.*, vol. 2, p. 1106). The Muslim sources are equally unanimous, however, in describing Chinggis's son Chaghatai as an enemy of Muslims (Juzjani, *op.cit.*, pp. 1107, 1144–1148; Khwand Amir, *op.cit.*, pp. 44).

20. Juzjani, *op.cit.*, pp. 1110–1115.

21. Boyle, *Successors*, p. 90.

22. Ibid., p. 220.

23. Owen and Eleanor Lattimore, *Silks, Spices and Empire*, New York: Dell, 1968, p. 68.

24. Boyle, *Successors*, pp. 184, 188.

25. Ata Malik Juvaini, *Tārīkh-i Jahān-Gushā*, tr. J.A. Boyle, *History of the World-Conqueror*, 2 vols., Manchester: Manchester University Press, 1958, vol. 1, 246; Boyle, *Successors*, pp. 176–177.
26. Boyle, *Successors*, p. 177; de Rachewiltz, *Papal Envoys*, pp. 100–101.
27. de Rachewiltz, *Papal Envoys*, p. 103.
28. Juzjani, *Tabaqāt-i Nāsirī*, vol. 2, pp. 1157–1158.
29. Ibid., 1160–1164.
30. de Rachewiltz, *Papal Envoys*, p. 120.
31. Ibid., p. 121.
32. She was executed in 1252 following Möngke's accession (Boyle, *Successors*, p. 215).
33. Peter Jackson and David Morgan, eds. and trans., *The Mission of Friar William of Rubruck*, London: Hakluyt Society, 1990, p. 42.
34. Ibid., p. 150.
35. Ibid., p. 151.
36. Ibid., pp. 163–164.
37. Ibid., p. 213.
38. Ibid., pp. 217, 220.
39. Leonardo Olschki, *Guillaume Boucher: A French Artist at the Court of the Khans*, Baltimore: Johns Hopkins Press, 1946, pp. 33–37.
40. Jackson and Morgan, *op. cit.*, p. 225.
41. Ibid., p. 171.
42. Ibid., p. 174.
43. Boyle, *Successors*, p. 207; Jackson and Morgan, *op. cit.*, pp. 173, 192. Möngke also kept on two Muslim scribes, Imad al-Mulk and Fakhr al-Mulk (Boyle, *Successors*, p. 222).
44. Boyle, *Successors*, p. 215.
45. Juzjani claims, implausibly, that Berke Khan converted Möngke to Islam at the event of the latter's succession (Juzjani, *op. cit.*, pp. 1181–1182).
46. Jackson and Morgan, *op. cit.*, p. 187.
47. Ibid., p. 228.
48. Juzjani claims these debates were instigated by the Christians and Buddhists in order to discredit the Muslims (Juzjani, *op. cit.*, pp. 1160–1163).
49. Jackson and Morgan, *op. cit.*, p. 229.
50. Ibid., p. 235.
51. Ibid., pp. 236–237.
52. Ibid.
53. E.A. Wallis Budge, tr., *The Monks of Kublai Khan*, London: Religious Tract Society, 1928, p. 223. Juzjani states that Baghdad was betrayed by Shi'is in the service of the caliph (Juzjani, *op. cit.*, pp. 1228–1252).
54. Jean Richard, "La conversion de Berke et les débuts de l'islamisation de la Horde d'Or," *Revue des études islamiques* 35 (1967), pp. 173–184.
55. Juzjani, *op. cit.*, pp. 1288–1290.
56. Ibid., p. 1291.

57. William Adam, "De modo sararcenos extirpandi," ed. Ch. Kohler, in *Receuil des historiens des Croisades, Documents Arméniens,* Paris: Imprimerie Nationale, 1902, vol. 2, p. 530, cited in DeWeese, *Islamization,* p. 141.
58. Polo, *Travels,* p. 119.
59. Khwand Amir, *Habīb al-siyār,* vol. 1, p. 38.
60. Boyle, *Successors,* p. 278.
61. Khwand Amir, *op. cit.,* p. 39.
62. Ibid., p. 39.
63. Leonardo Olschki, *Marco Polo's Asia,* Berkeley and Los Angeles: University of California Press, 1960, pp. 195, 198.
64. Rossabi, "Muslims," pp. 272–273. Rashid al-din mentions Khubilai's vizier Sayyid Ajall Sham al-Din 'Umar of Bukhara; his son Nasir al-Din, who was appointed governor of Qara-Jang; and grandson Abu Bakr, who was made governor of Zaytun (Boyle, *Successors,* pp. 287–288).
65. Rossabi, *Khubilai Khan,* p. 142.
66. Olschki, *Marco Polo's Asia,* pp. 198–199.
67. Rossabi, "Muslims," pp. 280–281.
68. Polo, *Travels,* pp. 133–135; Boyle, *Successors,* p. 293.
69. Polo, *Travels,* p. 135; Boyle, *Successors,* p. 294. Boyle notes that according to the Yüan Shih, however, Khubilai's restrictive edict occurred in 1280, prior to Ahmad's death.
70. Boyle, *Successors,* p. 294. See also A.C. Moule, *Christians in China before the Year 1550,* London: Society for Promoting Christian Knowledge, 1930, pp. 228–229.
71. Qur'an 9: 5. The verse in question refers to Muhammad's Meccan opponents; whether it condones the killing of polytheists in general is a matter of debate.
72. Boyle, *Successors,* p. 295. Khwand Amir states that the verse had earlier been brought to the attention of the Il-Khan Abaqa by "a vile Jew, intent upon doing the Muslims in" (Khwand Amir, *op. cit.,* p. 37).
73. Ibid., p. 294.
74. James Montgomery, tr., *The History of Yaballaha III,* New York: Columbia University Press, 1927, pp. 8–9.
75. Ibid., pp. 45–46.
76. Ibid., p. 46, note 21.
77. Khwand Amir, *op. cit.,* p. 67.
78. *History of Yaballaha III,* p. 50.
79. Khwand Amir, *op. cit.,* p. 74.
80. Ibid., pp. 74–75.
81. *History of Yaballaha III,* p. 75.
82. Ibid., p. 79.
83. On him see J.A. Boyle, ed., *Cambridge History of Iran,* vol. 5, Cambridge: Cambridge University Press, 1968, pp. 376–379, 380, 382–384. Rashid al-din says of Nawruz's earlier rebellion that "because of Nauruz, much damage

was done [in Khurasan] and many Muslims were killed" (Boyle, *Successors*, p. 141).

84. Khwand Amir, *op. cit.*, p. 81.

85. Khwand Amir, *op. cit.*, p. 82.

86. Boyle, *Successors*, p. 325. The conversions of Ghazan and Ananda seem to have persuaded Temür Khan that Islam was an acceptable religion, and to have encouraged further conversions at the Mongol court.

87. Budge, tr., *The Monks of Kublai Khan*, pp. 210–214.

88. Ibid., pp. 216–219.

89. Ibid., pp. 223–224.

90. Ibid., pp. 221–222.

91. Ibid., p. 225.

92. Ibid., p. 226.

93. Ibid., p. 229.

94. Ibid., p. 230.

95. Ibid., p. 231.

96. Ibid., pp. 234–238.

97. John of Marignolli, in Christopher Dawson, ed., *The Mongol Mission*, London and New York: Sheed and Ward, 1955, pp. 224–225.

98. Ibid., p. 226.

99. de Rachewiltz, *Papal Envoys*, p. 184.

100. Dawson, ed., *The Mongol Mission*, p. 237.

101. Ibid., p. 233.

102. Ibid., p. 237.

103. de Rachewiltz, *Papal Envoys*, p. 169.

104. Francis Rouleau, "The Yangchow Latin Tombstone As a Landmark of Medieval Christianity in China," *Harvard Journal of Asiatic Studies* 17/3–4 (1954), pp. 346–365.

105. Ibid., p. 189.

106. Ibid., p. 192.

107. Ibid., p. 195.

108. Fletcher suggests that since Islam arose among largely nomadic Arabs and Tibetan nomads had "adapted Tibetan Buddhism for nomadic consumption," these two traditions were the most appealing to the peoples of the steppes ("The Mongols: Ecological and Social Perspectives," p. 44). This argument, however, disregards the immense popularity of Nestorian Christianity in Inner Asia that lasted many centuries.

Chapter Seven

1. Grousset, *Empire of the Steppes*, p. 434. Similar views are expressed in Moffett, *Christianity in Asia*, pp. 480, 483–486, 504; G.W. Houston, "An Overview of Nestorians in Inner Asia," *Central Asiatic Journal* 24 (1980), p. 67; Bertold

Spuler, "The Disintegration of the Caliphate in the West," in P.M. Holt, et al., *Cambridge History of Islam*, 4 vols., Cambridge: Cambridge University Press, 1970, vol.1, p. 170; and G.W. Thacker, "A Nestorian Gravestone from Central Asia in the Gulbenkian Museum," *Durham University Journal* (March 1967), p. 100.

2. Khwand Amir, *Habīb al-siyār*, vol.1, pp. 229, 250, 260, 271–272; likewise over Hindu rulers in India (ibid., pp. 264, 266, 268–269) as well as plans to do the same to the Chinese (p. 292).

3. H. Moranville, *Mémoire sur Tamerlan et Sa Cour par un Dominicain en 1403*, Bibliothèque de l'école de Chartres, vol. 55, Paris, 1894, quoted in Moffett, *Christianity in Asia*, p. 486.

4. Khwand Amir, *op.cit.*, pp. 234, 249.

5. It is not impossible, given the long presence of Nestorianism among the steppe peoples, that some of Timur's nomadic rivals had Christian affinities, but nowhere do the sources mention this explicitly as a factor.

6. These come from two graveyards containing a total of some 610 tombstones dating from 858 to 1342. See Saeki, *Nestorian Documents and Relics*, pp. 408–419, and Thacker, "A Nestorian Gravestone."

7. Barthold, *Four Studies*, vol.1, p. 136.

8. Antoine Mostaert, "Ordosica," *Bulletin of the Catholic University of Peking* 9 (1934); cf. Henri Bernard, *La Découverte de nestoriens Mongols aux Ordos*, Tientsin: Hautes Études, 1935. The tribal name Erküt appears to be derived from the Persian *arkhūn*, or high priest (Saeki, *Nestorian Documents and Relics*, p. 426.

9. Palmer, *The Jesus Sutras;* Sébastien de Courtois, *Chrétiens d'Orient sur la route de la Soie: Dans les pas des nestoriens*, Paris: La Table Ronde, 2007.

10. L.E. Browne, *The Eclipse of Christianity in Asia from the Time of Muhammad Till the Fourteenth Century*, Cambridge: Cambridge University Press, 1933, p. 108.

11. Franck, *The Silk Road*, p. 259.

12. Bentley, *Old World Encounters*, p. 107.

13. I am grateful to Jerry Bentley for this observation.

14. Polo, *Travels*, pp. 235–237.

15. Lieu, *Manichaeism in Central Asia and China*, p. 194.

16. Ibid., p. 106.

17. Ibid., p. 133.

18. Ibid., p. 168.

19. Ibid., p. 180.

20. The history of the sect is given by a seventeenth-century source translated into French by Paul Pelliot, "Les traditions manichéennes au Fou-kien," *T'oung Pao* 22 (1934), pp. 193–208.

21. This relief and the temple that houses it are described in detail by Peter Bryder, "…Where the Faint Traces of Manichaeism Disappear," *Altorientalische Forschungen* 15/1 (1988), p. 203; see also Lieu, *Manichaeism in the Later Roman*

Empire, pp. 256–257, and Idem., *Manichaeism in Central Asia and China*, pp. 56–58, 188–195.

22. Lieu, *Manichaeism in Central Asia and China*, p. 58.

23. Bryder, "Traces," p. 207.

24. See Jiger Janabel, "From Mongol Empire to Qazaq Juzder: studies on the steppe political cycle (13–18 cc.)," unpublished Ph.D. dissertation, Harvard University, 1997.

25. The continual tension between steppe peoples who had converted to Islam and those who hadn't is a recurring theme in the *Habīb al-siyār;* for example, vol.1, pp. 97, 163, 234, 249, and elsewhere.

26. Muhammad Haydar Dughlat, *Tārīkh-i rashīdī,* tr. D. Ross, ed. N. Elias, New York: Praeger, 1970 [1895], p. 14.

27. Ibid., pp. 14–15.

28. Ibid., p. 52.

29. Ibid., pp. 57–58.

30. For more on this ethnonym see Golden, *Introduction,* pp. 176–177.

31. Barthold, *Four Studies,* vol.1, pp. 91–92; Joseph Fletcher, "Confrontations between Muslim Missionaries and Nomad Unbelievers in the Late Sixteenth Century: Notes on Four Passages from the Diya al-Qulub," in Walther Heissig, ed., *Tractata Altaica,* Wiesbaden: Otto Harrassowitz, 1976, pp. 170–171.

32. *Tārīkh-i Rashīdī,* pp. 125, 148.

33. Barthold, *Four Studies,* vol.1, p. 159.

34. Mahmud b. Amir Wali, *Bahr al-asrār fī manāqib al-akhyār,* cited in Golden, *Introduction,* p. 344.

35. Baldick, *Imaginary Muslims,* p. 174.

36. Thomas Oller interviewed and videotaped several of these Kazakh shamans, including a 14-year-old girl, during the course of visits to northwestern Mongolia in 1994 and 1995 (personal communication).

37. Some examples are mentioned in DeWeese, *Islamization,* p. 209; Fletcher, "Confrontations," p. 171; and Baldick, *Imaginary Muslims.*

38. Ibn Battuta, *Travels of Ibn Battuta,* tr. H.A.R. Gibb, 4 vols., Cambridge: Hakluyt Society, 1958–1994, vol.3, p. 568.

39. Ibid., p. 556.

40. The English merchant Anthony Jenkinson reports in 1558 that the Qazaqs and the Qyrgyz between them had completely cut off Silk Route trade with the East (Anthony Jenkinson, *The Voyage of Master Anthony Jenkinson,* London: Hakluyt Society, 1886, p. 86).

41. See Alam, "Trade, State Policy and Regional Change," pp. 202–227.

42. On this see Stephen Dale, *Indian Merchants and Eurasian Trade,* Cambridge: Cambridge University Press, 1994.

43. See Scott Levi, *The Indian Diaspora in Central Asia and its Trade, 1550-1900,* Leiden: E.J. Brill, 2002.

44. Frye, *Bukhara,* pp. 100–101; Bentley, *Old World Encounters,* p. 14.

Epilogue

1. Robert Nelson, *Economics As Religion*, University Park, PA: Penn State Press, 2001, p. 23.
2. See David Loy, "The Religion of the Market," *Journal of the American Academy of Religion* 65/2 (1997), pp. 275–290; also Richard C. Foltz, "The Religion of the Market: Reflections on a Decade of Discussion," *Worldviews: Environment, Culture, Religion* 11/2 (2007), pp. 135–154.
3. Jay McDaniel, "The Sacred Whole: An Ecumenical Protestant Approach," in John E. Carroll, Paul Brockelman, and Mary Westfall, eds., *The Greening of Faith: God, the Environment, and the Good Life*, Hanover, NH: University Press of New England, p. 105.
4. Harvey Cox, "The Market As God: Living in the New Dispensation," *Atlantic Monthly* (March 1999), pp. 18–23.
5. John B. Stuttard, *The New Silk Road: Secrets of Business Success in China Today*, New York: Wiley, 2000; Tim Ambler and Chris Styles, *The Silk Road to International Marketing: Profit and Passion in Global Business*, London: Financial Times and Prentice Hall, 2000.

Bibliography

Alam, Muzaffar, "Trade, State Policy and Regional Change: Aspects of Mughal-Uzbek Commercial Relations ca.1550-1750," *Journal of the Economic and Social History of the Orient* 37 (1994), pp. 202–227.

Allsen, Thomas, *Culture and Conquest in Mongol Eurasia*, Cambridge: Cambridge University Press, 2004.

———, review of Richard C. Foltz, *Religions of the Silk Road*, *Iranian Studies* 32/4 (1999), pp. 575–576.

Anthony, David W., *The Horse, the Wheel, and Language: How Bronze-Age Riders from the Eurasian Steppes Shaped the Modern World*, Princeton: Princeton University Press, 2007.

Armijo-Hussein, Jacqueline, "Sayyid 'Ajall Shams al-Din: A Muslim from Bukhara, Serving the Mongols in China, and Bringing 'Civilization' to Yunnan," unpublished Ph.D. dissertation, Harvard University, 1997.

Asmussen, Jes P., "The Sogdian and Uigur-Turkish Christian Literature in Central Asia before the Real Rise of Islam: A Survey," in *Indological and Buddhist Studies. Volume in Honour of Professor J.W. Jong on His Sixtieth Birthday*, Canberra: Australian National University, 1982, pp. 11–29.

———, *Manichaean Literature*, Delmar, NY: Scholars' Facsimiles and Reprints, 1975.

———, ed., *Xvastvanift: Studies in Manichaeism*, Copenhagen: Munksgaard, 1965.

Azarpay, Guitty, "A Jataka Tale on a Sasanian Silver Plate," *Bulletin of the Asia Institute*, new series, 9 (1995), pp. 99–125.

Bailey, Harold W., *The Culture of the Sakas in Ancient Iranian Khotan*, Delmar, NY: Columbia Lectures on Iranian Studies, 1982.

———, *Khotanese Buddhist Texts*, 2nd ed., Cambridge: Cambridge University Press, 1981 [1951].

Baldick, Julian, *Imaginary Muslims: The Uwaysi Sufis of Central Asia,* London and New York: I.B. Tauris, 1993.

Barfield, Thomas J., *The Perilous Frontier*, Oxford: Blackwell, 1989.

Barthold, W., *Turkestan Down to the Mongol Invasion*, 3rd ed., London: Luzac, 1987 [1928].

Barthold, W., "The Burial Rites of the Turks and Mongols," *Central Asiatic Journal* 14/1–3 (1970), pp. 195–227.

———, *Four Studies on the History of Central Asia*, tr,. V. and T. Minorsky, 3 vols., Leiden: Brill, 1962 [1958].

———, "Mesta do-Musulmanskogo kulta v Bukhare," *Vostochnye Zapiski*, 1 (1927), pp. 11–25.

Barber, E.J.W., *The Mummies of Urumchi*, New York: Norton, 1999.

Bazin, Louis and Peter Zieme, eds., *De Dunhuang à Istanbul*, Turnhout, Brepols, 2001.

Beal, Samuel, tr., *Buddhist Records of the Western World*, New Delhi: Oriental Reprints, 1969 [1888].

Beckwith, Christopher I., *Empires of the Silk Road: A History of Central Eurasia from the Bronze Age to the Present*, Princeton: Princeton University Press, 2009.

———, *The Tibetan Empire in Central Asia*, Princeton, NJ: Princeton University Press, 1987.

BeDuhn, Jason David, review of Richard C. Foltz, *Religions of the Silk Road*, *Journal of Chinese Religions* 29 (2001), pp. 294–296.

———, *The Manichean Body: In Discipline and Ritual*, Baltimore: Johns Hopkins University Press, 2000.

———, review of Hans-Joachim Klimkeit, *Gnosis on the Silk Road*, in *Journal of the American Oriental Society* 115/2 (1995), pp. 344–346.

Benjamin, Craig, *The Yuezhi: Origin, Migration and the Conquest of Northern Bactria*, Turnhout: Brepols, 2007.

Benjamin, Craig and Samuel Lieu, eds., *Walls and Frontiers in Inner-Asian History*, Turnhout: Brepols, 2000.

Bentley, Jerry, "Cross-Cultural Interaction and Periodization in World History," *American Historical Review* 101/3 (1996), pp. 749–770.

———, *Old World Encounters: Cross-Cultural Contacts and Exchanges in Pre-Modern Times*, New York: Oxford University Press, 1993.

Benveniste, Emile, "Le vocabulaire chrétien dans les langues d'Asie centrale," *L'Oriente Cristiano nella Storia della Civiltà*, Rome: Accademia Nazionale dei Lincei, 1964, pp. 85–91.

Ben-Zvi, I., *The Exiled and the Redeemed*, 3rd ed., Jerusalem: Ben Zvi, 1976, pp. 54–82.

Biruni, Abu Rayhan, *Athār al-baqiya*, tr. E. Sachau, *Chronology of Ancient Nations*, Lahore: Hijra International, 1983 [1879].

Boulnois, Luce, *The Silk Road: Monks, Warriors and Merchants*, New York: Norton, 2005.

Boyce, Mary, *Zoroastrianism: Its Antiquity and Constant Vigour*, Costa Mesa: Mazda, 1992.

———, *A History of Zoroastrianism*, 3 vols. to date, Leiden: Brill, 1975–.

Boyle, J.A., "The Thirteenth Century Mongols' Conception of the Afterlife," *Mongolian Studies* 1 (1974), pp. 5–14.

———, "Turkish and Mongol Shamanism in the Middle Ages," *Folklore* 83 (1972), pp. 184–193.

———, "A Form of Horse Sacrifice Among the 13th- and 14th-century Mongols," *Central Asiatic Journal* 10 (1965), pp. 145–150.

Bretschneider, Emilii, *Medieval Researches from Asiatic Sources*, 2 vols. in 1, Osnabruck: Biblio Verlag, 1987 [1875–1876].

Browne, L.E., *The Eclipse of Christianity in Asia from the Time of Muhammad Till the Fourteenth Century*, Cambridge: Cambridge University Press, 1933.

Bryder, Peter, "Cao'an Revisited," *Research into China Overseas Communication History* 16/2 (1989), pp. 35–42.

———, "...Where the Faint Traces of Manichaeism Disappear," *Altorientalische Forschungen* 15/1 (1988), pp. 201–208.

Budge, E.A.T. Wallis, tr., *The Chronography of Gregory Abu'l Faraj*, 2 vols., London: Oxford University Press, 1932.

———, tr., *The Monks of Kublai Khan: The History of the Life and Travels of Rabban Sawma*, London: Religious Tract Society, 1928.

Bulliet, Richard, *Conversion to Islam in the Medieval Period: A Study in Quantitative History*, Cambridge MA: Harvard University Press, 1980.

———, "Conversion to Islam and the Emergence of a Muslim Society in Iran," in Nehemia Levtzion, ed., *Conversion to Islam*, New York: Holmes and Meier, 1979, pp. 30–51.

———, "Naw Bahar and the Survival of Iranian Buddhism," *Iran* 14 (1976), pp. 140–145.

Chang, Hajji Yusuf, "The Hui (Muslim) Minority in China: An Historical Overview," *Journal of the Institute of Muslim Minority* Affairs 8/1 (1987), pp. 62–78.

Chaudhuri, K.N., *Asia before Europe: Economy and Civilisation of the Indian Ocean from the Rise of Islam to 1750*, Cambridge: Cambridge University Press, 1990.

Chavannes, E., "Le nestorianisme et l'inscription de Karabalassoun," *Journal Asiatique* (jan–fév. 1897), pp. 43–85.

Chavannes, E. and P. Pelliot, *Un traité Manichéen retrouvé en Chine*, Paris: Imprimérie Nationale, 1913.

Chou Yi-liang, "Tantrism in China," *Harvard Journal of Asiatic Studies* 8 (1945), pp. 241–272.

Christensen, A., "Die Moschee Makh in Buhara," *Orientalische Litteraturzeitung* 7 (1904), pp. 49–51.

Christian, David, *A History of Russia, Central Asia and Mongolia, Volume 1: Inner Eurasia from Prehistory to the Mongol Empire*, Oxford: Blackwell, 1998.

Christian, David and Craig Benjamin, eds., *Realms of the Silk Roads: Ancient and Modern*, Turnhout: Brepols, 2000.

———, *Worlds of the Silk Roads: Ancient and Modern*, Turnhout: Brepols, 1998.

Clark, Larry, "The Manichaean Turkic Pothi-Book," *Altorientalische Forschungen* 9 (1982), pp. 145–218.

Colless, Brian E., "The Nestorian Province of Samarqand," *Abr-Nahrain* 24 (1986), pp. 51–57.

Collins, J., "Persian Apocalypses," *Semeia* 14 (1979), pp. 207–217.

Curtin, Philip, *Cross-Cultural Trade in World History*, Cambridge: Cambridge University Press, 1984.

Dale, Stephen, *Indian Merchants and Eurasian Trade*, Cambridge: Cambridge University Press, 1994.

Dani, A.H. and V. Masson, eds., *History of the Civilizations of Central Asia*, vol. 1, Paris: UNESCO, 1992.

de Courtois, Sébastien, *Chrétiens d'Orient sur la route de la Soie: Dans les pas des nestoriens*, Paris: La Table Ronde, 2007.

de Goeje, M. J., *Bibliotheca Geografarum Arabicorum*, 8 vols., Leiden: Brill, 1895.

de la Vaissiére, Étienne, *Sogdian Traders: A History*, tr. James Ward, Leiden: Brill, 2005.

de Rachewiltz, Igor, *Papal Envoys to the Great Khans*, London: Faber and Faber, 1971.

DeWeese, Devin, *Islamicization and Native Religion in the Golden Horde*, State College PA: Penn State University Press, 1995.

Dughlat, Muhammad Haydar, *Tārīkh-i Rashīdī*, tr. D. Ross, ed. N. Elias, New York and Washington, D.C.: Praeger, 1970 [1895].

Dumézil, Georges, *Mythe et Epopée*, 3 vols., Paris: Gallimard, 1968–1973.

Dunlop, Douglas S., *History of the Jewish Khazars*, Princeton: Princeton University Press, 1954.

Eaton, Richard, *The Sufis of Bijapur, 1300-1700*, Princeton: Princeton University Press, 1978.

Eliade, Mircea, *Shamanism: Archaic Techniques of Ecstasy*, Princeton: Princeton University Press, 1964.

———, ed., *Encyclopedia of Religion*, 16 vols., New York: Macmillan, 1987.

Elverskog, Johan, *Buddhism and Islam on the Silk Road: A History of Cross-Cultural Exchange*, Philadelphia: University of Pennsylvania Press, 2010.

———, *Uygur Buddhist Literature*, Turnhout: Brepols, 1997.

Enoki, Kazuo, "Nestorian Christianism in Medieval Times," *L'Oriente Cristiano nella Storia della Civiltà*, Rome: Accademia Nazionale dei Lincei, 1964, pp. 45–77.

Erdy, Miklos, "Manichaeans, Nestorians, or Bird Costumed Humans in Their Relation to Hunnic Type Cauldrons in Rock Carvings of the Yenisei Valley," *Eurasian Studies Yearbook* 68 (1996), pp. 45–95.

Flattery, David S. and Martin Schwartz, *Hoama and Harmaline: The Botanical Identity of the Indo-Iranian Sacred Hallucinogen "Soma" and Its Legacy in Religion, Language, and Middle Eastern Folklore*, Berkeley: University of California Press, 1989.

Fletcher, Joseph, "The Naqshbandiyya in Northwest China," in B.F. Manz and Jonathan Lipman, eds., *Studies on Chinese and Islamic Inner Asia*, London: Variorum, 1995.

———, "The Mongols: Ecological and Social Perspectives," *Harvard Journal of Asiatic Studies* 46/1 (1986), pp. 11–49.

———, "Confrontations between Muslim Missionaries and Nomad Unbelievers in the Late Sixteenth Century: Notes on Four Passages from the Diya al-Qulub," in Walther Heissig, ed., *Tractata Altaica*, Wiesbaden: Otto Harrassowitz, 1976, pp. 167–174.

Foltz, Richard, *L'Iran creuset de religions: de la préhistoire à la Révolution islamique*, Québec: Les Presses de l'Université Laval, 2007. (Revised edition of *Spirituality in the Land of the Noble: How Iran Shaped the World's Religions*, Oxford: Oneworld Publications, 2004.)

———, "Does Nature Have Historical Agency?: World History, Environmental History, and How Historians Can Help Save the Planet," *TheHistory Teacher* 37/1 (2003), pp. 9–28.

———, "When Was Central Asia Zoroastrian?" *Mankind Quarterly* 38/3 (1998), pp. 189–200.

———, "Ecumenical Mischief under the Mongols," *Central Asiatic Journal* 42/2 (1998), pp. 42–69.

———, "Judaism and the Silk Route," *The History Teacher* (1998), pp. 9–16.

Forte, Antonino, "An Ancient Chinese Monastery Excavated in Kirgiziya," *Central Asiatic Journal* 38/1 (1994), pp. 41–57.

Franck, Irene M., *The Silk Road*, New York: Facts on File, 1986.

Frank, Andre Gunder and Barry Gills, eds., *The World System: From Five Hundred Years to Five Thousand*, London: Routledge, 1992.

Frye, Richard, *Bukhara, the Medieval Achievement*, Costa Mesa, CA: Mazda, 1997 [1971].

———, *The Heritage of Central Asia*, Princeton: Markus Weiner, 1996.

———, "The Fate of Zoroastrians in Eastern Iran," in Rika Gyselen, ed., *Au Carrefour des Religions: Mélanges offerts à Philippe Gignoux*, Bures-sur-Yvette: Groupe pour l'Étude de la Civilisation du Moyen-Orient, 1995.

———, "Comparative Observations on Conversion to Islam in Iran and Central Asia," *Jerusalem Studies in Arabic and Islam* 4 (1984), pp. 81–88.

———, *The Golden Age of Persia*, London: Weidenfeld and Nicolson, 1975.

———, ed., *Cambridge History of Iran*, vol. 5, *The Seljuk and Mongol Periods*, Cambridge: Cambridge University Press, 1968.

Gaulier, Simone, et al., *Buddhism in Afghanistan and Central Asia*, 2 vols., Leiden: Brill, 1976.

Gershevitch, Ilya, ed., *Cambridge History of Iran*, vol. 2, *The Median and Achæmenian Periods*, Cambridge: Cambridge University Press, 1985.

Gibb, H.A.R., *The Arab Conquests in Central Asia*, London: Royal Asiatic Society, 1923.

Gillman, Ian and Hans-Joachim Klimkeit, *Christians in Asia before 1500*, Richmond: Curzon Press, 1999.

Godbey, Allen H., "From Persia to China," in William C. White, *Chinese Jews*, 2nd ed., New York: Paragon, 1966, pp. 136–149.

Golden, Peter, *An Introduction to the History of the Turkic Peoples*, Wiesbaden: Otto Harrassowitz, 1992.

Gombrich, Richard, *Theravada Buddhism*, London: Routledge, 1988.

Grenet, Frantz, "Religious Diversity among Sogdian Merchants in Sixth-Century China: Zoroastrianism, Buddhism, Manichaeism, and Hinduism," *Comparative Studies of South Asia, Africa and the Middle East* 27/2 (2007), pp. 463–478.

——, "Bactria in the Avesta and in Zoroastrian Tradition,"in Ehsan Yarshater, ed., *Encyclopaedia Iranica*, vol. 3, Winona Lake, IN: Eisenbraun's 1988, pp. 343–344.

——, ed., *Cultes et monuments religieux dans l'Asie centrale préislamique*, Paris: Éditions du Centre national de la recherche scientifique, 1987.

——, *Les pratiques funeraires de l'Asie centrale sedentaire: De la conquete grecque à l'islamisation*, Paris: Éditions du Centre national de la recherche scientifique, 1984.

Grenet, Frantz and P. Bernard, eds., *Histoire et cultes de l'Asie centrale préislamique. Sources écrites et documents archéologiques*, Paris: Éditions du Centre national de la recherche scientifique, 1991.

Grenet, Frantz and Nicholas Sims-Williams, "The Historical Context of the Sogdian Ancient Letters," *Transition Periods in Iranian History, Studia Iranica*, cahier 5, Leuven: Peeters, 1987, pp. 101–122.

Grenet, Frantz and Zhang Guangda, "The Last Refuge of the Sogdian Religion: Dunhuang in the Ninth and Tenth Centuries," *Bulletin of the Asia Institute* 10 (1996), pp. 175–186.

Grousset, René, *The Empire of the Steppes*, tr. Naomi Walford, New Brunswick: Rutgers University Press, 1970.

Guidi, M., *La lotta tra l'Islam e il manicheismo*, Rome: Accademia Nazionale dei Lincei, 1927.

Hage, Wolfgang, *Syriac Christianity in the East*, Kottayam: St. Efrem Ecumenical Research Institute, 1988.

Haloun, G. and W. Henning, trs., "The Compendium of the Doctrines, and Styles, of the Teachings of Mani, the Buddha of Light," *Asia Major* 3/2 (1952), pp. 184–221.

Hambly, Gavin, *Central Asia*, London: Weidenfeld and Nicolson, 1969.

Haneda, Akira, "Introduction: Problems of the Turkicization, Problems of Islamization," *Acta Asiatica* 34 (1978), pp. 1–21.

Harmatta, Janos, ed., *History of the Civilizations of Central Asia*, vol. 2, Paris: UNESCO, 1994.

Harrison, Paul, "Searching for the Origins of the Mahayana: What Are We Looking For?" *The Eastern Buddhist* 28/1 (1995), pp. 48–59.

——, "The Earliest Chinese Translations of Mahayan Sutras: Some Notes on the Works of Lokaksema," *Buddhist Studies Review* 10/2 (1993), pp. 135–177.

——, "Who Gets to Ride in the Great Vehicle? Self-Image and Identity among the Followers of the Early Mahayana," *Journal of the International Association of Buddhist Studies* 10/1 (1987), pp. 67–90.

Harvey, Peter, *An Introduction to Buddhism: Teachings, History and Practices*, Cambridge: Cambridge University Press, 1990.

Hedin, Sven, *The Silk Road: Ten Thousand Miles through Central Asia*, London: I.B. Tauris, 2009.

Heissig, Walther, *The Religions of Mongolia*, Berkeley: University of California Press, 1980.

Henning, W.B., "A Sogdian God," *Bulletin of the School of Oriental and African Studies* 28/2 (1965), pp. 242–254.

————, "The Book of Giants," *Bulletin of the School of Oriental and African Studies* 11 (1943-1946), pp. 52–74.

————, "Mani's Last Journey," *Bulletin of the School of Oriental and African Studies* 10 (1939–1942), pp. 941–953.

Herodotus, *The Histories*, tr. Aubrey de Sélincourt, rev. A.R. Burn, New York: Penguin, 1972.

Herzfeld, Ernst, *Zoroaster and His World*, 2 vols., New York: Octagon Press, 1974 [1947].

Hinüber, Oskar von, "Expansion to the North: Afghanistan and Central Asia," in Heinz Bechert and Richard Gombrich, eds., *The World of Buddhism*, London: Thames and Hudson, 1984, pp. 99–107.

Hiskett, Mervyn, *The Course of Islam in Africa*, Edinburgh: Edinburgh University Press, 1994.

Hodgson, Marshall, *The Venture of Islam*, 3 vols., Chicago: University of Chicago Press, 1974.

Hoffman, H., "Kalacakra Studies: I," *Central Asiatic Journal* 13 (1969), pp. 52–73.

Hopkirk, Peter, *The Great Game*, Tokyo: Kodansha International, 1992.

————, *Foreign Devils on the Silk Road*, Amherst, MA: University of Massachusetts Press, 1984 [1980].

Horner, I.B., tr., *Milinda's Questions*, 2 vols., London: Luzac & Co., 1969 [1963].

Houston, G.W., "An Overview of Nestorians in Central Asia," *Central Asiatic Journal* 24 (1980), pp. 60–68.

Hunter, Erica C.D., "The Church of the East in Central Asia," *Bulletin of John Rylands University Library of Manchester* 78/3 (1996), pp. 129–142.

————, "Syriac Christianity in Central Asia," *Zeitschrift für Religions- und Geistesgeschichte* 44/4 (1992), pp. 362–368.

————, "The Conversion of the Kerait to Christianity in A.D. 1007," *Zentralasiatische Studien* 22 (1989–1991), pp. 143–163.

Huili, *The Life of Hsuan-Tsang*, tr. Li Yung-hsi, Peking: Chinese Buddhist Association, 1959.

Ibn Battuta, *The Travels of Ibn Battuta*, tr. H.A.R. Gibb, 4 vols., Cambridge: Hakluyt Society, 1958–1994.

Ibn Khurdadbih, *Kitāb al-masālik wa'l-mamālik*, tr. C. Barbier de Meynard, "Le Livre des Routes et des Provinces par Ibn Khordadbeh," *Journal Asiatique* 6/5 (1865), pp. 5–127, 227–280, 446–527.

Ibn Miskawayh, *Tajārub al-umam*, tr. D.S. Margoliouth, Oxford: Oxford University Press, 1920–1921.

Ibn Nadim [Abu'l-Faraj Muhammad ibn Ishaq al-Warraq], *Fihrist al-'ulūm*, tr.
B. Dodge, *The Fihrist of al-Nadim: A Tenth Century Survey of Muslim Culture*, 2
vols., New York: Columbia University Press, 1970.

Janabel, Jiger, "The Islamization of Southern Qazaqstan in the Ninth Century,"
paper presented at the American Historical Association annual conference,
1998.

————, "From Mongol Empire to Qazaq Juzder: Studies on the Steppe Political
Cycle (13–18 cc.)," unpublished Ph.D. dissertation, Harvard University, 1997.

Jenkinson, Anthony, *The Voyage of Master Anthony Jenkinson*, London: Hakluyt
Society, 1886.

Juliano, Annette L. and Judith Lerner, eds., *Nomads, Traders and Holy Men along
China's Silk Road*, Turnhout: Brepols, 2002.

Juvaini, Ata Malik, *Tārīkh-i jahān gushā*, tr. J.A. Boyle, *History of the World
Conqueror*, Seattle: University of Washington Press, 1997 [1958].

Juzjani, Minhaj al-Din, *Tabaqāt-i Nāsirī*, 2 vols., tr. H.G. Raverty, Osnabrück:
Biblio Verlag, 1991 [1881].

Kashgari, Mahmud, *Dīvān lughāt al-türk*, tr. R. Dankoff and J. Kelly, 3 vols.,
Cambridge MA: Dept. of Near Eastern Languages and Civilizations, 1982–
1985.

Khazanov, Anatoly, *Nomads and the Outside World*, Cambridge: Cambridge
University Press, 1984.

Khwand Amir, *Habīb al-siyār*, vol. 3, tr. W.M. Thackston, Jr., 2 vols., Cambridge
MA: Dept. of Near Eastern Languages and Civilizations, 1994.

Klimkeit, Hans-Joachim, *Gnosis on the Silk Road*, San Francisco: Harper, 1993.

————, "Christian Art on the Silk Road," in Thomas W. Gaehtgens, ed., *Kunstlerischer
Austaush: Akten des XXVIII Internationalen Kongresses für Kunstgeschichte, Berlin,
15-20 Juli 1992*, Berlin: Akademie Verlag, 1993, pp. 477–488.

————, "Jesus' Entry into Parinirvana: Manichaean Identity in Buddhist Central
Asia," *Numen* 33 (1986), pp. 225–240.

————, "Christian- Buddhist Encounter in Medieval Central Asia," in
G.W. Houston, *The Cross and the Lotus*, Delhi: Motilal Banarsidass, 1985,
pp. 9–24.

————, *Manichaean Art and Calligraphy*, Leiden: Brill, 1982.

————, "Christians, Buddhists and Manichaeans in Medieval Central Asia,"
Buddhist-Christian Studies 1 (1981), pp. 46–50.

Koshelenko, G., "The Beginnings of Buddhism in Margiana," *Acta Antiqua
Academiae Scientarum Hungaricae* 14 (1966), pp. 175–183.

Kuzmina, Elena, *The Prehistory of the Silk Road*, Philadelphia: University of
Pennsylvania Press, 2008.

Kyuzo, Kato, "Cultural Exchange on the Ancient Silk Road," *Senri Ethnological
Studies* 32 (1992), pp. 5–20.

Lamotte, Etienne, *History of Indian Buddhism*, Louvain and Paris: Peters Press,
1988.

Lang, D.M., "St. Euthymius the Georgian and the Barlaam and Ioasaph Romance," *Bulletin of the School of Oriental and African Studies* 17 (1977), pp. 306–325.

Lattimore, Owen and Eleanor, *Silks, Spices and Empire*, New York: Dell, 1968.

Law, David, *From Samaria to Samarkand*, Lanham MD: University Press of America, 1992.

le Coq, Alexander von, *Die buddhistische Spätantike in Mittelasien*, vol. 2, *Die manichäischen Miniaturen*, Berlin: D. Reimer,1923.

―――, *Buried Treasures of Chinese Turkestan*, London: Allen & Unwin, 1928.

Leslie, Donald D., *Islam in Traditional China: A Short History*, Canberra: Canberra College of Advanced Education, 1986.

―――, *The Survival of the Chinese Jews*, Leiden: Brill, 1972.

LeStrange, Guy, *The Lands of the Eastern Caliphate*, Cambridge: Cambridge University Press, 1930.

Lieu, S.N.C., *Manichaeism in Central Asia and China*, Leiden: Brill, 1998.

―――, *Manichaeism in the Later Roman Empire and Medieval China*, Tübingen: Mohr, 1992 [1985].

Litvinsky [Litvinskii], B.A., ed., *History of the Civilizations of Central Asia*, vol. 3, Paris: UNESCO, 1996.

―――, "Central Asia," in G.P. Malalasekera, ed., *Encyclopaedia of Buddhism*, vol. 4, fasc. 1, Columbo: Government of Ceylon, 1979, pp. 21–52.

Litvinskii, B.A., and I.R. Pichikian, "The Hellenistic Architecture and Art of the Temple of the Oxus," *Bulletin of the Asia Institute*, new series, 8 (1994), pp. 47–66.

Liu, Ts'un-yan, "Traces of Zoroastrian and Manichaean Activities in pre-T'ang China," in *Selected Papers from the Hall of Harmonious Winds*, Leiden: Brill, 1976, pp. 2–55.

Liu, Xinru, *Silk and Religion*, Delhi: Oxford University Press, 1996.

―――, "Silks and Religions in Eurasia, c.A.D. 600-1200," *Journal of World History* 6 (1995), pp. 25–48.

―――, *Ancient India and Ancient China, Trade and Religious Exchanges AD 1-600*, New Delhi: Oxford University Press, 1988.

Liu, Xinru and Lynda Norene Shaffer, *Connections across Eurasia: Transportation, Communication, and Cultural Exchange on the Silk Roads*, New York: McGraw-Hill Higher Education, 2007.

Livshits, V., "The Sogdian Letters from Mt. Mugh," *XXV International Congress of Orientalists*, Moscow, 1960.

Loewenthal, Rudolf, *The Jews of Bukhara*, Washington, D.C.: Central Asian Collectanea, 1961.

MacKenzie, David Neil, "Mani's Sabuhragan," *Bulletin of the School of Oriental and African Studies* 42 (1979), pp. 500–534, and 43 (1980), pp. 288–310.

―――, "Christian Sogdian Notes," *Bulletin of the School of Oriental and African Studies* 33/1 (1970), pp. 116–124.

Maenchen-Helfen, O., "Manichaeans in Siberia," in *Semitic and Oriental Studies Presented to William Popper,* Berkeley: University of California Press, 1951, pp. 311–326.

Mair, Victor, ed., *The Bronze Age and Early Iron Age Peoples of Eastern Central Asia,* Washington, D.C.: Institute for the Study of Man, 1998.

———, "Old Sinitic *Myag, Old Persian Magus, and English 'Magician,'" *Early China* 15 (1990), pp. 27–47.

Mallory, J.P., *In Search of the Indo-Europeans: Language, Archaeology, and Myth,* London: Thames and Hudson, 1989.

Mallory, J.P. and D.Q. Adams, *The Oxford Introduction to Proto-Indo-European and the Proto-Indo-European World,* New York: Oxford University Press, 2006.

Mallory, J.P. and Victor H. Mair, *The Tarim Mummies: Ancient China and the Mystery of the Earliest Peoples from the West,* London: Thames and Hudson, 2000.

Margoliouth, D.S., "An Early Judeo-Persian Document from Khotan in the Stein Collection, with Other Early Persian Documents," *Journal of the Royal Asiatic Society* (1903), pp. 735–761.

Messina, Giuseppe, *Cristianismo, buddhismo manicheismo nell'Asia antica,* Rome: Nicola Ruffolo, 1947.

Mingana, Alphonse, "The Early Spread of Christianity in Central Asia and the Far East," *Bulletin of the John Rylands Library* 9 (1925), pp. 297–371.

Minorsky, V., "Tamin ibn Bahr's Journey to the Uighurs," *Bulletin of the School of Oriental and African Studies* 12 (1948), pp. 275–305.

Moffett, Samuel H., *A History of Christianity in Asia,* vol. 1, San Francisco: Harper, 1992.

Montgomery, J.A., *The History of Yaballaha III, Nestorian Patriarch of His Vicar Bar Sawma,* New York: Columbia University Press, 1927.

Mostaert, Antoine, *Ordosica, Bulletin of the Catholic University of Peking* 9, Peking: Catholic University, 1934.

Moule, A.C., *Christians in China before the Year 1550,* London: Society for Promoting Christian Knowledge, 1930.

Narshakhi, Abu Bakr Muhammad, *Tārīkh-i Bukhārā,* tr. Richard N. Frye, *History of Bukhara,* Princeton: Markus Weiner, 2007[1954].

Nattier, Jan, "The Heart Sutra: A Chinese Apocryphal Text?" *International Journal of Buddhist Studies* 15/2 (1992), pp. 153–223.

———, "Church Language and Vernacular Language in Central Asian Buddhism," *Numen* 37/2 (1990), pp. 195–219.

———, "The Meanings of the Maitreya Myth: A Typological Analysis," in Alan Sponberg and Helen Hardacre, eds., *Maitreya, the Future Buddha,* Princeton: Princeton University Press, 1988, pp. 23–47.

Neusner, Jacob, *Aphrahat and Judaism: The Christian-Jewish Argument in Fourth-Century Iran,* Leiden: Brill, 1971.

———, "Rabbi and Magus in Third-Century Sasanian Babylonia," *History of Religions* 6 (1966), pp. 169–178.

Olschki, L., "Manichaeism, Buddhism and Christianity in Marco Polo's China," *Zeitschrift der schweizerischen Gesellschaft für Asienkunde* 5/1–2 (1951), pp. 1–21.

Outram, Alan K., et al., "The Earliest Horse Harnessing and Milking," *Science* (March 6, 2009), pp. 1332–1335.

Palmer, Martin, *The Jesus Sutras: Rediscovering the Lost Scrolls of Taoist Christianity*, New York: Ballantine, 2001.

Peake, Harold and Herbert John Fleure, *The Steppe and the Sown*, New Haven: Yale University Press, 1928.

Pelliot, Paul, *Recherches sur les Chrétiens de l'Asie centrale et d'Extrême-Orient*, Paris: Imprimérie nationale, 1973.

———, "Neuf notes sur des questions d'Asie centrale," *T'oung Pao* 26 (1929), pp. 201–265.

———, "Les traditions manichéennes au Fou-kien," *T'oung pao* 22 (1923), pp. 193–208.

———, "Chrétiens de l'Asie centrale et d'Extrême-Orient," *T'oung Pao* 15 (1914), pp. 623–644.

———, "Les influences iraniennes en Asie Central et en Extrême-Orient," *Revue d'Histoire et de Littérature Réligieuses* (1912), pp. 97–119.

Pestalozza, Uberto, "Il manicheismo presso i Turchi occidentali ed orientali," *Rendiconti del Reale Instituto Lombardo di Scienze e Lettere*, 2nd series, 67 (1934), pp. 417–497.

Phillips, E.D., "The Argippaei of Herodotus," *Artibus Asiae* 23 (1960), pp. 124–128.

Piacentini, Valeria Fiorani, *Turchizzazione ed islamizzazione dell'Asia Centrale (VI-XVI secolo d. Cr.)*, Milan: Società Editrice Dante Alighieri, 1974.

Plano Carpini, John of, *The Journey of Friar John of Pian de Carpini*, in Manuel Komroff, ed., *Contemporaries of Marco Polo*, New York: Dorset, 1989 [1928].

Poliakov, Sergei P., *Everyday Islam: Religion and Tradition in Rural Central Asia*, Armonk, NY: M.E. Sharpe, 1992.

Pollock, Michael, *Mandarins, Jews and Missionaries*, Philadelphia: Jewish Publication Society, 1980.

Polo, Marco, *The Travels*, tr. Ronald Latham, New York: Penguin, 1959.

Pourshariati, Parvaneh, *Decline and Fall of the Sasanian Empire: The Sasanian-Parthian Confederacy and the Arab Conquest of Iran*, London: I.B. Tauris, 2008.

Pritsak, Omeljan, *The Origin of Rus*, vol. 1, Cambridge, MA: Harvard University Press, 1981.

———, "The Khazar Kingdom's Conversion to Judaism," *Harvard Ukrainian Studies* 2 (1978), pp. 261–281.

Pulleyblank, E.G., "Han China in Central Asia," *International Historical Review* 3 (1981), pp. 278–286.

———, "A Sogdian Colony in Inner Mongolia," *T'oung Pao* 46 (1952), pp. 317–356.

Puri, B.N., *Buddhism in Central Asia*, Delhi: Motilal Banarsidass, 2000 [1987].

Rabinowitz, L., *Jewish Merchant Adventures: The Study of the Radanites*, London: E. Goldston, 1948.

Rashid al-din Fadhlullah, *Jāmi' al-tawārīkh*, tr. J.A. Boyle, *The Successors of Genghis Khan*, New York: Columbia University Press, 1971.

Reischauer, Edwin O., *Ennin's Diary: The Record of a Pilgrimage to China in Search of the Law*, New York: Ronald Press, 1955.

Richard, Jean, "Le Christianisme dans l'Asie Centrale," *Journal of Asian History* 16 (1982), pp. 101–124.

———, "La conversion de Berke et les débuts de l'islamisation de la Horde d'Or," *Revue des études islamiques* 35 (1967), pp. 173–184.

Risso, Patricia, *Merchants and Faith: Muslim Commerce and Culture in the Indian Ocean*, Boulder, CO: Westview, 1995.

Rondelez, V., "Un évêché en Asie Centrale au XIVe siècle," *Neue Zeitschrift für Missionswissenschaft* 7 (1951), pp. 1–17.

Rossabi, Morris, *Voyager from Xanadu: Rabban Sauma, First Eastern Emissary to the West*, New York: Kodansha, 1992.

———, "The 'Decline' of Central Asian Caravan Trade," in James Tracy, ed., *The Rise of Merchant Empires: Long-Distance Trade in the Early Modern World, 1350-1750*, Cambridge: Cambridge University Press, 1990.

———, *Khubilai Khan: His Life and Times*, Berkeley and Los Angeles: University of California Press, 1988.

———, "The Muslims of the Early Yüan Dynasty," in John D. Langlois, ed., *China under Mongol Rule*, Princeton: Princeton University Press, 1981, pp. 258–299.

Rouleau, Francis, "The Yangchow Latin Tombstone As a Landmark of Medieval Christianity in China," *Harvard Journal of Asiatic Studies* 17/3–4 (1954), pp. 346–365.

Rubruck, William, *The Mission of Friar William of Rubruck*, Peter Jackson and David Morgan, eds., London: Hakluyt Society, 1990.

Russell, James R., "Zoroastrianism as the State Religion of Ancient Iran," *Journal of the K.R. Cama Oriental Institute* 53 (1986), pp. 74–142.

Saeki, P.Y., *The Nestorian Documents and Relics in China*, 2nd ed., Tokyo: Academy of Oriental Culture, 1951.

Schafer, Edward H., *The Golden Peaches of Samarkand: A Study of T'ang Exotics*, Berkeley: University of California Press, 1962.

———, "Iranian Merchants in T'ang Dynasty Tales," *Semitic and Oriental Studies Presented to William Popper*, Berkeley: University of California Press, 1951, pp. 403–422.

Schopen, Gregory, "Notes on the Cult of the Book in Mahāyāna," *Indo-Iranian Journal* 17/3–4 (1975), pp. 147–181.

Schwartz, Martin, "Studies in the Texts of Sogdian Christians," unpublished Ph.D. dissertation, University of California, Berkeley, 1967.

Scott, David, "Buddhist Responses to Manichaeism," *History of Religions* 35 (1995), pp. 148–162.

———, "The Iranian Face of Buddhism," *East and West* 40 (1990), pp. 43–77.

——, "Manichaean Responses to Zoroastrianism," *Religious Studies* 25 (1989), pp. 435–458.

——, "Manichaean Views of Buddhism," *History of Religions* 25/2 (1985), pp. 99–115.

Shaked, Shaul, "First Man, First King: Notes on Semitic Iranian Sycretism and Iranian Mythological Transformations," in *Gilgul: Essays on Transformation, Revolution and Permanence*, Leiden: Brill, 1987, pp. 238–256.

——, "Iranian Influence on Judaism: First Century B.C.E. to Second Century B.C.E," in W.D. Davies and Louis Finkelstein, eds., *Cambridge History of Judaism*, vol. 1, Cambridge: Cambridge University Press, 1984, pp. 308–325.

——, ed., *Irano-Judaica*, Jerusalem: Ben-Zvi Institute, 1982.

Shaked, Shaul and Amnon Metzer, eds., *Irano-Judaica* , 6 vols. to date, Jerusalem: Ben-Zvi Institute, 1990–.

Shizuka, Sasaki, "A Study on the Origin of Mahayana Buddhism," *The Eastern Buddhist* 30/1 (1997), pp. 79–113.

Shkoda, V.G., "The Sogdian Temple: Structure and Rituals," *Bulletin of the Asia Institute* 10 (1996), pp. 195–206.

Sims-Williams, Nicholas, *Bactrian Documents, Part 2*, London: Khalili Collections, 2007.

——, ed., *Indo-Iranian Languages and Peoples*, Oxford: Oxford University Press, 2002.

——, *Bactrian Documents from Northern Afghanistan, Part 1: Legal and Economic Documents*, Oxford: Oxford University Press, 2001.

——, *Sogdian and other Iranian Inscriptions of the Upper Indus*, 2 vols., London: School of Oriental and African Studies, 1989–1992.

Sinor, Denis, ed., *Cambridge History of Early Inner Asia*, Cambridge: Cambridge University Press, 1990.

Stavisky, B.Ya., "Kara Tepe in Old Termez: A Buddhist Religious Centre of the Kushan Period on the Bank of the Oxus," in J. Harmatta, ed., *From Hecataeus to Al-Huwarizmi: Bactrian, Pahlavi, Sogdian, Persian, Sanskrit, Syriac, Arabic, Chinese, Greek and Latin Sources for the History of Pre-Islamic Central Asia*, Budapest: Academiai Kiado, 1984, pp. 95–135.

Stein, M. Aurel, *Ruins of Desert Cathay*, 2 vols., New York: Dover, 1987 [1912].

Subtelny, Maria, "The Cosmic Cock: Zoroastrian Mythological Elements in the Islamic Ascension Narrative," paper presented at the 7th International Society for Iranian Studies biennial conference, Toronto, July 31–August 3, 2008.

Sundermann, W., "Lo studio dei testi iranici di Turfan," in Gherardo Gnoli, ed., *Iranian Studies*, Rome: Istituto italiano per il Medio ed Estremo Oriente, 1985, pp. 199–234.

Tabari, Abu Ja'far Muhammad b. Jarir, *Ta'rīkh al-rusūl w'al-mulūk*, 3 vols., ed. M.J. de Goeje, Leiden: Brill, 1879–1901.

Tajadod, Nahal, *Les Porteurs de Lumière: l'épopée de l'église perse*, Paris: Albin Michel, 2008 [1993].

Tajadod, Nahal, *A l'Est du Christ : vie et mort des chrétiens dans la Chine des Tang*, Paris: Omnibus, 2000.

———, "A Linguistic Voyage through Manichaeism and Chinese Zoroastrianism," *Diogenes* 171 (1995), pp. 63–73.

———, *Mani: le Bouddha de lumière*, Paris: Cerf, 1991.

Thacker, T.W., "A Nestorian Gravestone from Central Asia in the Gulbenkian Museum," *Durham University Journal* (March 1967), pp. 94–107.

Thackston, Wheeler M., Jr., tr., *Naser-e Khosraw's Book of Travels*, Albany: SUNY Press, 1986.

Thubron, Colin, *Shadow of the Silk Road (P.S.)*, New York: Harper Perennial, 2008.

Torday, Laszlo, *Mounted Archers: The Beginnings of Central Asian History*, Durham: Durham Academic Press, 1997.

Trinkhaus, K. Maurer, "Mortuary Ritual and Mortuary Remains," *Current Anthropology* 25/5 (1984), pp. 674–678.

Upasak, C.S., *History of Buddhism in Afghanistan*, Varanasi: Central Institute of Higher Tibetan Studies, 1990.

Uray, G., "Tibet's Connections with Nestorianism and Manichaeism in the 8th–10th Centuries," *Wiener Studien zur Tibetologie und Buddhismuskunde* 10 (1983), pp. 399–429.

Utas, Bo, "The Jewish-Persian Fragment from Dandan-Uiliq," *Orientalia Suecana* 17 (1968), pp. 123–126.

Utz, David A., "Arshak, Parthian Buddhists, and 'Iranian' Buddhism," in *Buddhism Across Boundaries: Chinese Buddhism and the Western Regions*, John McRae and Jan Nattier, eds., Sanchung: Fo Guang Shan Foundation for Buddhist and Culture Education, 1999, pp. 446–470.

———, "A Sogdian Thaurnaturgical Text from Dunhuang and the Origins of Inner Asian Weather Magic," in *Historical Themes and Current Change in Central and Inner Asia*, Michael Gervers and Wayne Schlepp, eds. (Toronto Studies in Central and Inner Asia 3), Toronto: University of Toronto, 1998, pp. 101–121.

———, *A Survey of Buddhist Soghdian Studies*, Tokyo: Reiyukai Library, 1980.

Vasary, Istvan, " 'History and Legend' in Berke Khan's Conversion to Islam," in Denis Sinor, ed., *Aspects of Altaic Civilization III*, Bloomington, IN: Research Institute for Inner Asian Studies, 1990, pp. 230–252.

Walter, Mariko Namba, *Tokharian Buddhism Buddhism in Kucha: Buddhism of Indo-European Speakers in Chinese Turkestan before the 10th century C.E.*, Philadelphia: University of Pennsylvania, 1998.

Whitfield, Roderick, *Cave Temples of Mogao: Art and History on the Silk Road*, Los Angeles: Getty Publications, 2000.

Whitfield, Susan, *Life along the Silk Road*, Los Angeles: University of California Press, 2000.

Whitfield, Susan, and Ursula Sims-Williams, eds., *The Silk Road: Trade, Travel, War and Faith*, Chicago: Serindia, 2004.

Widengren, Geo, *Mani and Manichaeism*, London: Weidenfeld and Nicolson, 1965.

Wilford, John Noble, "New Finds Suggest Even Earlier Trade on Fabled Silk Road," *New York Times* (March 16, 1993), pp. C1, C8.

Williams, A.V., "Zoroastrians and Christians in Sasanian Iran," *Bulletin of the John Rylands Library* 78/3 (1996), pp. 37–53.

Williams, Paul, *Mahayana Buddhism: The Doctrinal Foundations*, London: Routledge, 1989.

Wink, André, *Al-Hind: The Making of the Indo-Islamic World*, vol. 1, Leiden: Brill, 1990.

Winston, D., "The Iranian Component in the Bible, Apocrypha, and Qumran: A Review of the Evidence," *History of Religions* 5 (1966), pp. 183–216.

Wood, Frances, *The Silk Road*, Berkeley: University of California Press, 2002.

Wriggins, Sally Hovey, *Xuanzang: A Buddhist Pilgrim on the Silk Road*, Boulder, CO: Westview Press, 1996.

Yarshater, Ehsan, ed., *Cambridge History of Iran*, vol. 3, *The Seleucid, Parthian, and Sasanian Periods*, Cambridge: Cambridge University Press, 1983.

———, ed., *Encyclopaedia Iranica*, London: Routledge & Kegan Paul and Costa Mesa, CA: Mazda Publishers, 1985–.

Yüan, Ch'en, *Western and Central Asians in China under the Mongols,* tr. Ch'ien Hsing-hai and L. Carrington Goodrich, Nettetal: Steyler Verlag, 1989.

Yule, Henry and H. Cordier, *Cathay and the Way Thither*, 4 vols., London: Hakluyt Society, 1937 [1913–1916].

Zaehner, R.C., *The Dawn and Twilight of Zoroastrianism*, New York: Putnam, 1961.

Zhou, Xijuan, "Manichaean Monasteries under the Khocho Uyghurs," *International Journal of Central Asian Studies* 8/1 (2003), pp. 129–146.

———, "The Transformations of Manichaeism under the Khocho Uyghurs," *Journal of Central Asian Studies*, 5/2, (2001), pp. 2–15.

Zieme, Peter, ed., *Aspects of Research into Central Asian Buddhism*, Turnhout: Brepols, 2008.

Zürcher, Erik, *The Buddhist Conquest of China*, Leiden: Brill, 1959.

Index

Abaqa Khan, 119, 159 n 72
Abbasid Empire, 16, 77, 89, 95
Abu Muslim, 89, 90, 95
Achæmenid Empire, 16, 28–29, 31
Afghanistan, 14, 24, 40, 43–44, 107, 145 n 34, 147 n 6
Agni, deity, 28; town, 55
Ahmad, finance minister to Mongols, 118–119
Ahmad Yasavi, 134
Ahriman, 27, 31, 73
Ahura Mazda, 21, 27–29, 35, 59, 73
ahuras, 27
Alamut, 99
Alans, 124–125
Alexander the Great, 43, 65
Alexandria, school of, 61
Ali b. abi Talib, 89, 98
Ali Sultan, 125, 128
Allsen, Thomas, 13
Almaliq, 125
Alopen, 68, 83
Altaic languages, 24, 26
Altin Tepe, 29
Amesha Spenta, 29
Amitabha, 46, 52, 82
Amu Darya, 14
An Lushan, 77, 79, 102
An Shigao, 49–50
Andrew of Longjumeau, 112
Andrew of Perugia, 124
Angra Mainyu, *see* Ahriman

Antioch, school of, 61
apocalypticism, 32
apostasy, 86, 89, 94
Arabic language, 16–18, 77, 86, 97, 98, 134, 151 n 16, 153 n 46
Arabs, 9, 65, 77, 86–90, 120, 123, 132, 154 n 2
Aramaic script, 15
Arbil, 123
Arghun Khan, 119–120, 122
Argippaei, 25
arhat, 38–39, 42, 53
Armenians, 112–114, 123–124
art, 6; Buddhist, 7, 44–46, 53; funerary, 25; Islamic, 16; Manichaean, 80
Ashoka Maurya, 37–38, 40, 43, 48
Assyrian inscriptions, 28; conquest of Israel, 30
astronomy/astrology, 50, 65, 70–71
asura see *ahura*
Augustine, St., 6, 75
Avalokitesvara, 46, 80
Avesta, 26–30, 32, 35, 153 n 46
Avignon, 126
Azerbaijan, 26, 91

Babak, 91
Babylonians, 30
Bactria, 14, 27, 31, 43–44, 89
Bactrian texts, 29; language, 43
Bactrians, 13, 14, 44, 47, 55, 62

Baghdad, 15, 61, 67, 70, 76, 89, 90,
96, 99, 100, 112, 116, 119, 122,
158 n 53
Bahram I, 71
Bahram II, 63
Bahram V, 63
Baidu Khan, 120–121
Balash, 64
Balkh, 11, 43, 55, 89, 95, 98
Bamiyan, 40, 55, 147 n 6
baptism, 67–68, 129
Bar Hebraeus, 67
Bardaisan, 62
Barlas tribe, 128
Barmak family, 89, 95
Batinites, see Seveners, Shi'ite sect
Batu Khan, 105
Bentley, Jerry, 13, 88, 137
Berke Khan, 116, 158 n 45
Berlin, 7
Bezeklik, 82
Bible, 33, 59, 137
Black Sea, 23
bodhisattva, 42, 44–46, 82
Bogomils, 75
Bön religion, 57
Boucher, Guillaume, 114
Brahmanism, 52
Buddha, 37–8, 39, 40, 41–2, 43, 44,
45, 46, 49, 52, 53, 54, 73, 81, 82,
83, 84, 131
Buddhism, 7–10, 21, 22, 29, 37–58,
65, 66, 69–71, 76, 79–82, 89, 93,
95, 103–104, 130, 133; in China,
12, 49–52, 58; Japanese, 46, 52–53;
under Mongols, 106–109, 113, 115,
122; spread of, 10, 13–15, 17, 41,
45, 47; survival under Islam, 96,
100, 106
Buddhist texts, 15, 39, 46, 51;
councils, 38, 40, 45; relics, 38, 45,
54; schools, 39–42
Bukhara, 11, 16, 17, 25, 29, 31, 55,
57, 94, 96, 99–100, 102, 104, 129

Bulgars, 100, 156 n 39
Bulghai, Mongol secretary, 114
bull, worship of, 28–29; sacrifice of, *see*
sacrifice, animal
Byzantine empire, 9, 63, 86–87, 100,
142 n 9; church, 61, 64

caliphate, 16, 86, 89, 99
camels, 11
Cao'an, 131
Caspian Sea, 2, 97–98
Cathar movement, 75
Catholicism, 9, 107, 111, 123–126,
128–130
Central Asia, bilingualism in, 24;
Buddhism in, 21, 39–41, 47;
Chinese control, 49, 135; Christians
in, 22, 62, 67, 127–130; Islam in,
13, 15–17, 91–92, 135; Israelite
presence in, 30–31; Manichaeans in,
7, 75; modern governments, 1, 14,
135; social history of, 2–3, 23
Chaghatai Khan, 109–110, 157 n 19
Chalcedon, Council of, 61–62
chan, 50, 53, see also *zen*
Chang'an (Xi'an), 54, 68, 78, 95,
102, 131
Chariots, 24–25, 149 n 41
charisma, 12, 18, 56, 89, 92, 93,
101, 134
Chengdu, 54
China, frontiers of, 23; study of
Buddhism in, 39; trade with, 1, 4,
31, 33–34, 45, 47, 101
Chinese scholars, 7; language, 15,
34, 35, 50–51, 53, 69; texts, 4, 26,
46, 49–50, 54–55, 68–69, 75, 77,
83–84, 103
Chinggis Khan, 101, 105–109, 112,
132, 157 n 19
Chinqai, Mongol secretary, 111, 114
Christian texts, 66, 69
Christianity, in China, 9, 68–70,
129–130; as proselytizing religion, 17

Christians, 12, 19, 22, 42, 55, 59, 60, 63–65, 67, 70, 73, 88, 107–109, 111–113, 115–117, 120, 122–124, 126–131, 134, 158 n 48; captive, 63, 114

Constantinople, 61, 64

Crusaders, 98, 105, 112

Ctesiphon, 61, 76

Cyril, Patriarch of Alexandria, 61

Cyrus, 30–31

daēva, 27, 145 n 19

Damascus, 77, 87, 116

Daniel, Book of, 32

Daoism, 53, 70, 82, 107, 131

Darius I, 29

David, Israelite king, 30, 33

Dayuan, 4

deva, see daēva

devil, 27, 30–31, 83; see also satan

Dharmaguptaka school, 39–40, 42, 47

dhimmī communities ("peoples of the Book"), 88, 94

dhyana, see chan

diophysitism, 60–61

divination, 25, 114

doctrinal disputes, 59–60, 64

Dominican monks, see Monks

donkeys, 11, 109

Dumézil, Georges, 24

Dunhuang, 7, 20, 29, 54–55, 69, 143 n 35

East Asia, 1, 9, 14, 33, 35, 50, 56, 97, 126

East Turkestan, 6–7, 9, 135; see also Xinjiang

Ecbatana, see Hamadan

Egypt, 4, 6, 16, 34, 87, 98, 112, 116, 119, 135

Eightfold Path, 37, 82

elect, Manichaean monks, 71, 73–75

Elias, Metropolitan of Marv, 67

Elias III, Nestorian Patriarch, 67

Eljigidei, 112

Elkesaites, 71

England, 7, 142 n 16

Enlightenment, 38, 41, 43, 53

Ennin, Japanese monk, 79, 142 n 20

Ephesus, Council of, 61

eschatology, 33

Esfahan, 30

esotericism, 12, 52, 73, 75, 76, 98

Esther, Book of, 31–32

Ezekiel, Book of, 32

Fatimid dynasty, 98–99

Faxian, 12, 50, 54

Ferdowsi, Abu'l-Qasim, 26

fire temples, 57, 95–96; worship, 24–25, 28, 44, 56, 63, 78, 93

Four Noble Truths, 37

Franciscan monks, see Monks

Fraoshkart, 32

Fravardigan, 32

Fujian province, 22, 131, 135

Gandhara, 42–45, 48

Gandhari, see Prakrit languages

Gathas, 26, 29

Gaykhatu Khan, 120, 122

Genghis Khan, see Chinggis Khan

George, Öngöt prince, 123–124

Georgians, 113, 128

Germany, 7, 142 n 16

Ghazan Khan, 120–123, 160 n 86

ghazāt, 133

ghāzī, 128

Ghaznavid dynasty, 92, 100

ghost festival, 35

Gnosticism, 73, 152 n 35

Golden Horde, 112, 116

Greek texts, 28, 32; influence in India, 43–45; influence in Iran, 65; influence in Sogdiana, 29, 65; myths, 25, 35, 43, 45; rule in Palestine, 33; writers, 25

Gundeshapur, 65

Gür-khan, 103, 105, 156 n 46
Güyük Khan, 111–112, 115

hadīth, 93
Hamadan, 30, 122
Han dynasty, 3, 4, 33, 34, 35, 49, 96
haoma, 27, 144 n 18
Hasan-i Sabah, 99
hearers, Manichaean laity, 71, 75
heaven, 26, 31, 35, 78, 83, 91, 117,
    150 n 66; *see also* paradise
Hebraic religion, 17, 59; *see also*
    Israelites
hell, 31, 35, 90
Hellenism, 31, 33
Herodotus, 25, 144 n 11
Hormizd IV, 64
horses, 3, 4, 11, 24–5, 26, 46, 49,
    141 nn 4 & 6, 153 n 54
horse-sacrifice, *see* sacrifice, animal
Hui Muslims, 101–3
Huili, 56–7
Hülegü Khan, 108, 115–6, 122

Ibn Battuta, 134
Ibn Khurdadbih, 97–98
idolatry, 55, 94–96, 109, 113, 117,
    120, 121, 125, 132–133, 150 n 60
Il-Khan dynasty, 108–109, 119–121,
    159 n 72
India, 1–4, 7, 12, 14, 19, 24–26, 33,
    37–38, 40–41, 43–58, 70, 100,
    109–110, 124, 135–136, 138
Indian Ocean, 13, 97, 142 n 22
Indo-Aryan, 24–25, 28, 57
Indo-European, 2–4, 14, 20, 24–27,
    32, 44, 48
Indus River, 57, 71
Innocent IV, pope, 110–111
Iran, 1, 26–28, 30, 32, 35, 53, 57,
    62–65, 68, 71, 77, 87–91, 94–99,
    106, 115, 121, 128–129, 135, 138,
    142 n 9; Christianity in, 62–65;
    Parthian rule in, 16, 27–28, 31, 47–48

Iranian religion, 14, 28–29, 31–32,
    57, 62, 68, 90, 145 n 28; languages,
    16, 43
Iranians, 13, 20, 24–26, 28, 32, 34–35,
    48, 87, 89, 94
Islam, 6, 8–9, 12–13, 15–18, 22,
    31, 55, 65, 73, 85–105, 107–109,
    111, 116–117, 119–122, 126–129,
    132–133, 135, 137–138, 150 n 60,
    158 n 45, 160 nn 86,108, 162 n 25;
    popular expressions of, 18–19, 93,
    101, 127; spread of, 13, 17, 19,
    55, 92
Islamic law, 16, 55, 92–93, 121; see
    also Sharia law
Isma'ilis, *see* Seveners, Shi'ite sect
Israelites, 20, 27, 30–32, 35, 71; in
    Central Asia, 30; in China, 34

Jäbä, Mongol general, 106
Jamshid, 29
Jaxartes, *see* Syr Darya
Jayhun, *see* Amu Darya
Jerusalem, 30, 32, 112, 116, 119
Jesus Christ, 46, 60–62, 69, 90, 113,
    117, 137–138; in Manichaeism, 73,
    81–83
Jewish communities, 17, 30–31,
    33, 63
Jews of Babylonia, 30–32, 62
jihād, 87
jizya, 88, 95, 122
Job, Book of, 31
John of Marignolli, 125
John of Montecorvino, 123–125, 130
John of Plano Carpini, 107, 110–111
Judah, kingdom of, 30
Judaism, 7, 8, 17, 27, 31, 70, 97–98;
    in China, 33; decline of, 17;
    definition vis-à-vis Christianity, 60
Juvaini, Ata Malik, 106, 110
Juzjani, Minhaj al-Din, 109–112,
    116, 156 n 46, 157 n 19,
    158 nn 45,48,53

Kaifeng, 33–34, 95
Kanishka I, 45
Karakorum mountains, 50–51, 54
Kartir, 63, 71
Kashgar, 11, 50, 65, 67, 99–100, 106
Kashmir, 45, 48, 50, 51, 54, 58
Kavad, 64, 66, 91
Kazakh, 133–134, 162 n 36
Kazakhstan, 2, 67, 113, 128, 133,
  141 n 4
Kebek, Mongol ruler, 134
Kerait, 67, 108, 129
Khanbaliq, 118, 123–125
Khazars, 97–98
Khizr Khwaja, 132–133
*Khoja*s, 101
Khotan, 11, 39, 48, 51, 54, 55, 58
Khotanese language, 15
Khubilai Khan, 108, 115, 117–119,
  121, 126, 159 n 69
Khurasan, 15, 30, 79, 89, 99, 123,
  160 n 83
Khurram-dīniyya, 91; *see also* Mazdak
Khusrow I, 91
Khwand Amir, 106, 110, 117,
  159 n 72
Khwarazm, 27, 55, 105
Kitbuqa, 115–116
Korean pilgrims, 12, 47
Körgüz Küregen, *see* George, Öngöt
  prince
Kosheng, 107
Kucha, 11, 48, 50, 55, 133
Küchlük, 106, 108, 156 n 2
Kumarajiva, 50
kumiz, 68
Kurds, 123
Kushan empire, 40, 42, 44–47, 50, 62,
  65, 147 n 2
Kyrgyz, 133
Kyrgyzstan, 51, 55, 128

Ladakh, 57, 150 n 67
Lanzhou, 70

Laozi, 69, 131
Lattimore, Owen, 110
le Coq, Albert von, 5, 7
Li Guangli, Han general, 4
light, as religious symbol, 28, 46,
  52, 73, 75, 78–80, 82, 83,
  130, 131
Lokaksema, 50
Louis IV, King of France, 112, 114
Luoyang, 49, 50, 54, 70, 77, 78, 95

Magi, 29, 59, 63–64, 71, 77, 90, 91,
  153 n 46
Mahadeva, five theses of, 38
Mahasanghika, 38, 39–40, 41, 48,
  147 n 6
Mahayana, 9, 39, 40, 41–42, 46, 48,
  50, 51, 52, 81
Maitreya, 46
Makh temple, 29, 96
Mandaeans, 73
Mani, 70–76
Manichaean texts, 6–7, 15, 17, 75, 81,
  83–84
Manichaeism, 6, 42, 46, 59–66,
  152 n 35; Buddhist influences on,
  71; in Central Asia, 9, 29, 57, 77; in
  China, 9, 22, 70, 79–80, 90, 99, 103,
  130–131, 135, 153 nn 42,46,54; as
  official religion, 9, 22, 77–78, 129; as
  proselytizing religion, 71, 75, 80–81;
  spread of, 12, 13, 74
Mansur, Abbasid Caliph, 89
mantra, 52
Mar Ammo, 80–81
Mar Makikha, 116, 122
Mar Yaballaha, *see* Yaballaha III,
  Nestorian Patriarch
Maragha, 120, 122, 123
Marv, 11, 31, 47, 50, 67
Mary, mother of Jesus, 61
Massagatae, 25, 147 n 11
Maurya dynasty, 37, 147 n 2
mawlā, 88

Mazdak, 91
Mazdakites, see *Khurram-dīniyya*
Mecca, 55, 85, 86, 159 n 71
Medes, 27, 30, 87
Mediterranean, 1, 5, 6, 10, 14, 15, 33, 44, 45, 64, 72, 75, 96, 97, 98, 109, 123
Menander, *see* Menandros
Menandros, 44
merchants, 8, 13, 16, 35, 49, 60, 67, 85, 107, 125, 128, 130, 132, 134; Buddhist, 37, 43, 147 n 2; Chinese, 4; Iranian, 68, 95; Jewish, 34, 97; Muslim, 99, 102, 108; Sogdian, 14, 15, 51, 57, 65, 67, 94; as transmitters of culture, 70
merit, in Buddhism, 40, 42, 46, 52, 81, 82
Merkit, Mongol tribe, 108
Mesopotamia, 27, 28, 29, 30, 62, 70, 71, 77, 87, 89, 97
messianism, 31, 46, 82
Ming code, 80
Ming dynasty, 131
Mingdi, Han emperor, 34
miracles, 62, 111, 134
Miran, 48
missionaries, 12, 19, 90, 138; Buddhist, 40, 43, 46, 48, 49, 50, 52, 53; Christian, 9, 67, 68, 69, 116, 128, 129, 130; Manichaean, 78, 80; Muslim, 92, 99, 101, 134
Mithra, 27, 28, 46
monasteries, 22; Buddhist, 42, 43, 45, 47, 54, 56, 95; Manichaean, 80, 153 n 54; Nestorian, 66, 69, 120
Möngke Khan, 108, 110, 112, 114–115, 117, 122, 158 n 32,43,45
Mongol period, 8, 68, 80, 95, 100, 102, 104
Mongolia, 3, 12, 26, 77, 108, 110, 112, 129, 162 n 36
Mongols, 66, 67, 70, 99, 101, 103–126

Monks, Buddhist, 12, 35, 37–38, 42, 46–56, 58, 69, 70, 75, 76, 79, 84, 109–110, 115; Christian, 69–70, 75, 107, 110, 112, 113, 114, 117, 123, 125; Daoist, 6, 107; Manichaean, 71, 74–75, 78, 80, 153 n 54
monophysitism, 61–62
moon, worship of, 26, 28–29, 78
Moses, 27, 90, 117
Mu'awiya, 89
Muhammad, 55, 80, 85–86, 89, 90, 101, 150 n 6, 159 n 71
mules, 11
Muqanna', 90–91
Muslim traders, *see* merchants, Muslim
mysticism, 16, 32

Nagasena, 44
Naiman, Mongol tribe, 105–106, 108
Najm al-din Kubra, 134
Nalanda, 51
Nanai, Sogdian goddess, 30
Naqshbandi Sufi order, 101, 127
Narseh I, Sasanian emperor, 64
Narshakhi, 90–91, 94, 96
Nasir-i Khusrow, 99
Naw Bahar, 95
Nawruz, Il-khan general, 120–123, 159–160 n 83
Nestorian Christianity, 7, 14, 21, 61–70, 81, 82, 84, 99, 100; disappearance of, 70, 129–131; evidence of, 22, 66; under Mongols, 103, 107, 108, 111–116, 119–125, 128, 134, 160 n 108, 161 n 5; spread of, 9, 13
Nestorian monument, 82
Nestorius, 61
nikaya, 39, 42, 48, 50
nirvana, 53, 81
Nizam al-Mulk, Seljuk vizier, 99, 155 n 34
Nizaris, Sevener Shi'ite sect, 99
nō rūz, 29

nomads, 2, 4, 14, 18, 23, 24, 44, 47, 65–68, 78, 92, 93, 100, 127, 128, 132, 134–135, 160 n 108, 161 n 5

Oghul Qaimish, 112
Ögödei Khan, 109–111, 128, 157 n 19
Öngöts, 108, 119, 123, 129
Orkhon River, 26, 78
Ormazd, see Ahura Mazda
Oxus river, see Amu Darya
Özbek Khan, 116

paintings, see art
Pakistan, 41, 43, 44, 54, 71
Palestine, 12, 30, 33, 35, 60, 62
Pali texts, 40, 42
Pamir Mountains, 27, 55
paper, technology of, 15
paradise, 28, 31, 52, 82, 90; see also heaven
Parthian, 13, 21, 27, 28, 44, 47–48, 49, 50, 71, 80, 87, 149 n 47, 154 n 2; empire, 16, 31, 47, 62, 63, 65; texts, 15, 62, 75, 80, 81
pax mongolica, 5, 101
Pelliot, Paul, 5, 69, 153 n 58
Persian language, 7, 11, 16, 17, 18, 26, 75, 77, 89, 94, 95, 96, 97, 101, 145 n 19, 153 n 46, 161 n 8; empires, 16, 29, 30–31, 33, 61, 63, 87
Persians, 9, 13, 16, 27, 31, 34, 62, 66, 75, 77, 86, 94, 97, 99, 101, 102, 106, 109, 111, 112, 154 n 2
Phags-pa, 118, 126
Poliakov, Sergei, 18
Polo, Marco, 5, 107, 117, 118, 131
prajñā, 40
Prajnaparamita literature, 42
Prakrit languages, 15, 40, 45
Prester John, 105, 109, 112
Pure Land, 9, 52, 54
Purim, 32

Qalmaqs, 133
Qara Balghasun (Ordu Baliq), 78
Qara Shahr, 54
Qara-khanid dynasty, 92, 99, 100, 103
Qara-khitai, 67, 103, 104, 105
Qocho, 79, 80, 153 n 54
Qom, 106
Quanzhou, 131; see also Zaytun
Qur'an, 17, 19, 55, 87, 88, 93, 117, 119, 126, 132, 134, 159 n 71
Qusam ibn Abbas, 134

Rabban Sauma, 12, 107, 119–120
rabbinical tradition, 27–28, 60, 98
Radanites, 96–97
Ragnarök, 32
raiding, 2, 4, 23, 47, 86–87, 100, 132
Rashid al-din, 109–111, 117–118, 157 n 16, 159 nn 64,83
Rayy, 106
razzia, 86; see also raiding
rebellions, 16, 77, 79, 86, 89, 102, 106, 123, 159 n 83
Revelation, Book of, 32–33
revelations, to Mani, 71, 74; to Muhammad, 85
Richthofen, Ferdinand von, 1
Rig Veda, 2, 24, 27
Roman sources, 31; Catholics, 107, 128, 130; church, 64; empire, 17, 31, 59, 60, 64, 75, 77, 96–97
Russians, 1, 14, 113, 116, 135

Sa'ad al-Dawla, Jewish vizier to Mongols, 120
Sabeans, 64, 71
sacrifice, animal, 24, 25, 26, 27, 57, 144 n 16
saffron, 12
Sahara desert, 13
Sakas, 14, 25, 28, 29, 44, 65, 144 nn 8,11

salvation, in Buddhism, 42, 52; in Gnosticism, 73; in Manichaeism, 75, 81; *see also* soteriology
Samanid dynasty, 16, 65, 96, 99–100, 155 n 35
Samarkand, 11, 15, 20, 31, 47, 55, 56, 65, 79, 95, 96, 104, 116, 129, 134
samsāra, 42, 81
sangha, 37–38, 71
Sanskrit, 7, 13, 26, 41, 45, 50, 51, 54, 55, 82, 95
Saoshyant, 46
Sartaq, 112, 116
Sarvastivada, 39, 40–42, 47, 48, 50
Sasanian empire, 16, 27, 28, 30, 50, 56, 57, 61, 63–64, 65, 66, 71, 77, 87, 89, 90, 91, 94, 95, 96, 130, 149 n 47, 154 n 2; art, 44
satan, 31; *see also* devil
Satoq Bughra Khan, 99–100, 155 n 35
Sayhun, *see* Syr Darya
Scandinavian mythology, 32
schisms, Buddhist, 38, 39, 147 n 5; Manichaean, 76
Scythians, *see* Sakas
Seleucid empire, 43, 47, 87
Seljuks, 92, 99, 100
Semirechye, *see* Seven Rivers region
Seven Rivers region, 67, 128, 133
Seveners, Shi'ite sect, 98–99
Shāh-nāmeh, 26, 90
shamanism, 22, 66–68, 78, 97, 100, 106, 128, 134, 151 n 16, 162 n 36
Shapur I, 63, 71
Shapur II, 63
Sharia law, 13, 101
Shi'ism, 89, 98, 106, 158 n 53
Shimnu, Sogdian devil, 30
Shiva, 29, 45
shrines, Buddhist, 95; Daoist, 6; Manichaean, 131; Muslim, 12, 18–19, 96

shu'biyya movement, 77
Siddhartha Gautama, *see* Buddha
silk, 4, 5, 10, 12, 31, 33, 34, 47, 49, 77, 97, 133, 142 n 9
Siyavash, cult of, 25, 57
slaves, 30, 97, 109, 112, 113, 118
Sogdian language, 14, 15, 16, 35, 46, 51, 69; "ancient letters," 20, 29; texts, 15, 29, 66, 75, 80, 81; *see also* merchants, Sogdian
Sogdiana, 31, 57, 65, 89–90, 94, 150 n 64; *see also* Transoxiana
Solomon, Israelite king, 30
soma, see *haoma*
Song dynasty, 3, 131, 150 n 61
Sorghaghtani Begi, 108
soteriology, 46, 52
Southeast Asia, 39, 136
Soviet archaeologists, 47; period, 18–19
Sri Lanka, 39
Stein, Sir Marc Aurel, 5, 6–7, 15, 20, 96
steppes, 1–4, 9, 18, 23–26, 44, 47, 68, 77, 100, 103, 105–108, 126–130, 132–134, 136, 160 n 108, 161 n 5, 162 nn 24,25
Sthavira, 38; *see also* Theravada
stupa, 43, 45, 57, 76
Sübödei, Mongol general, 106
Sufis, 12, 19, 92–93, 96, 101, 116, 127–128, 132, 134
Sukhavati, 52
sun, worship of, 25, 28, 46, 63, 78, 81
Sunni, 99–100, 106, 128, 132
Syr Darya (Jaxartes, Sayhun), 14
Syria, 16, 61, 85, 87, 111
Syriac language, 60, 63, 66–67, 69, 75, 105, 113

Tabari, Muhammad b. Jarir, 96
Tabiti, Sogdian goddess, 25
Tajikistan, 14, 18
Takla Makan, 4, 48, 55
Talas, 55; Battle of, 9

Tamerlane, *see* Timur Gurgan
Tang dynasty, 13, 33, 35, 51, 52, 68–70, 76, 77–79, 95, 102, 115
Tangri, Turkish sky god, 26, 66, 106
Tantra, 52
Taoism, *see* Daoism
Tarim Basin, 15, 26, 48, 50–51, 58, 66, 78, 79, 96, 99, 100, 101, 133
Tashkent, 46, 55
Tatars, 108
Taxila, 43
Temujin, *see* Chinggis Khan
Tenduc, *see* Kosheng
Termez, 55
Theravada, 39, 40, 42, 147 n 4
Tibet, 1, 53, 57–58
Tibetan empire, 58
Tibetans, 58, 102, 118, 126, 160 n 108
Timothy I, Patriarch of Baghdad, 67
Timur Gurgan (Tamerlane), 127–128, 161 n 5
Tirmidh, *see* Termez
Tocharian language, 15, 44, 48, 149 n 41; people, 4, 149 n 4; *see also* Yuezhi
Töregene, 111
translation of texts, 17–18, 46, 50, 53–54, 66, 69, 82
Transoxiana, 14, 27, 50, 55, 99, 101, 134; *see also* Sogdiana
Tughluq Temür, 132
Tughshada, 89, 94
Tun-huang, *see* Dunhuang
Turfan, 11, 54, 66, 81–82, 133
Turkish language, 15, 18, 24, 26, 66, 75, 78, 81, 97, 149 n 41; religion, 67, 78, 93, 97
Turks, 6, 21, 25, 65, 66, 67, 77, 79, 90, 92, 97, 99, 100, 101, 105, 106, 107, 123, 127, 129, 132; funerary practices, 26
Turpan, *see* Turfan

Uighurs, 6, 22, 77–82, 102, 109, 114, 117–118, 149 n 41
Umayyads, 77, 87–89
Ural Mountains, 26
Uzbekistan, 4, 14, 19

vegetarianism, 2, 75, 79, 131
vihara, 45, 46, 95, 148 n 33
vinaya, 38, 39, 42
Vishnu, 43
Vishtaspa, (mythical?) Iranian king, 27, 32

waqf, 128
Warner, Langdon, 5
"White Cloud", Buddhist sect, 80
"White Lotus", Buddhist sect, 80
William of Rubruck, 107, 112, 130
women, role as educators, 18–20, 93
Wu, Zhou Empress, 76
Wudi, Han emperor, 3–4

Xi'an, *see* Chang'an
Xinjiang, 6, 7, 26; *see also* East Turkestan
Xiongnu, 4, 26
Xuanzang, 6, 12, 43, 46, 48, 51, 54–57, 150 n 59
Xuanzong, 68

Yaballaha III, Nestorian Patriarch, 107, 119–123
Yaghnobi language, 14
Yahweh-worshippers, 21
yaks, 11
Yasavi Sufi order, 101, 127, 134
Yazdigerd I, 64
Yazdigerd III, 95
Yima, *see* Jamshid
Yogacara, 55
Yo-Yo Ma, 2
Yuan dynasty, 102; *see also* Mongols

Yuezhi, 4, 44; *see also* Tocharian
Yunnan province, 102

Zaytun, 125, 131, 159 n 64; *see also*
    Quanzhou
zen, 40, 50, 53; see also *chan*
Zhang Qian, 3

Zoroastrian religion, 6, 7, 13, 14, 21,
    22, 26, 27, 29, 30, 44, 46, 56, 59,
    64, 65, 88, 89, 94–95, 150 n 66; in
    China, 69–70, 95; as state religion,
    27, 56–57, 63, 77, 79, 90; texts,
    17, 26
Zurvan, 46, 73

CPSIA information can be obtained
at www.ICGtesting.com
Printed in the USA
LVHW022157101220
673855LV00015B/269